"This is a ground-breaking book that challenges the VAWG prevention and response orthodoxy. Evidence from the online-surveys, field work and document reviews are used to build a VAWG Prevention and Response Framework that can be adapted and applied across sectors, in both development and humanitarian emergency contexts. Case studies from across the world provide detailed examples of what works, focusing too on what does not and the blinkered gender-blind approaches that are too often applied."

— *Maureen Leah Chirwa, Health Systems Research and Management Specialist, founder of a woman established research firm, Prime Health Consulting and Services in Malawi*

PREVENTION OF VIOLENCE AGAINST WOMEN AND GIRLS

Prevention of Violence Against Women and Girls argues that women and girls are vulnerable across all areas of society, and that therefore a commitment to end violence against women and girls needs to be embedded into all development programmes, regardless of sectorial focus.

This book presents an innovative framework for sensitisation and action across development programmes, based on emerging best practices and lessons learnt, and illustrated through a number of country contexts and a range of programmes. Overall, it argues that SDG 5 can only be achieved with a systematic model for mainstreaming an end to violence against women and girls, no matter what the priorities of the particular development programme might be. Demonstrating how the approach can be applied across contexts, the authors explore cases from the energy sector, health and humanitarian intervention, and from countries as varied as South Sudan, Myanmar, Rwanda, Nepal, and Kenya.

Drawing on nearly three decades of experience working on gender, health, and violence against women programmes as both practitioners and academics, the authors present key lessons which can be used by students, researchers, and practitioners alike.

Tamsin Bradley is a social anthropologist and applied researcher who has worked for over 20 years to end violence against women and girls by researching evidence around what works to end it. She is currently Professor of International Development at the University of Portsmouth and has projects across South Asia and Africa. She has published four monographs, two edited volumes, and many journal articles.

Janet Gruber is a social anthropologist, a development practitioner, and academic. In a career spanning 25 years she has worked on VAWG prevention and response, gender equality, health and rights, and access to justice. Janet has worked in humanitarian emergencies, in conflict and fragile state environments, and in development settings. Janet has a PhD from Cambridge University and is currently Gibbs Research Fellow at Newnham College, Cambridge. Publications include book chapters and journal articles on Mainstreaming of VAWG prevention, HIV & AIDS in conflict and fragile states, refugee return, and gender equality.

Rethinking Development

Rethinking Development offers accessible and thought-provoking overviews of contemporary topics in international development and aid. Providing original empirical and analytical insights, the books in this series push thinking in new directions by challenging current conceptualizations and developing new ones.

This is a dynamic and inspiring series for all those engaged with today's debates surrounding development issues, whether they be students, scholars, policy makers and practitioners internationally. These interdisciplinary books provide an invaluable resource for discussion in advanced undergraduate and postgraduate courses in development studies as well as in anthropology, economics, politics, geography, media studies and sociology.

Southern-Led Development Finance
Solutions from the Global South
Edited by Diana Barrowclough, Kevin P. Gallagher and Richard Kozul-Wright

Introducing Forced Migration
Patricia Hynes

Mobile Technology and Social Transformations
Access to Knowledge in Global Contexts
Edited by Stefanie Felsberger and Ramesh Subramanian

Prevention of Violence Against Women and Girls
Mainstreaming in Development Programmes
Tamsin Bradley and Janet Gruber

For more information about this series, please visit: www.routledge.com/Rethinking-Development/book-series/RDVPT

PREVENTION OF VIOLENCE AGAINST WOMEN AND GIRLS

Mainstreaming in Development Programmes

Tamsin Bradley and Janet Gruber

LONDON AND NEW YORK

First published 2022
by Routledge
2 Park Square, Milton Park, Abingdon, Oxon OX14 4RN

and by Routledge
605 Third Avenue, New York, NY 10158

Routledge is an imprint of the Taylor & Francis Group, an informa business

© 2022 Tamsin Bradley and Janet Gruber

The right of Tamsin Bradley and Janet Gruber to be identified as authors
of this work has been asserted by them in accordance with sections
77 and 78 of the Copyright, Designs and Patents Act 1988.

All rights reserved. No part of this book may be reprinted or reproduced
or utilised in any form or by any electronic, mechanical, or other
means, now known or hereafter invented, including photocopying and
recording, or in any information storage or retrieval system, without
permission in writing from the publishers.

Trademark notice: Product or corporate names may be trademarks
or registered trademarks, and are used only for identification and
explanation without intent to infringe.

British Library Cataloguing-in-Publication Data
A catalogue record for this book is available from the British Library

Library of Congress Cataloging-in-Publication Data
Names: Bradley, Tamsin, author. | Gruber, Janet, author.
Title: Prevention of violence against women and girls : mainstreaming
in development programmes / Tamsin Bradley and Janet Gruber.
Description: 1 Edition. | New York : Routledge, 2021. |
Series: Rethinking development | Includes bibliographical
references and index.
Subjects: LCSH: Women—Violence against. | Girls—Violence against. |
Gender mainstreaming.
Classification: LCC HV6250.4.W65 B723 2021 (print) |
LCC HV6250.4.W65 (ebook) | DDC 363.32082—dc23
LC record available at https://lccn.loc.gov/2021010865
LC ebook record available at https://lccn.loc.gov/2021010866

ISBN: 978-0-367-23588-8 (hbk)
ISBN: 978-0-367-23584-0 (pbk)
ISBN: 978-0-429-28060-3 (ebk)

DOI: 10.4324/9780429280603

Typeset in Bembo
by codeMantra

For dearest Ottilie, in the hope that she and all other girls will grow into women in a world free from violence

To Megan I am already so proud of you, keep pushing for what you know is right.

CONTENTS

List of figures	*xi*
List of tables	*xiii*
Acknowledgements	*xv*

	Introduction	1
1	Theorising violence against women and girls	14
2	VAWG mainstreaming – a framework for action	35
3	Women, internal displacement, and violence in Nepal and Myanmar	58
4	Focus on VAWG in humanitarian emergencies: the scale of the problem and responses	72
5	VAWG prevention and response in humanitarian emergencies: an overview of current approaches and gaps in knowledge	98
6	VAWG and conflict: focus on women, peace, and security	118
7	The rule of law, women's rights, and VAWG prevention and response	140

x Contents

8   How to mainstream VAWG across sectors: two examples
from modern slavery and sustainable energy programming   166

9   Funding for VAWG prevention and response: gaps and
opportunities   187

    Conclusion: the Covid-19 pandemic and implications for
VAWG prevention and response and gender equality   201

Index   *215*

FIGURES

1.1	The ecological model	16
1.2	Intersectional dimensions and the ecological model	17
2.1	Intervention and mechanism process	41
2.2	With this knowledge in place…	42
2.3	The ecological model	43
2.4	Questions to guide the creation of an enabling environment to support action against VAWG	45
2.5	Questions to guide understanding of what kind of social norm change interventions might be appropriate	46
2.6	Questions to guide increasing social perceptions of the value and benefit of women's full and equal participation in life	47
2.7	Theory sequence linked to the VAWG Mainstreaming Framework	48
4.1	IDPs in 2019	77

TABLES

2.1	The power quartet	40
2.2	Critical and reflective questions to ask throughout the design stage	42
2.3	Using the ecological model for access to justice programming	44
3.1	Number of participants from each site (female and male)	66
5.1	Using the ecological model in humanitarian emergencies	109
8.1	Applying the ecological model in approaches to respond to energy need	171
8.2	Applying the ecological model to modern slavery contexts	183

ACKNOWLEDGEMENTS

Our thanks go to a trio of former and current Routledge staff members. Firstly to Louisa Vahtrick, former Anthropology Editor, who gave the initial encouragement for the book when we three discussed the idea at the 2016 Association of Social Anthropologists of the UK's conference at Durham University. Helena Hurd, Editor, Development Studies, continued the support. Matthew Shobbrook, Editorial Assistant, Environment and Sustainability and Development Studies, has been a real tower of strength and patience, working closely with us during the development of the book; his inputs and professional focus are very much appreciated.

Massive thanks go to George Byrne for his professionalism and patience copy editing the volume. The book would not be as strong as it is without his dedication and hard work.

INTRODUCTION

This volume argues that now is the time for a truly concerted effort to bring an end to violence against women and girls (VAWG). In the past decade, we have seen an increased global focus on ending VAWG in all its forms. However, given the extent and scope of violence, which reaches into the lives of so many women and girls across the world, a siloed approach to programming is no longer sufficient. If we are to finally see any real reductions in overall global levels of violence, VAWG must be addressed across development and humanitarian emergency sectors, including, but not limited to, Women, Peace, and Security (WPS), health, and sustainable energy programming.

As the chapters in this volume show, regardless of the development context or the primary humanitarian issue being addressed, violence can also be responded to – and indeed should be – because VAWG is everywhere. It cuts across development sectors and intersects with issues of gender, access, and vulnerability. The rallying cry of the Sustainable Development Goals is to *Leave no one behind*, and to do so requires developing a closer understanding of who the most marginal are as well as how they are marginalised. We know that those most vulnerable to violence also tend to be least able to gain access to support, advocacy and resources, and this can further erode women's resilience, even where they have agency and courage.

As we discuss in this Introduction, the notion of 'gender mainstreaming' has become a ubiquitous feature of development. Gender programming has become a central component of development planning and is based on the understanding that power relations underpin a person's ability to resist harm and claim access to resources, education and employment, and health services. Women and girls fare less well because of how gender operates and shapes these power relations. Increasingly, we know that certain groups of men and boys are also systematically excluded from opportunities. Violence is a mechanism used by many, either to

DOI: 10.4324/9780429280603

2 Introduction

maintain power structures that benefit them or to express deep frustration at the injustices that leave them unable to live a life of dignity. For this reason, VAWG is an ever-present force that operates to maintain structures of power and a status quo that benefits the very few. While gender mainstreaming has pointed the spotlight on these structural inequalities and the power dynamics behind them, it has failed to transform them in a sustained and meaningful way. This volume argues that it is now necessary to focus on VAWG because violence is the key means through which gender inequalities are embedded and upheld in society.

Before we develop this central argument further, let us first review how VAWG is defined for the purposes of this volume.

Definitions of violence

This volume uses the VAWG definition applied in the United Nations (UN) Declaration on the Elimination of Violence Against Women (DEVAW), which is:

> any act of gender-based violence that results in, or is likely to result in, physical, sexual or psychological harm or suffering to women, including threats of such acts, coercion or arbitrary deprivation of liberty, whether occurring in public or in private life.
>
> *(UN, 1993)*

However, across the globe, definitions of violence vary substantially; violence is a concept used to categorise certain forms of interpersonal behaviour, and, as such, it is subject to sociocultural interpretation. Some acts and structures viewed as violent in the Global North may not be viewed as such elsewhere, and opinions about whether and how to challenge them will, therefore, vary. This diverse understanding of violence also applies to academic research, which frequently operates with different definitions according to discipline (gender studies, law, peace studies, etc.). This lack of clarity across contexts and academic fields can lead to difficulty in cross-cultural approaches to programme and policy design. Research on VAWG requires a broad definition of violence, which recognises that it is both a physical and a psychological phenomenon, and that it operates on multiple levels, from the personal to the macro-structural.

One major development partner's contribution to tackling VAWG is the global programme funded by the UK Department for International Development (DFID) – *What Works to Prevent Violence Research and Innovation Programme*, Phase I, 2016 – early 2020 (hereafter, 'What Works')[1] – which supported projects and evaluations in more than 20 countries in Africa and Asia. What Works applied a VAWG vantage point gained from the application of an ecological model (Heise, 1998, 2011; see also Scriver, Duvvury, Ashe, Raghavendra, & O'Donovan, 2015); the approach is discussed in detail in this volume, especially in Chapter 2. This theoretical perspective facilitates the understanding of violence as multidimensional, with linkages between personal, situational, sociocultural (structural) and global factors.

We argue that a mainstreaming framework needs to refine the social ecology perspective through the addition of intersectional analysis and a VAWG spectrum. In combination, these perspectives allow for a more complex and nuanced understanding of why violence happens to emerge. Within this analysis, strategies and effective action can be identified.

The global prevalence of VAWG

In order to make the argument that VAWG must now be mainstreamed across development programmes as forcefully as possible, we need to present current prevalence rates that clearly evidence the scale of the problem. Our data demonstrate that VAWG is a global challenge and that it can and does occur at any stage of a woman's life.

The following cross section of data (taken from the UN Women website) demonstrates the scale and breadth of the problem. It is estimated that 35% of women worldwide have experienced physical and/or sexual intimate partner violence (IPV) or sexual violence by a non-partner (not including sexual harassment) at some point in their lives. Some national studies show that upwards of 70% of women have experienced physical and/or sexual violence from an intimate partner in their lifetime. Evidence also shows that women who have experienced physical or sexual IPV report higher rates of depression, are more likely to have an abortion and are at an increased risk of acquiring HIV when compared to women who have not.

Similar to data from other regions, in all four countries of a multi-country study from the Middle East and North Africa, men who witnessed their fathers using violence against their mothers, and men who experienced some form of violence at home as children, were significantly more likely to report perpetrating IPV in their adult relationships. For example, in Lebanon, the likelihood of perpetrating physical violence was more than three times higher among men who had witnessed their fathers beating their mothers during childhood than those who had not.

It is estimated that of the 87,000 women around the world who were intentionally killed in 2017, more than half (approximately 50,000) were killed by partners or family members, and more than a third (approximately 30,000) were killed by their current or former intimate partner. This means that 137 women across the world are killed by a partner or member of their own family every day.

Adult women account for nearly half (49%) of all human trafficking victims detected globally, and women and girls together account for 72%, with girls representing more than three quarters of all child trafficking victims. More than four out of every five trafficked women and nearly three out of every four trafficked girls are trafficked for the purpose of sexual exploitation.

Child marriage is an important factor with regard to VAWG; it often results in early pregnancy and social isolation, interrupts schooling, limits a girl's opportunities, and increases her risk of experiencing domestic violence. During

4 Introduction

the past decade, the global rate of child marriage has declined, with South Asia seeing the most significant shift from 49% to 30%. Nonetheless, 12 million girls under 18 are married each year, and in sub-Saharan Africa – where this harmful practice is most common – almost four out of ten young women were married before their eighteenth birthday. It is estimated that there are 650 million women and girls in the world today who were married before the age of 18. This means that, although some change has occurred, many women of all ages remain in relationships that began, and the power relationships of which were established, when they were children.

In the 30 countries with representative data on prevalence, at least 200 million women and girls aged 15–49 have undergone female genital mutilation (FGM). In most of these countries, the majority of girls were cut before age 5. More than 20 million women and girls in just seven countries (Egypt, Sudan, Guinea, Djibouti, Kenya, Yemen, and Nigeria) have undergone FGM perpetrated by a health care provider. Alongside patterns of migration and population movement, FGM is becoming a practice with global dimensions, particularly among migrant and refugee women and girls.

Girls and young women face particular risks with regard to VAWG. It has been estimated that 15 million adolescent girls (aged 15–19) worldwide have experienced forced sex (which includes forced sexual intercourse or other sexual acts) at some point in their life. In the vast majority of countries, adolescent girls are most at risk of forced sex by a current or former husband, partner, or boyfriend. But according to data from 30 countries, only 1% has ever sought professional help.

Childhood bullying is a global issue, with one out of three students (aged between 11 and 15 years) having been bullied by their peers at school on at least one day in the past month. Girls and boys are equally likely to experience bullying, but boys are more likely to experience physical bullying than girls, and girls are more likely to experience psychological bullying, particularly being ignored, ostracised, or subject to nasty rumours. Girls also report being made fun of because of how their face or body looks more frequently than boys. In addition to bullying, school-related gender-based violence (SRGBV) is a major obstacle to universal schooling and the right to education for girls.

In a multi-country study from the Middle East and North Africa, between 40% and 60% of women said that they had experienced street-based sexual harassment (mainly sexual comments, stalking/following, or staring/ogling), and between 31% and 64% of men said that they had carried out such acts at some point in their lives. Younger men, men with more education, and men who experienced violence as children were more likely to engage in street sexual harassment.

It should be noted that in educational settings and in the workplace, in private, in public and online, VAWG is present across developing contexts, including in 'developed' nations. For example, 23% of female university students reported having experienced sexual assault or sexual misconduct in a survey across 27 universities in the USA in 2015. Rates of reporting to campus officials, law enforcement, or others ranged from 5% to 28%, depending on the specific type of behaviour.

Online harassment is a growing concern; in the European Union (EU), one in ten women in the report has been experiencing cyber-harassment since the age of 15 (including having received unwanted, offensive, sexually explicit emails or SMS messages, or offensive, inappropriate advances on social networking sites). The risk is the highest among young women between 18 and 29 years of age.

Harassment and psychological violence in the workplace and online also overlap. For example, 82% of women parliamentarians who participated in a study conducted by the Inter-parliamentary Union in 39 countries across five regions reported having experienced some form of psychological violence (ranging from remarks, gestures, and images of a sexist or humiliating sexual nature to threats of violence and/or mobbing) while serving their terms. They cited social media as the main channel through which such psychological violence is perpetrated; nearly half of those surveyed (44%) reported having received death, rape, assault, or abduction threats against them or their families. Sixty-five per cent had been subjected to sexist remarks, primarily by male colleagues in parliament, from opposing parties and also their own. Results from an Australian national survey show that almost two out of five women (39%) aged 15 and older who have been in the workforce in the last five years have experienced sexual harassment in the workplace during that period, compared to one in four (26%) of their male counterparts. Conversely, in almost four out of five cases (79%), one or more of the perpetrators were male.

Despite these shocking statistics, the UN Women has highlighted that, in many parts of the world, programming to prevent and respond to VAWG is inadequate or non-existent. The website states that:

> In the majority of countries with available data, less than 40 per cent of the women who experience violence seek help of any sort. Among women who do, most look to family and friends and very few look to formal institutions and mechanisms, such as police and health services. Less than 10 per cent of those women seeking help for experience of violence sought help by appealing to the police.
>
> *(UN Women, 2020)*

Clearly, then, there is a disparity between the realities of violence in the lives of women and girls and the efforts being made to reduce it. There has been a global shift towards countries adopting laws against various forms of VAWG (for example, at least 144 countries have passed laws on domestic violence, and 154 have laws on sexual harassment), but as UN Women highlights, even when laws exist, this does not mean that they are always compliant with international standards and recommendations or implemented (see Chapter 7 for further discussion).

6 Introduction

Legislation in and of itself is not sufficient to bring about the transformation needed. Instead, those working in the VAWG space call now for a holistic approach that includes lobbying of politicians and judicial officials to hold them to account and to ensure that laws are properly implemented. It also includes an array of different approaches to prevent VAWG, and services to respond when prevention has failed. Such approaches need to be connected and coordinated at various levels with the facilitation of lesson sharing across contexts. We argue in this volume that pushing for a mainstreaming approach to VAWG will hugely contribute towards achievement of this more holistic approach.

How might VAWG mainstreaming differ from gender mainstreaming?

Gender mainstreaming as an approach emerged following the fourth World Women's Conference held in Beijing in 1995. Following the conference, organisations across the development sector were encouraged to incorporate gender into their internal and external structures. As pointed out by Moser and Moser (2005), this did not happen seamlessly and faced many challenges, not least due to the confusion as to what mainstreaming gender should mean in practice. Gender was often interpreted as the need to include women, but theoretical work understands gender more as a unit of analysis used to unpack power relations in order to ensure the most marginalised can access opportunities and services (de Waal, 2006).

Studies such as those conducted by Meer (2005) and Mannell (2012) point to the gap between what was promised by donors and governments to support the integration of gender and the realities that left 'gender units' and 'gender focal points' often underfunded and without the visibility needed to make any real political inroads. In practice, though, gender mainstreaming has all too often been implemented in the form of training, which is designed to encourage organisations to better account for the needs of women in their planning and activities. But there is little evidence that having the tools to end, or at least confront, the systematic inequalities that women and girls face necessarily translated into increased motivation to do so. What is evident, however, is that without significant and sustained commitment, gender inequalities will not be reversed.

Walby (2005) saw gender mainstreaming as a critical feminist tool in triggering a change in power dynamics. Something, then, has been lost in the translation of gender mainstreaming into the workings of organisations; in some cases, it is now seemingly reduced to simple head counting (i.e. documenting how many men and women are reached by a project) or sometimes ignored altogether. This situation is a far cry from the feminist tool to mobilise around women's rights envisaged at the Beijing conference. Perhaps part of the problem is that we have seen something of a backlash against the term 'gender mainstreaming' because it has been identified by those outside of the feminist movement as a feminist tool (Tiessen, 2007). Development practitioners that do not operate with a feminist lens have perhaps failed to understand the value in using such a framework for the benefit of both men and women, as well as whole communities. Or rather, as Mannell (2012) points out, the relational dimension to gender is a critical part of understanding how power dynamics negatively affect the lives of women and many men. So, feminism also must not be interpreted as solely focusing on women. More appropriately, the feminist lens allows for gender to be applied critically as a relational concept for the deconstruction of power, and this requires a focus on both men and women.

In recent years, it has been argued that gender alone is not enough – that not all men and women will experience marginalisation and not to the same degree. There is a need to combine gender with an intersectional focus that drills down into who specifically is the most vulnerable to particular risks at any given time. In response to this, VAWG programming has, for a long time, incorporated considerations of race, social class/caste, age, and disability in order to identify who is most at risk and where/how to channel resources for maximum impact.

How might a switch to VAWG mainstreaming help to overcome these issues?

As the data presented above attest, VAWG in its various forms remains the major barrier to the empowerment of women and achieving the goal of gender equality. As such, if ending violence was made an integrated goal of all programming, it might well provide a much clearer and effective focus than the language of gender mainstreaming currently does. In addition to offering a more clearly defined goal, ending violence is both emotive and hard to disagree with and, therefore, it may well serve to generate greater commitment within organisations.

VAWG mainstreaming may also help to address a worrying contradiction: violence in general, but especially VAWG, is known to spike in humanitarian emergencies. However, attention to VAWG prevention and response is all too often not a priority at such times. As will be seen in Chapter 9, there are extreme shortfalls in funding for VAWG prevention and response activities in humanitarian emergencies. Working to mainstream VAWG focus into humanitarian response is an important step towards overcoming these shortfalls (see further Chapters 4 and 5). In our Conclusions, we return to this issue with reference to the invisibility of VAWG during the Covid-19 (SARS-CoV-2) pandemic. Numerous reports are emerging across the globe that suggest surges in FGM, child marriage, trafficking and domestic abuse have taken place since the pandemic began. Yet, dedicated funding to respond is lacking and, while spikes were predicted by VAWG activists, very few examples of preventative measures can be identified. Making VAWG a mainstreamed part of programme planning, implementation, and monitoring activities will help to overcome this invisibility, and it should also mean that funding will automatically be allocated to activities that serve to prevent and mitigate violence. This clear objective is a key strength of VAWG mainstreaming as it makes translating the approach into practice relatively straightforward.

8 Introduction

What does a VAWG mainstreaming approach look like?

In order to illustrate what a VAWG Mainstreaming Framework looks like, we have developed a tool, which is framed around a series of questions covering each stage of the development process from design, to implementation, to the monitoring and evaluation of an intervention (for more details, see Chapter 2). These questions are intended to provoke reflection and create space for practitioners to think through the implications (positive and negative) for any proposed programme. One such question is whether there are specific activities connected with the development focus that may represent insecurity and vulnerability for women and girls? For example, in relation to water, sanitation, and hygiene (WASH), going to the toilet may involve significant risk if the toilet block is far from home and is unlit. We argue that regardless of what the focus of the programme or intervention is, there will always be elements and activities that pose a potential risk to women and girls. Identifying from the start what these might be allows for timely and appropriate consideration of how such risk might be mitigated, rather than addressing the issues as they arise. In many cases, the mitigation might cost very little if planned for early. To continue with our example, reducing the risk of violence in a WASH intervention might simply involve positioning a toilet block in a safe, well-lit area, which is much more cost-efficient than moving the toilet block and/or addressing instances of violence as they happen. The approach we propose is not least about sensitising all to the high prevalence of different forms of violence and the intersections between violence and broader development concerns.

In this volume, we combine the exploration of country contexts with the consideration of different development and humanitarian emergency sectors. We critically apply the social ecology model alongside an intersectional approach in order to understand where and how violence emerges in relation to specific issues. These include environmental displacement, humanitarian emergency, the WPS Agenda, the rule of law, modern slavery (particularly regarding readymade garments and commercial sexual exploitation), sustainable energy, funding mechanisms, and VAWG-specific programming. In order to do so, we have reviewed the situation in many countries and offer a degree of comparison and synthesising of evidence. We review the contexts of countries and continents, including Africa and South Asia (e.g. South Sudan, Rwanda, Kenya, Nepal, Myanmar, India, and Bangladesh), while also referring to evidence and initiatives from the UK, Latin America, and elsewhere. In doing so, we intend to underscore the importance of contextualising VAWG as well as demonstrating that VAWG is a global challenge and one that requires an urgent and sustained response.

Chapter summaries

In Chapter 1, we take a theoretical look at the conceptualisation of gender and feminism in the design of VAWG programming. We review the influential social ecology model and argue that an adapted version works well as a VAWG mainstreaming tool. In this chapter, we present a political economy and intersectional lens as important dimensions to the adapted model we propose. We apply the lens to several country contexts (South Sudan, Zambia, Ghana, South Africa, Pakistan, and Nepal) in order to demonstrate the importance of identifying how the distinct history and political-economic make-up of a country shapes the environment in which certain types of VAWG are more or less prevalent and in which certain interventions are more or less likely to work. Part of this analysis has to involve consideration of the social and cultural norms that legitimise VAWG. While these norms are fundamentally shaped by patriarchy, the ways in which they will play out in a given context will differ. We end this chapter by arguing that sensitisation to the ecology of violence needs to drive development programming and is at the heart of the mainstreaming approach we advocate.

Chapter 2 builds upon the first chapter by focusing on how we envisage a VAWG Mainstreaming Framework operating in practice. We expand the central argument of the volume: that if we are finally to end VAWG, then this commitment needs to be embedded into all development and humanitarian emergency programmes, regardless of sectoral focus. Women and girls are vulnerable across the board, and recognition of this reality is the first step. The VAWG Mainstreaming Framework proposed in this chapter clarifies how to position a VAWG lens at the centre of development programming, irrespective of sector and priorities. We provide further evidence of the need for such a lens and then present the various stages of the approach. Finally, the chapter sets out how the framework should be applied in practice and in two programme areas: micro finance and HIV/Aids. These two examples serve to demonstrate its applicability across development issues.

Chapter 3 is based on primary data collected as part of a project exploring links between women, violence, and environment-forced displacement in Myanmar and Nepal. In both contexts, displacement has occurred as a result of specific events (earthquakes in Nepal and cyclones in Myanmar), which have compounded annual patterns of displacement triggered by flooding. Quantitative and qualitative data demonstrate that instances of VAWG, already very common in both countries, increase in the wake of forced displacement. IPV in particular increases, partly due to the stress experienced as a result of homes being destroyed and livelihoods being lost. The data also point to a lack of acknowledgement among key stakeholders that violence represents an urgent issue that needs to be responded to as part of the relief efforts. The evidence presented in this chapter once again supports the volume's argument that VAWG must be mainstreamed in humanitarian emergency efforts. To conclude the chapter, we offer an overview of how this could be approached in this context.

Chapter 4 is the first of two chapters that discusses VAWG prevention and response in the context of humanitarian emergencies. We begin by setting out definitions of what constitutes a 'humanitarian emergency', which leads into an examination of the impact of these events, including the numbers of people whose lives are disrupted, affected, and often changed forever. We consider the different ways in which VAWG and gender-based violence (GBV) are described by those responding to a humanitarian emergency, and the implications of such imprecision. By looking at a number of key global initiatives, we provide an overview of the extent to which the global community succeeds in providing support and redress to VAWG survivors in the extraordinarily challenging environment of a humanitarian emergency. Focus here is on multi-partner and multilateral efforts.

Chapter 5 continues the focus on humanitarian emergencies. We shift our focus to the current priorities, as well as some of the gaps, in humanitarian emergency response planning and support efforts and the implications of this for VAWG. One issue considered in relation to the 'humanitarian aid architecture' is the extent to which structures, ways of theorising, and ways of implementing assistance effectively address (or fail to address) VAWG. We look at why so much of the literature is still gender blind, and again consider what that means for effective approaches to VAWG prevention and response. The current hot topic of localisation is reviewed, as are the extent to which intersectionality and opportunities for social norm change specific to VAWG are, or are not, part of a humanitarian emergency response. We review the literature and identify gaps in knowledge and conclude with a preliminary application of our proposed VAWG Mainstreaming Framework to the context of humanitarian emergencies.

Chapter 6 considers responses to VAWG in conflict and post-conflict situations, using the example of the emergence and development of the WPS Agenda since the ground-breaking UN Security Council Resolution (UNSCR) 1325 in 2000. At the core of this chapter is how civil society, primarily women's rights advocates, was the driving force behind the creation of the WPS Agenda and how this impetus continues to resonate throughout WPS action. We critically examine UNSCR 1325 and nine further WPS Resolutions, as well as UNSCR 2272, which addresses sexual exploitation and abuse by the UN peacekeepers. We then turn our attention to 1325/WPS National Action Plans and the International Criminal Court and what these have achieved to date. Gaps in the WPS Agenda are considered in detail and the adequacy or otherwise of targeted funding to support WPS is reviewed, as are two conflict-related sexual violence (CRSV) initiatives: UN Action and the UK-funded Prevention of Sexual Violence in Conflict Initiative (PSVI).

Chapter 7 addresses the rule of law, which includes international mechanisms, principles and national laws, how individual countries address such matters and whether any such actions have led to reduction of VAWG, and wider gender inequality. We shine a spotlight on actions such as the 1979 Convention on the Elimination of All Forms of Discrimination Against Women (CEDAW), Beijing 1995 and the degree of SDG focus on VAWG. We look at the due diligence principle and how that informs legal efforts to prevent and respond to VAWG. National-level laws that prohibit and criminalise what continues to be widely defined as 'domestic violence' are considered in terms of their reach, efficacy, and genuine gender focus. Femicide, the gaps between legal instruments (policy) and social norms (practice) are considered, as is the current situation regarding legal and state responsiveness to VAWG in the UK. We include an extended case study of Rwanda, its governmental and legal responses to VAWG and societal norms and barriers to its reduction. The chapter concludes with consideration of a number of gaps in both evidence and response.

Chapter 8 returns to the VAWG Mainstreaming Framework and offers further sectoral examples of how it can be applied. We draw on two sets of primary qualitative data collected as part of the evaluation for a sustainable energy programme in Kenya and from a programme targeted at ending modern slavery in Bangladesh and India. The focus on sustainable energy helps to illustrate how VAWG intersects with development programming regardless of focus. Research presented in this chapter highlights, for example, the risk of rape associated with women collecting wood in refugee camps in Kenya. Minimising the need for firewood collection through the provision of better solar cooking options is one way to mitigate this while maintaining a focus on sustainable energy. A mainstreaming approach allows for this and other instances to be identified and incorporated into the delivery of the intervention. In relation to modern slavery, which is in itself an act of violence, a VAWG lens makes it possible to see how various forms of violence intersect and become gendered in an environment of bonded or forced labour (e.g. work-based harassment, insecurity travelling to and from work, 'domestic violence' due to overcrowding and insanitary living arrangements). Programming to promote and achieve better working conditions needs to focus on prevention of such violence.

Chapter 9 looks at the inadequacy of funding dedicated to VAWG prevention and response in both development and humanitarian emergency assistance. To highlight such shortfalls, the UN Office for the Co-ordination of Humanitarian Affairs (UN OCHA) estimates that 1% of all funding for humanitarian emergencies worldwide is dedicated to 'sexual and gender-based violence prevention and response activities' (2019 data).

Much funding for VAWG prevention and response is categorised in aggregate under 'gender equality'. While total sums may appear huge, further examination (e.g. of data generated by UN OCHA) throws up issues of concern (see, e.g., UN OCHA, 2019). These include wasted opportunities for tracking spend vis-à-vis reach and effectiveness – for gender equality interventions and even more so for VAWG-focused work. We critically examine these issues and also existing funding modalities, as well as newer actions, such as the Risk-informed Early Action Partnership (REAP) set up in 2019. We consider new players and new approaches (e.g. public-private partnerships) in the gender equality and VAWG fields, and we address a number of existing and emerging challenges. We end by discussing where next for funding advocacy.

For reasons solely of space, we have been unable to include a chapter on advocacy in this volume. Our work on advocacy specific to VAWG prevention and response has led us to reconsider what advocacy and activism are, what they require, what they seek to do, and the ongoing challenges and current areas of focus. We note the immense contributions made during the past decades by civil society organisations (CSOs) (including women's rights organisations – WROs)

12 Introduction

and women's movements across the world to VAWG prevention and response advocacy. These are often small organisations that are underfunded with short-term, precarious money flows, and their work frequently receives far too little notice.

We shall seek to publish our text on the subject of advocacy in a peer-reviewed and open access journal in 2021, linking our proposed VAWG Mainstreaming Framework to advocacy and activism on VAWG prevention and response. Examples will be given of successful global, sectoral, national, and community-led advocacy initiatives. Our sectoral focus will be on health and advocacy[2]. Much has been achieved in the past 50 years in terms of gender equality and women's rights, including the right to live free from violence. Yet, the need for vigilance remains. Backlash and retrograde actions are ever-present dangers, as is exemplified by the Trump administrations further tightening of the Mexico City Protocol, the so-called 'Global Gag Rule'. In the paper, we shall conclude by examining a few of the gaps identified by advocates, activists, practitioners, policymakers, and academics in VAWG prevention and response.

Notes

1 Phase II of What Works will go ahead, funded under the auspices of the Foreign, Commonwealth and Development Office, into which DFID was merged in late 2020.
2 The advocacy paper will provide in-depth review of the Rwanda *Isange* One-Stop Centres and the South African *Thuthuzela* Care Centres. Both initiatives seek to provide comprehensive health and psychosocial services, access to appropriately trained police officers and legal support. Chapter 7 does not include discussion of the *Isange* OSC programme as part of the Rwanda case study, for reasons of chapter focus as well as space constraints.

References

de Waal, M. D. (2006). Evaluating gender mainstreaming in development projects. *Development in Practice, 16*(2), 209–214. https://doi.org/10.1080/09614520600562454

Heise, L. (1998). Violence against women: An integrated, ecological framework. *Violence Against Women, 4*(3), 262–290. https://doi.org/10.1177/1077801298004003002

Heise, L. (2011). *What Works to Prevent Partner Violence? An Evidence Overview.* DFID. http://strive.lshtm.ac.uk/resources/what-works-prevent-partner-violence-evidence-overview

Mannell, J. (2012). 'It's just been such a horrible experience.' Perceptions of gender mainstreaming by practitioners in South African organisations. *Gender & Development, 20*(3), 423–434. https://doi.org/10.1080/13552074.2012.731753

Meer, S. (2005). Freedom for women: Mainstreaming gender in the South African liberation struggle and beyond. *Gender & Development, 13*(2), 36–45. https://doi.org/10.1080/13552070512331332285

Moser, C., & Moser, A. (2005). Gender mainstreaming since Beijing: A review of success and limitations in international institutions. *Gender and Development, 13*(2), 11–22. https://doi.org/10.1080/13552070512331332283

Scriver, S., Duvvury, N., Ashe, S., Raghavendra, S., & O'Donovan, D. (2015). *Conceptualising Violence: A Holistic Approach to Understanding Violence against Women and Girls* (Working Paper). What Works to Prevent Violence against Women and Girls. https://www.whatworks.co.za/resources/evidence-reviews/item/85-conceptualising-violence-a-holistic-approach-to-understanding-violence-against-women-and-girls

Tiessen, R. (2007). *Everywhere/Nowhere: Gender Mainstreaming in Development Agencies*. West Hartford, CT: Kumarian Press.

UN. (1993). *Declaration on the Elimination of Violence against Women* (General Assembly resolution 48/104 of 20 December 1993). United Nations. https://www.ohchr.org/EN/ProfessionalInterest/Pages/ViolenceAgainstWomen.aspx

UN OCHA. (2019). *Gender-Based Violence: A Closer Look at the Numbers*. https://www.unocha.org/story/gender-based-violence-closer-look-numbers

UN Women. (2020). *Facts and Figures: Ending Violence against Women*. https://www.unwomen.org/en/what-we-do/ending-violence-against-women/facts-and-figures

Walby, S. (2005). Gender mainstreaming: Productive tensions in theory and practice. *Social Politics: International Studies in Gender, State & Society, 12*(3), 321–343. https://doi.org/10.1093/sp/jxi018

1

THEORISING VIOLENCE AGAINST WOMEN AND GIRLS

Introduction

In recent years, there has been a rapid growth in global awareness of violence against women and girls (VAWG), which is illustrated by the visibility of international campaigns such as #MeToo, #HeforShe, and the annual '16 Days of Activism'. It has made this moment in history feel like a particularly important time for programming that seeks to end VAWG, and the momentum to achieve change feels more sustainable, now, than at any point in the past. These movements have provided further evidence of the crucial role of end-VAWG programming, and, along with the shocking spikes in violence triggered by Covid-19 lockdowns,[1] they have given renewed impetus to providing support at a much greater scale. As such, 'scaling up' interventions to end VAWG now represent a key challenge. The translation of this crucial moment into practical transformation in countries with exceptionally high prevalence rates is dependent on a multitude of different factors. While no overarching set of criteria can explain VAWG across the globe, a growing body of research across multiple disciplines, geographical locations, and cultural spaces means that we are increasingly able to learn lessons regarding what works in different contexts. With the help of continued rigorous research and the application of certain tried and tested frameworks, we can apply such lessons and effective approaches to other contexts. As such, this chapter sets out the theoretical discourses that have influenced and shaped approaches to VAWG programming. We argue that, despite the increased focus at the global level on the relationship between gender and violence, scaled interventions to end VAWG require more careful and precise targeting of resources backed by evidence of what works best at the local level.

In this chapter, we set out the interconnected theoretical approaches that have influenced (positively and less so) our work on the VAWG Mainstreaming

DOI: 10.4324/9780429280603-1

Framework. The chapter is structured as follows: first, we provide a brief overview of the ways in which attention to VAWG prevention and response have been shaped by feminist theory and activism since the 1970s, which is deeply rooted in earlier actions for gender equality. We then address the ecological model, which has been particularly informative in our work on VAWG Mainstreaming and various adaptions of which have been developed to widen its scope. We present an adapted version of the ecological model, designed to help practitioners to pinpoint who the most vulnerable are in any given situation.[2] We then shift our focus to social norms, embedded as these are in the social and ecological contexts of people's lives. We consider the use of political economy analysis (PEA) and political analysis (PA): two distinct, but inter-related, theoretical approaches to development and humanitarian assistance. These all too often neglect issues of gender in political, economic, and power analyses; we argue that such gaps matter and must be rectified. In highlighting the importance of a political approach to understanding VAWG, we give six country examples (Ghana, Zambia, South Africa, Pakistan, Nepal, and South Sudan).

Feminist approaches to VAWG prevention since 1970: operationalising gender in VAWG programming

Interventions to prevent and end VAWG are informed by a set of theoretical approaches that link gendered power dynamics to household and community relationships. While development programmes with elements that focus on women and girls, including the violence they endure, have existed longer, 'gender mainstreaming' has been around since the 1980s. It refers to a process that seeks to ensure that actions within and across different development sectors also promote gender equality. Gender mainstreaming was initially heralded as an effective way to understand and respond to social inequalities, and 40 years on, gender is now broadly considered to be a necessary part of the design, implementation, monitoring, and evaluation of development programmes. But despite this, gendered violence persists, which casts doubt on the extent to which 'mainstreaming' has truly been achieved (Mukhopadhyay, 2016). As such, a VAWG lens must also be mainstreamed into development programming in order to drive deep structural change.

Feminist theory has provided a lens through which to understand how gender relations and the power that weaves through them legitimise VAWG. And in order to shed light on why, even in the wake of gender mainstreaming, women and girls continue to experience so much violence, since the late 1970s feminist theorists have developed models to explain VAWG. These invariably focus on patriarchy as the foundation for male oppression of women (Dobash & Dobash, 1979). For example, the phrase 'the personal is the political' was used to emphasise the need to address VAWG (and specifically Intimate Partner Violence – IPV) at the level of policy, not to see it as a private 'domestic' matter. Policy and legal remedies have been seen as mechanisms to bring violence into the public sphere (Maguigan, 2003), but, as Walker (1979) stated, no single route would be adequate in responding to and ending VAWG. Instead, a multi-level systematic approach is needed, combining legal responses with safe exit options and campaigns to challenge gender stereotypes that render women submissive and inferior to men. Logically, then, a gendered perspective is fundamental to VAWG programming, both to inform its design and to monitor structural shifts in patterns of inequality.

Phase I of the DFID-funded What Works to Prevent VAWG programme (2016–2020) demonstrated how critical it is to link VAWG and gender, not just to understand why it happens, but also to shape future programming in ways that maximise opportunities to end VAWG.

The adapted ecological model

The most often applied framework for understanding why and how violence persists in the lives of women is Heise's (1998) ecological model (see also Heise, 2011, and for the expansion of the ecological model to the global level, see Fulu & Miedema, 2015). The model depicted below divides the constructed environment into different spheres that interlock in ways that can help to explain why violence happens. It demonstrates that activism with the goal of changing or reversing patterns of violence needs to happen at each social level. The outer sphere of the model is the socio-cultural level, within which the values that shape social norms that legitimise violence against women are situated. These then shape the gendered relationships at community and household levels and influence the behaviour of perpetrators at the individual level as well as the experiences of survivors (Figure 1.1).

Arguably, however, these spheres cannot sufficiently explain why some groups of women seem to be more vulnerable to violence than others. An array of intersecting factors come into play that can determine the extent of risk a woman

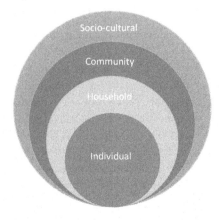

FIGURE 1.1 The ecological model.

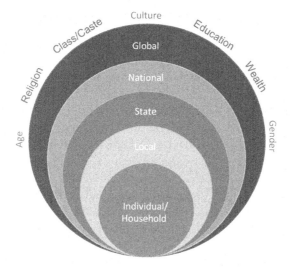

FIGURE 1.2 Intersectional dimensions and the ecological model.

might face, while her resilience can be linked to the coping mechanisms she can access that enable her to mitigate and reduce those risks.

Figure 1.2 shows the differing horizontal and vertical intersectional dimensions that cut across the various spheres of the ecological model and help us to understand the relative experiences and identify the resources available to different women across contexts.

These dimensions include, but are not limited to, class, caste, religion, culture, age, gender, socio-economic status, and levels of disability. The practical application of this intersectional ecological model, then, can help to inform a more nuanced understanding of the multiple levels and layers through which violence is perpetrated and legitimised. The weaving of an intersectional lens through the model also helps practitioners to ensure that no marginalised group is left behind. In Chapter 2, we provide a detailed, stage by stage consideration of how to apply the ecological model in the context of our proposed VAWG Mainstreaming Framework. But here, we move to consider the norms that underpin specific gendered relations that render women and girls vulnerable to violence.

Social norms

The previous section outlined the social ecology model, which helps us unpick the operationalisation of violence in our daily lives. However, what the model does not do is fully appreciate how it is sustained. How and why do the gendered power structures within each of its spheres remain intact? The answer put simply is the existence of gendered social norms that influence the lens through which we see the world and how we behave within it. Before moving into an analysis

18 Theorising violence

of how social norms are maintained, it is important to be clear about what we are referring to. Bradley (2020) offers a detailed summary of how social norms are defined and the various theoretical perspectives developed to help explain them. Essentially, 'a social norm is a perception of where a social group is or where the social group ought to be on some dimension of attitude or behaviour' (Ball, Paluck, Poynton, & Sieloff, 2010, p. 9). Norms are linked to sanctions that are put in place at various levels and that operate to maintain a collective normative view or perception. Campaigns to end VAWG continue to be underpinned by a critical focus that seeks to understand how norms are changed. According to Harper and Marcus (2014), change happens when a new norm becomes more widely adopted than an old one, but what is needed to trigger the rise of new norms is far from clear. For many working to end VAWG, these triggers have become the most critical issue. This is because VAWG programmes tend to be founded on the belief (or rather the *hope*) that if we understand the causes of violence better, we can act to end it.

This 'knowledge, attitudes, and practice' (KAP) strategy is focused very much on changing individual behaviours, but research has shown that the linear process of individual change that was envisaged simply does not materialise (see e.g., Westoff, 1988). Thus, despite concerted efforts, rates of VAWG remain stubbornly high. Moreover, new forms of violence frequently emerge, sometimes as a result of apparent progress towards gender equality, such as a backlash against women achieving well in the workplace or assuming roles traditionally in the domain of men (see True, 2012). As Bradley (2020) argues, knowledge alone is not sufficient: perpetrators of VAWG continue their violence even in contexts where there is a high level of acceptance that violence is wrong. Female Genital Mutilation (FGM) is a pertinent example: a family may commit publicly to stopping it but then continue the practice privately. In our research, we have seen countless examples across multiple contexts of women who remain in violent situations, despite having the knowledge and even the attitude that violence is 'wrong' and that it is not 'normal' (see, e.g., Bank, Michau, Horn, Dutt, & Zimmerman, 2015). For example, in Chapter 3, mothers-in-law emerge as the most numerous perpetrators of violence, which is contrary to the data that typically highlights the prevalence of IPV in particular. The irony is that many of the mothers-in-law who are now perpetrators of violence will likely have suffered domestic abuse as children, young wives, and mothers. At certain points in their lives, then, women are also part of the cycle of propagating gendered norms around violence.

We agree with those scholars who state that understanding the link between social norms and violence is critical (Heise, Ellsberg, & Gottmoeller, 1999). However, in line with Bradley (2020), we argue that caution is necessary when using some of the approaches found within social norm theory. Individual behaviours are defined as 'normative' because they are applied by a significant number of people within a given context. The behaviours are then linked to cultural views around why they continue. For example, a man hitting his wife

Theorising violence **19**

because he believes all men do this is a social norm, while believing that not to do so would bring his masculinity into question is a cultural view. Social sanctions also operate to ensure that particular 'accepted' behaviours can flourish without conflict or contradiction. In some contexts, violence can persist because women do not want to report it and bring shame to their family. Instead, women accept abuse as normative rather than risk shaming those on whom they are often dependent.

Attempts to reverse norms can be categorised into two main approaches. First is the creation and use of social movements to drive a different discourse and transformation, and second is the promotion of positive role models. These can range from global celebrities to community and/or religious leaders, who, through their adoption and promotion of new norms, are thought to be able to influence their community (see Bedri & Bradley, 2017). These two approaches are presented in a highly optimistic light. In its report on social norms, UNICEF stated that when programmes are holistic and community-based, enshrining human rights is likely to occur, which will be followed by the transformation of social norms (Mackie, 2000; Mackie, Moneti, Shakaya, & Denny, 2015). This implies a somewhat linear set of processes that will magically generate the change desired. But the more likely reality is that embedded power relations will maintain ways of thinking through a complex system of violently imposed sanctions and stigma that adapts to political and economic change. Attention also needs to focus on the influence of the political and economic context (which we come to below), because even when new ideologies emerge that support an end to localised violence, transformation is often slow or non-existent. Violence will only end when there is a commitment to confronting it throughout the social ecology across global, national, local, and individual levels.

As Bradley (2020) argues, an excessive focus on social norms/mind-sets is unable to come to grips with what sustains violence or what can end it because such approaches cannot unpack the dynamic interaction of social relationships, power, institutions, and the environmental dimensions that shape perceptions, attitudes, and behaviours. In other words, social norm theory alone fails to help us understand how the norms that exist result in the dominance of patriarchy. What role do they play in the construction of relationships and institutional structures? We know that violence exists both in a structural institutional sense through the exclusion of women from many domains and positions, and in a physical sense through various acts of abuse across public and private spaces. As such, mapping the various locations and levels of violence is important, but to go beyond this, Bradley, Martin, and Parliwala (forthcoming) suggest a combination of approaches and models. For example, Bourdieu's concept of *habitus* (1977) pushes us to focus on the dynamics of the different spheres and types of relationships that sustain violence. *Habitus* conceptualises social life as a constantly changing series of relationships held together by structures that are imposed by norms, power, and authority. *Habitus* can be both an organising tool and a theoretical lens through which to understand the social realities for different groups of women and to capture how change manifests and impacts. Understanding the complexity of how different forms of violence feed on each other and link to symbolic, structural, and behavioural dimensions is critical if violence is to be replaced with gender equality. However, in drawing on the idea of *habitus*, Bradley, Martin, and Parliwala recognise the need to exercise analytical caution to move beyond linear or circular assumptions. Contradictions can be seen at all levels, including individual viewpoints and ideologies – and they are constantly in flux. Thus, governments will shift commitment on human rights, depending on economic priorities and political will, or an individual woman may challenge violence in the workplace but accept her husband beating her at home. Appreciating how and where individual agency emerges in a sustained form and feeds into collective action for change is critical.

Applying Bourdieu's theory, we begin to see certain gendered behaviours and perceptions as symbolic violence, because of how they ultimately render women as inferior and vulnerable. Connell's (1995) argument regarding the need to appreciate how power operates shows how power relations are often concealed, meaning that violence may not clearly manifest itself. Relating experiences to *habitus* makes it possible to understand the intersections of the symbolic and physical realities of how violence plays out, regardless of how and when agency is exercised. The symbolic and physical realities become embedded in the *habitus* of individuals, leading them to accept violence as an integral part of society, and potentially perpetuate it further.

As Bradley (2020) points out, the notion that men should be the main bread winners, meaning that women can only work in lower paid roles that require fewer skills and thereby cannot challenge the breadwinning status of husbands, is pervasive. Women who travel in public without husbands are often considered shameful and are believed to be likely to cheat and are, therefore, 'asking' for harassment: this is a widely held belief. That women should expect to be beaten if they fail to perform their household chores correctly, regardless of whether they also work, is often taken for granted. We can continue to draw out the norms that clearly need to change if transformation is to occur but understanding how and why these expectations are maintained requires much closer consideration of context. Behaviours might be expressed at the individual level, but they are forced and reinforced by wider spheres and structures and by the relationships that bind different spheres together. In relation to the focus of this volume, we argue that gender norms shape every aspect of social life, which means any development intervention is playing into an environment in which power relations are already rigidly enforced. It is therefore essential that practitioners think through the implications of an intervention on and for the lives of the most vulnerable, even if they are not the primary focus of it. Increasing awareness of the potential harm an intervention may unintentionally bring is as important as maximising all opportunities to challenge the gender norms that sanction VAWG.

In addition to a focus on the different organisational spheres of life depicted by the social ecological model and reflecting on how and where VAWG plays out within and between them, there is also a need to identify and challenge the ideologies that sustain them. In other words, the relationships between ideological, religious, and political spheres, and the household cannot be overlooked. In light of this, attempts to disrupt such relationships have moved the end VAWG sector into engaging with men more systematically. Working with groups of men in specific locations is popular, with many interventions applying the Stepping Stones behavioural change programme. However, the evidence that such programmes bring sustainable change is somewhat flimsy because, we argue, they do not necessarily manage to dismantle patriarchal views that endorse VAWG (see, e.g., Gibbs, Jewkes, & Sikweyiya, 2017).

We firmly believe that 'underpinning' norms will shift only when women have a level of resilience and collective agency that is strong enough to respond to the backlash that change often brings. We also argue throughout this volume that dismantling these underpinning norms will only happen if the existence of VAWG as an embedded part of the lives of women and girls is properly acknowledged, which must be accompanied by a commitment to challenging it at every opportunity. That is to say, there is a need for a VAWG lens to be mainstreamed across and within all development sector programming.

The coloniality and hegemony of power: challenges from feminism[3]

Inattention to power is evident in approaches to social norm or mind-set change, which frequently bypass issues of authority. Yet, structures of authority exist to maintain a system in which an elite minority benefits at the expense of many. We argue that attention needs to be focused on the way that power layers itself through each dimension of life because individuals will only be successful in bringing about change if they can counter the power that suppresses them through the legitimisation of violence. This necessitates joint action at various levels.

Quijano first developed the concept of the 'coloniality of power' to describe the power and hegemonic control that emerged during the colonial era, the structures and systems of which continue to wield extraordinary influence (see Quijano, 2000). Hegemonic control in this context indicates how the era of Empire and colonisation further solidified constructs of superiority, power, and control, based on a Eurocentric, white, and male perception of how the world and its peoples should be ordered and controlled. Apportioning oneself such power also confers the power to objectify, oppress, and consider others as inferior. Both the coloniser and the colonised can and do adopt such beliefs and behaviours. Lugones has expanded this to focus on issues of gender: just as the coloniality of power positions people according to ideas of race, identity, and inferiority, so too does it define gender roles and relations and imposes values and norms (Lugones, 2008, 2010, 2016). Again, the coloniality of power is seen as acting to enable, increase, and reify gender and other inequalities that exist within societies, as well

22 Theorising violence

as those imposed from without. Lugones' work has been instrumental in furthering and enriching discussion of gender and violence; she argues that articulations of gender, sexuality, and race need to be understood through the prism of colonialism and its multiple and continuing effects – coloniality of the mind persists.

As we have argued with regard to intersectionality, consideration of coloniality and hegemony of power sheds light on the ways in which people are categorised and 'managed' within structures and systems. Such structures of control link into hierarchies of knowledge and resources, and control of them. When considering VAWG prevention and response, it is apparent that (too) much of the discourse and ownership of knowledge and resources is anchored in the Global North. Awareness of such imbalance has led to calls for the 'decolonisation of knowledge', and by extension, a re-balancing of access to, and control over, resources. As we describe throughout this book, financial allocations for VAWG prevention and response are extraordinarily inadequate, while access to funding for such interventions represents an often-insurmountable barrier for southern civil society organisations and networks. Furthermore, data collection, production of knowledge, and crucially use of such information continue to be profoundly influenced and shaped by the male ordering of the world (Criado-Perez, 2019 provides powerful examples of the impacts of such narrowness of vision).

Decolonisation of knowledge allows for deep focus on intersectionality. This has the potential to expose how imposed and/or externally defined knowledge and its control fail to address, let alone come near to understanding, how issues of gender inequality and VAWG are shaped by hegemonic and patriarchal structures. Here again, Lugones' views resonate: the 'presence' of dominant groups, beliefs, and norms necessitates the 'absence' of the other, of nuance, and of awareness of multiple intersections of identity (Lugones, 2008).

Context is everything: political economy analysis (PEA)

Moving from the social and cultural spheres into the political and power arena (although all are tightly enmeshed with each other and all have profound impacts on responses to VAWG), we discuss an often-used theoretical approach in development policy and practice: PEA. PEA examines the political and power structures in society and how relative proximity to, and engagement in, these will shape people's expectations, incentives, and behaviours. PEA gauges how access, or not, to political power structures will often guide responses to development challenges. This is as true for those who provide development (and humanitarian) assistance from an external perspective as it is for those who are either national and local implementers or actual recipients of aid. In some recent literature, PEA is re-defined as Political Analysis (PA), which is stated to address the political space as a more contingent area of power, agency, and process. Advocates of this approach describe PA as clarifying how existing local, national, and global political and power structures may, and often will, shape and determine how individuals and groups act with or against those systems, and what their options may be to act strategically, organise, or resist. Among the key differences is that PA is often expressed as a more local focus and that it places greater emphasis on acknowledging people's individual agency (see Hudson & Leftwich, 2014).

Despite its broad application in development practice, in recent years, PEA (and also PA) has been challenged by academics and some development practitioners because of its often complete gender blindness. Power structures, actors, agency, and formal and informal access routes to systems of power are debated and analysed in the literature as though 'people' everywhere are the same: they are seen in aggregate. Matters such as gender roles and relations, relative inequality, patriarchal systems (and very much also VAWG and the power and socio-political structures inherent in enabling such violence) appear to be viewed as irrelevant to any political and power analysis (for examples of gender-blind PEA/PA documents, see, e.g., Hudson & Marquette, 2015).

Challenging unequal power structures is increasingly seen as integral to any effective use of PEA/PA, in terms of genuinely informing and supporting gender-transformative development policy and practice. Development practitioners focusing on the intersections between PEA/PA, gender, and power point out that these links are too frequently ignored. This leads to insufficient work being done on the gender aspects of social, political, and economic power, and how these influence society, social norms, and unequal gender relations, which, in turn, limits attention to such matters in development and humanitarian assistance (see Haines & O'Neil, 2018). Patterns of violence, including conflict and war, are both shaped by and contribute to gender inequality. The Women's International League for Peace and Freedom (the oldest global women's peace and rights movement, founded in 1915) has argued that war, violence, and conflict all have their roots in, and contribute to, gender inequality. Yet, policies and international instruments to a large extent continue to ignore gender power relations that perpetuate violence and inequality, preferring to assume a level playing field (see further Cockburn, 2010, 2013).

As the focus on VAWG prevention and response has increased over the past two decades, calls for a feminist approach to PEA have also gained momentum, not only with regard to *prevention* of violence against women, but to its *eradication*. In the Women, Peace and Security (WPS) sphere and the wider development context, Jacqui True has been among the leading proponents of a feminist political economy approach to violence against women. She warns of the troubling absence of gender-focused analysis of political and economic processes, which she argues helps to perpetuate inequalities, as expressed through armed conflict, responses to humanitarian emergencies, and globalisation, for example (True, 2010; see also Davies & True, 2018, for an in-depth analysis of PEA/PA in the primary context of WPS).

The VAWG Mainstreaming Framework and a gendered PEA/PA

Much of the literature and actions on VAWG, whether sectoral or across sectors, fail to consider gender aspects of a PEA/PA approach. One reason for this is likely to be the existing political structures and systems within which the framers and

24 Theorising violence

funders of most VAWG prevention and response initiatives work. Just a few examples of such obstacles are the individual UN agency mandates, the politicised nature of much development aid (for example, the restrictions on sexual and reproductive health and rights actions by the US government in 2017 through the 'Global Gag Rule'; see CHANGE, 2018, and also Chapter 9), and the far too numerous politicians who are all too willing to respond to the perceived pressure to act against 'waves' (even 'hordes') of possible migrants, including refugees and asylum seekers. As such, we assert here that, whether work is described as PEA or PA, it will remain incomplete and inadequate if it does not address gender inequalities in access to and relations within the corridors of debate. Addressing the place and role of such spaces is contingent upon the meaningful participation, empowerment, and engagement of women and girls in framing, addressing, and acting upon VAWG.

In essence, much non-feminist or 'gender-blind' PEA/PA perpetuates 'business as usual' in terms of existing structures of power; it is almost inconceivable that any such analysis can ignore patriarchal systems and inequality based on gender and other 'difference', such as ethnicity, religion, and sexuality. And yet, it so often does. Whose voices are to be heard and whose agency supported if analysis proceeds at the level of aggregate 'people'? And whose definitions of political processes at any level are to hold sway? A truly feminist and egalitarian analysis of political and economic context would surely discuss the extent to which socio-cultural norms and patterns of inequality and oppression are interwoven and shaped by intersectional systems of power. Though linked to existing approaches to PEA/PA, this would have much wider relevance. To overlook gender in such analyses is to ignore that which is a central component of all power relations and structures and is both a cause and a manifestation of persistent inequality.

Country case studies

To summarise our discussion so far, the application of the ecological model, and taking lessons from intersectionality and the coloniality of power, tells us that the prevalence of different forms of VAWG is heavily reliant on the political economy of any given context. Thus, it is necessary for the adapted ecological model that we propose to be fully contextualised with reference to specific examples. Here, we review different legal and regulatory environments across a number of countries in which the prevalence of VAWG is exceptionally high. From these, we can see how very different operating contexts can and do have significant implications for the likely uptake of evidence on what works. We have selected six country examples in order to demonstrate how the model might be applied in order to illustrate the critical need for acknowledging and responding to the specifics of each situation and setting. The countries selected are Ghana, Zambia, South Africa, Pakistan, Nepal, and South Sudan. Comparison between these contexts also helps us to better understand why an intervention might work well in one place, but not in others.[4]

Theorising violence **25**

In all selected contexts, levels of VAWG are high, but what differs is the strength of the wider enabling environment (e.g. the existence of a robust set of legislative measures, capacity to implement prevention activities, and a responsive and transparent justice system) and the size of the economy. In each of the countries, legislation to promote gender equality and reduce some types of violence exists in some form. However, the political will to implement this legislation and the comparative visibility and strength of civil society working on VAWG differ greatly between contexts. A further dimension that adds complexity and uniqueness to different situations is the level of ethnic, religious, and cultural diversities, which shapes gendered values and beliefs and, in turn, has an impact on the likely effectiveness of specific interventions.

In terms of the economy, Ghana and Zambia are classed as lower-middle-income countries, and both have very high levels of normalised violence, especially IPV. The Ghanaian government has passed and/or amended several laws that protect the rights of women and girls, largely in response to calls for action on VAWG by activists, Non-governmental Organisations (NGOs), and the global community. These include laws providing for criminalisation of practices such as FGM and discrimination based on sex, and the 2007 Domestic Violence Act (Act 732). Widowhood rights have been addressed and, in 1998, the Women and Juveniles' Unit (WAJU) of the Ghana Police Service (currently named the Domestic Violence and Victim Support Unit - DOVVSU) was created in order to respond to domestic violence. Ghana is now about to launch a 'one stop centre' (OSC) approach. The DOVVSU of the Ghana Police Service in the capital, Accra, will be the location of the first centre. In 2008, the National Policy and Plan of Work was established in order to implement the Domestic Violence Act coordinated by the Ministry of Gender, Children and Social Protection (MoGCSP). But sources indicate that while reporting of domestic violence cases has increased, it has not correlated with an increase in prosecutions and convictions: an inadequately resourced formal justice system and a lack of logistical capacity continue to undermine access to justice (see, e.g., Adu-Gyamfi, Donkoh, & Addo, 2014). The October 2014 Shadow CEDAW Report noted that prosecutors have 'inadequate' skills to convict perpetrators of domestic violence and that the 'state's provision for access to justice is insufficient and ineffective in the key areas of prosecution, punishment and attrition' (CEDAW, 2014).

In Zambia, as with Ghana, there is an Anti-Gender-Based Violence Act (Anti-GBV Act), which was passed in 2010 and revised in 2011. Fast track GBV courts were also launched as part of the UNDP Joint Programme on GBV (March 2012–January 2016). Fifteen were created in 2016 in Kabwe, Central Province, and in Lusaka. According to the Zambian government, the courts were established in order to increase access to justice for victims. Such actions are needed: Kishor and Johnson's 2004 multi-country study found that Zambia had the highest prevalence of IPV, with 48% of ever-married women experiencing it at some point in their lives. Yet, less than half of abused women and girls (only 46%) sought help, and cited various personal, economic, and social

26 Theorising violence

concerns, especially fear of stigma as their reason for not doing so. Underpinning these high levels of VAWG are very high levels of gender inequality. The Global Gender Gap (GGG) Index ranks Zambia 116th of 145 countries (WEF, 2019a). In response to this, CARE Zambia and the European Union (EU) expanded efforts through the Coordinated Response to Sexual and Gender Based Violence in Zambia project, which ran from September 2007 to December 2011. The *A Safer Zambia* or ASAZA project also sought to reduce the incidence of VAWG through greater understanding of the types and triggers of violence and offered support for survivors, including through stronger justice mechanisms.

The Constitution of South Africa recognises that gender equality can only be achieved through dismantling patriarchal ideologies that perpetuate women's oppression, and the country's legislative and policy framework is aligned to international conventions. The Domestic Violence Act No 116 of 1998 (DVA) and the Criminal Law Sexual Offences and Related Matters Act No 32 of 2007 (SOA) are two prominent laws relating to VAWG. The National Gender Policy Framework, the Employment Equity Act (EEA), and the Promotion of Equality and Prevention of Unfair Discrimination Act (PEPUDA) directly address gender equality (Freedom House, 2017). South Africa's legal system guarantees equality to all people, and in sub-Saharan Africa, South Africa ranks third highest for gender equality, behind Rwanda and Namibia. But these statistics hide huge internal levels of inequalities, which have disproportionate impacts on women and girls (Dimitrova-Grajzl & Obasanjo, 2019). As with Ghana and Zambia, high levels of corruption and failure to implement gender legislation mean that levels of VAWG remain high. These three country contexts point to the reality that, even when a strong legislative framework and gender inclusion policies exist, little will change unless the political will and capacity exist to implement them.

Since Pakistan's independence in 1947, successive governments have approached poverty reduction through seeking rapid Gross Domestic Product (GDP) growth rates. The country adopted Import Substitution Industrialisation (ISI) and later neo-liberal economic policies, which together are thought to have fuelled a wealth gap and increased the economic vulnerability of many (DW, 2016). Pakistan was ranked 151st of 153 countries in the 2019 GGG Index Report (WEF, 2019b). There is very little research that maps differences between states of the country in terms of gender inequality and VAWG. However, in 2015, Punjab State passed a law criminalising all forms of violence against women, including domestic, emotional, psychological, economic, and sexual violence. This Act established a toll-free abuse reporting phone hotline for women to report abuse or violence and provided shelters for women and children. The Parliamentary Assembly intends to investigate reports of abuse, and then deploy Global Positioning System (GPS) bracelets to track perpetrators. While undoubtedly a positive move, action by a single state needs to be contextualised against the troubling reality of VAWG in Pakistan. There are many thousands of reported cases of violence against women every year, ranging from domestic violence, rape, acid attacks, and sexual assault, to kidnappings and honour killings.

An Aurat Foundation Study in 2013 found that there were 5,800 reported violent crimes against women in Punjab State alone. Research on gender and VAWG in Pakistan often cites the highly conservative religious-political environment as the primary contributing factor that hinders the creation and implementation of laws against VAWG (Bradley & Kirmani, 2015). This also has implications for the impact that civil society can have because the campaigns of women's organisations are not supported by a robust legal framework at the national level and there is a lack of continuity in legislation from one state to another.

Sustained periods of conflict engender unique and highly complex contexts in which VAWG, in many different forms, invariably increases. Here, we consider the actions taken to prevent this in two countries that have recently experienced periods of internal conflict, looking first at Nepal.

In Nepal, multiparty democracy was introduced as a result of decades of political struggle. Slow economic progress is thought to have fuelled the ten years of Maoist insurgency (1996–2006). The peace solution led to a transition from a monarchy to a federal republic, which was established in 2008. In 2020, Nepal has a Gender Inequality Index (GII) value of 0.452, with a ranking 142 out of 189 countries (UNDP, 2020). Acknowledging the deeply rooted problem of IPV in Nepal, the Nepali government passed the Domestic Violence Act in 2009, and since then, a few cases of IPV have been brought into courts or into the public domain. But despite some significant steps towards ending VAWG having apparently been taken, many women remain at risk of violence. This is exacerbated by the caste system, which creates differences in levels of vulnerability, with Dalit women being significantly more likely to suffer from multiple forms of violence. It is estimated that around 66% of women who have experienced physical or sexual violence do not seek help (Ministry of Health, Nepal, 2017). This is partly due to insufficient safe shelters and a lack of awareness among women regarding their rights, which despite the passing of the Domestic Violence Act have contributed to conviction rates remaining very low. The limited capacity to guarantee full and effective investigation of cases also remains a serious problem in preventing cases of violence against women in Nepal, meaning that there is little to discourage perpetrators. The main challenge, then, is to ensure that laws and policies are fully implemented and that access to justice is strengthened (Robins, 2011). That said, it is important to note that there is very little global evidence that legislation on its own acts as a deterrent to perpetrators of VAWG, even when it is implemented effectively and when survivors have access to justice.

South Sudan gained its independence in 2011 after 50 years of civil war with what is now Sudan. The Sudan People's Liberation Movement (SPLM) signed the first Comprehensive Peace Agreement in 2005, providing the basis for South Sudan's eventual independence in July 2011. But even after independence, peace was short-lived, and in December 2013, a new wave of conflict, this time internal to newly independent South Sudan, broke out. The dispute opened up along largely (but not solely) ethnic lines as the ruling presidential party was made up of the Dinka ethnic majority, while the opposition consisted primarily of

28 Theorising violence

the second largest grouping, the Nuer. The conflict that unfolded saw tens of thousands killed and 3 million people displaced, both to neighbouring countries and also internally, with around 200,000 people being forced to move into UN 'Protection of Civilian Camps' (PoCs), which were set up within South Sudan's borders. In August 2015, a new peace agreement was signed but violence broke out again within a year. The conflict saw the opening up of an oppositional power vacuum, and the installation of a new Vice President in August 2016 from the Juba-based faction of the SPLM In Opposition (SPLM IO). A further peace agreement was signed in Khartoum in June 2018.

In addition to political conflict, the country is plagued by inter-communal tensions, primarily fuelled by the drive to accumulate wealth through cattle. This economic reality sees violence erupt through cattle raiding, which happens alongside women and girls being abducted for marriage. Approximately 65% of women and girls in South Sudan report having experienced sexual violence, and 33% of this is the result of non-partner abduction linked to cattle raiding and displacement (Ellsberg et al., 2020). Women and girls are subjected to a number of other cultural practices that are in themselves violent, such as FGM (although this is prohibited under two laws in South Sudan) (28TooMany, 2018) or that lead to violence, including bride-price, child marriage, polygamy, and wife inheritance (Longman & Bradley, 2015). South Sudan's law prohibits rape and other sexual violence, but marital rape is not recognised by legislation, and convictions are very low with a judicial system that barely functions. There is an Access to Justice (A2J) programme funded by the EU that has explored the use of paralegals and mobile courts, but such programmes struggle to make inroads due to the sheer scale of the problem. The design and implementation of effective and sustained responses to VAWG is made extremely challenging by the national context, and, as a result, INGO interventions tend to focus on psycho-social support and livelihood programmes (Samuels, Jones, & Abu Hamad, 2017).

The link between traditional values and beliefs and VAWG

Our overview of the situation in the six countries above highlights how the intersection of traditional and cultural practices that embed and normalise gender inequalities present a major barrier to ending, or even achieving significant reduction in, VAWG. These practices shape the attitudes that permeate every level of society, influencing the political will of key stakeholders to implement legislation. It is unrealistic to think that the prevailing patriarchal norms that underpin gendered relations are not shared by the political elite. Thus, shifting these norms is clearly urgent and understanding the entry points for change is a critical step towards doing so. At the global level, campaigns such as the #MeToo movement and '16 Days of Activism' have undoubtedly helped to highlight the pervasiveness of VAWG and have drawn attention to the need to bring an end to the normalisation of violence. But across contexts, the visibility and impact of these campaigns differ considerably. For example, in Juba, the capital of South

Sudan and the urban hub of the humanitarian response, a relatively small, tight-knit, and coordinated VAWG network exists, consisting of practitioners working on protection and GBV, and global campaigns are responded to at this level. But in a conflict-ridden context with enormous internal diversity, they fail to reach far outside Juba, where the women and girls most at risk of violence are often located.

Security risks and the reach of VAWG campaigning and programming

In Pakistan, campaigning is muted by the tensions and security risks associated with the dominance of ultra-conservative religious views on gender that make it dangerous for activists to speak out on issues relating to VAWG (Bradley & Kirmani, 2015). In South Africa and Ghana, campaigns have greater traction but political will has still, until relatively recently, been weak. Nepal, with its new federal system and growing women's movement, is beginning to see higher levels of mobilisation and campaigning on issues of VAWG. Social mobilisers and women's organisations have helped to bring campaigns to vulnerable groups, but the impact is limited by the lack of an enabling environment. Even when visibility for VAWG as a human rights issue is achieved through media and community campaigns, without political will, country practitioner capacity to respond, and sufficient resourcing, little sustainable change will occur.

In the contexts explored above, national government commitments to support interventions that are donor-funded are present. And, in all contexts apart from South Africa, governments have supported the implementation of national gender action plans that are often coordinated by departments with a gender and/or women remit. In reality, these plans tend to be driven by the UN agencies and INGOs rather than by government or the Civil Service. In many cases, the UN employees will work inside gender ministries to support and strengthen the capacity of civil servants (e.g. in Zambia and South Sudan) to deliver the action plans. In countries where there is significant distrust of the foreign aid sector, such as Pakistan, implementation even with donor funding is challenging. Thus, there is often a disconnect between global campaigns and the realities of making things happen on the ground. Cynically, national governments might sometimes be happy to agree to endorse global declarations on ending VAWG and even accept national action plans because they come with the promise of donor funding. Lack of political will across VAWG contexts is also evident in poorly resourced gender ministries. Arguably, many Departments of Gender only exist now as a result of the pressure brought to bear by global conventions such as CEDAW and action on SDG 5. Often, these departments receive significantly less government funding than other ministries. Strengthening capacity at this level and forging connections with strong civil society groups and other government departments and the judiciary are critical factors in the drive to end VAWG.

South Africa stands apart from the other five countries discussed above and is an interesting context to explore and learn from. The levels of campaigning

30 Theorising violence

across the country appear to be greater and more coordinated, and are generally better funded, than in the other country contexts. The data on levels and prevalence of VAWG are robust, and concern over growing inequalities fuelling more civil unrest has also created a moment in which pressuring the South African government to act on VAWG is finally working. How has it been possible to see such scale of government commitment?

Conclusions

As will be seen throughout this book, our VAWG Mainstreaming Framework approach foregrounds a gendered and feminist lens. It is based upon an acknowledgement and understanding of the intrinsic inequalities of 'business as usual' power relations. The framework recognises interconnectedness, and in doing so allows for attention to be brought to the urgencies that arise as a result of intersectional vulnerabilities. The framework also addresses the challenges of hegemonic masculinity (see, e.g., Christensen & Jensen, 2014; Connell, 1987, 2014; Connell & Messerschmidt, 2005). The mainstreaming of VAWG is based on the principle that all voices must be given equal space and time and seeks to facilitate this, rather than discussions being dominated by the most powerful. It is also devised in a manner that allows proper attention to be given to social processes, for good and ill, as well as 'intentionality', i.e. people's perceived and/or actual goals and objectives and what the achievement of those might bring about in terms of relations of power, for example, and how they are encapsulated within gendered social norms. Thus, the Framework seeks to avoid further imposition of any coloniality of power or hegemonic structure.

Another aspect of our Framework is that through its development of the ecological model, it draws attention to how people in extreme circumstances, such as a humanitarian emergency, can be more or less resilient, and in doing so considers how relative resilience might conceivably be a marker for pivot points for positive change.

Application of a trans-generational (i.e. horizontal) perspective to our framework and approach enables a potentially deeper embedding of VAWG prevention and response, especially when linked to the ideal of household and community support to all ages, with mutual benefits. In addition, if older members of the household or community continue to inspire respect and trust in the young, there might conceivably be opportunities for older people to be supported to mediate and moderate negative social norms around VAWG. It is likely that, for many, this will require deep personal and group introspection, as well as challenging individually held and powerful beliefs, attitudes, and behaviours.

Key learning for VAWG programming

- Behavioural change interventions must disconnect the values and beliefs that entrench gender inequality and legitimise VAWG;

Theorising violence **31**

- Internal diversity must be mapped in order to effectively design behavioural change interventions that can respond to the specific beliefs and practices that sustain VAWG in different parts of a country;
- The realities of security risks for activists in highly conservative contexts need to be responded to within VAWG programming.

Notes

1 See the Conclusions for analysis of evidence to date on how the Covid-19 pandemic is having multiple, adverse impacts on VAWG prevention and on people's overall resilience, coping mechanisms – and how vulnerabilities have increased.
2 For further discussion of how this links into our VAWG Mainstreaming Framework, see Chapter 2.
3 This chapter section has been informed by Banerjee and Connell (2018), Bulbeck (1998), Connell (1987, 2014), Connell and Messerschmidt (2005), Crenshaw (1995), Criado-Perez (2019), Christensen and Jensen (2014), Faris and Jayasekara (2019), Lugones (2008, 2010, 2016), Mfecane (2019), Quijano and Ennis (2000), Tuhiwai Smith (2012), Wedgwood (2009).
4 See Chapter 7 for further discussion of international and national Rule of Law and legislative measures to address VAWG.

References

28TooMany. (2018). *South Sudan: The Law and FGM.* Thomas Reuters Foundation. https://www.28toomany.org/static/media/uploads/Law%20Reports/south_sudan_law_report_v1_(may_2018).pdf
Adu-Gyamfi, S., Donkoh, W. J., & Addo, A. A. (2016). Educational reforms in Ghana: Past and present. *Journal of Education and Human Development, 5*(3), 158–172. https://doi.org/10.15640/jehd.v5n3a17
Ball, L., Paluck, E. L., Poynton, C., & Sieloff, S. (2010). *Social Norms Marketing Aimed at Gender Based Violence: A Literature Review and Critical Assessment.* International Rescue Committee.https://www.alignplatform.org/resources/social-norms-marketing-aimed-gender-based-violence-literature-review-and-critical
Banerjee, P., & Connell, R. (2018). Gender theory as southern theory. In B. Risman, C. Froyum, & W. Scarborough (Eds.). *Handbook of the Sociology of Gender* (pp. 57–68). Springer. https://doi.org/10.1007/978-3-319-76333-0_4
Bank, A., Michau, L., Horn, J., Dutt, M., & Zimmerman, C. (2015). Prevention of violence against women and girls: Lessons from practice. *The Lancet, 385*(9978), 1672–1684. https://doi.org/10.1016/S0140-6736(14)61797-9
Bedri, N., & Bradley, T. (2017). Mapping the complexities and highlighting the dangers: The global drive to end FGM in the UK and Sudan. *Progress in Development Studies, 17*(1), 24–37. https://doi.org/10.1177/1464993416674299
Bradley, T. (2020). *Global Perspectives on Ending Violence against Women and Girls.* London: Zed Books.
Bradley, T., & Kirmani, N. (2015). Religion, gender and development in South Asia. In E. Tomalin (Ed.). *The Routledge Handbook of Religions and Global Development* (pp. 229–244). London: Routledge.
Bradley, T., Martin, Z., & Parliwala, R. (2021). Conceptualising subjectivities and rationalities in understanding gendered violence- processes of social and cultural change. *Progress in Development Studies, 21*(2), 181–195. https://doi.org/10.1177/14649934211012910.

32 Theorising violence

Bourdieu, P. 1977. *Outline of a Theory of Practice*. Translated by Richard Nice. New York: Cambridge University Press.

Bulbeck, C. (1998). *Re-Orienting Western Feminisms: Women's Diversity in a Post-Colonial World*. Cambridge University Press. https://doi.org/10.1017/CBO9780511552151

CEDAW. (2014). *NGO Shadow Report to 6th & 7th Periodic Report of Ghana on Convention on the Elimination of All Forms of Discrimination against Women (CEDAW)*. CEDAW. https://tbinternet.ohchr.org/Treaties/CEDAW/Shared%20Documents/GHA/INT_CEDAW_NGO_GHA_18396_E.pdf

CHANGE. (2018). *Prescribing Chaos in Global Health: The Global Gag Rule 1984–2018*. Center for Health and Gender Equality.

Christensen, A. D., & Jensen, S. Q. (2014). Combining hegemonic masculinity and intersectionality. *NORMA: International Journal for Masculinity Studies, 9*(1), 60–75. https://doi.org/10.1080/18902138.2014.892289

Cockburn, C. (2010). Gender relations as causal in militarization and war: A feminist standpoint. *International Feminist Journal of Politics, 12*(2), 139–157. https://doi.org/10.1080/14616741003665169

Cockburn, C. (2013). War and security, women and gender: An overview of the issues. *Gender & Development, 21*(3), 433–452. https://doi.org/10.1080/13552074.2013.846632

Connell, R. (1987). *Gender and Power*. Allen and Unwin. https://doi.org/10.1177/027046768800800490

Connell, R. (1995). *Masculinities*. Polity Press.

Connell, R. (2014). Margin becoming centre: For a world-centred rethinking of masculinities. *NORMA: International Journal for Masculinity Studies, 9*(4), 217–231. https://doi.org/10.1080/18902138.2014.934078

Connell, R., & Messerschmidt, J. W. (2005). Hegemonic masculinity: Rethinking the concept. *Gender & Society, 19*(6), 829–859. https://doi.org/10.1177/0891243205278639

Crenshaw, K. (1995). Mapping the margins: Intersectionality, identity politics, and violence against women of color. In G. Peller, K. Crenshaw, K. Thomas, & N. Gotanda (Eds.). *Critical Race Theory* (pp. 357–383). The New Press.

Criado-Perez, C. (2019). *Invisible Women: Exposing Data Bias in a World Designed for Men*. Penguin Books. https://www.penguin.co.uk/books/111/1113605/invisible-women/9781784706289.html

Davies, S., & True, J. (Eds.) (2018). *The Oxford Handbook on Women, Peace and Security*. Oxford University Press. https://doi.org/10.1093/oxfordhb/9780190638276.001.0001

Dimitrova-Grajzl, V., & Obasanjo, I. (2019). Do parliamentary gender quotas decrease gender inequality? The case of African countries. *Constitutional Political Economy, 30*(2), 149–176. https://doi.org/10.1007/s10602-018-09272-0

Dobash, R. E., & Dobash, R. P. (1979). *Violence against Wives*. New York: Free Press.

DW. (2016, November 3). *Why Is the Gender Gap Widening in Pakistan?* DW: Made for Minds. https://www.dw.com/en/why-is-the-gender-gap-widening-in-pakistan/a-36245560

Ellsberg, M., Ovince, J., Murphy, M., Blackwell, A., Reddy, D., Stennes, J., Hess, T., & Contreras, M. (2020). No safe place: Prevalence and correlates of violence against conflict-affected women and girls in South Sudan. *PLoS One, 15*(10), e0237965. https://doi.org/10.1371/journal.pone.0237965

Faris, D., & Jayasekara. P. (2019). *Towards Decolonising Knowledge in the Violence Prevention Field*. The Prevention Collaborative. https://prevention-collaborative.org/resource/towards-decolonising-knowledge-in-the-violence-prevention-field/

Freedom House. (2017). *Freedom in the World South Africa*. https://freedomhouse.org/country/south-africa/freedom-world/2017

Fulu, E., & Miedema, S. (2015). Violence against women: Globalizing the integrated ecological model. *Violence against Women, 21*(12), 1431–1455. https://doi.org/10.1177/1077801215596244

Gibbs, A., Jewkes, R., & Sikweyiya, Y. (2018). "I tried to resist and avoid bad friends" the role of social contexts in shaping the transformation of masculinities in a gender transformative and livelihood strengthening intervention in South Africa. *Men and Masculinities, 21*(4), 501–520. https://doi.org/10.1177/1097184X17696173

Haines, R., & O'Neil, T. (2018). *Putting Gender into Political Economy Analysis: Why It Matters and How to Do It* (Briefing May 2018. Practitioners' Guidance Note). Gender and Development Network. https://gadnetwork.org/gadn-news/2018/5/9/putting-gender-in-political-economy-analysis-why-it-matters-and-how-to-do-it

Harper, C., & Marcus, R. (2014). *Gender Justice and Social Norms - Processes of Change for Adolescent Girls: Towards a Conceptual Framework, 2* (ODI Report). Overseas Development Institute.https://www.odi.org/sites/odi.org.uk/files/odi-assets/publications-opinion-files/8831.pdf

Heise, L. (1998). Violence against women: An integrated, ecological framework. *Violence Against Women, 4*(3), 262–290. https://doi.org/10.1177/1077801298004003002

Heise, L. (2011). *What Works to Prevent Partner Violence? An Evidence Overview.* DFID. http://strive.lshtm.ac.uk/resources/what-works-prevent-partner-violence-evidence-overview

Heise, L., Ellsberg, M., & Gottemoeller, M. (1999). Ending Violence against Women. *Population Reports, 27*(4), 1–1.

Hudson, D., & Leftwich, A. (2014). *From Political Economy to Political Analysis* (DLP Research Paper; No. 25). Developmental Leadership Program, University of Birmingham UK. www.dlprog.org/publications/from-political-economy-to-political-analysis.php

Hudson, D., & Marquette, H. (2015). Mind the gaps: What's missing in political economy analysis and why it matters. In OECD: *A Governance Practitioner's Notebook: Alternative Ideas and Approaches.* https://www.oecd.org/dac/accountable-effective-institutions/governance-practitioners-notebook.htm

Kishor, S., & Johnson, K. (2004). *Profiling Domestic Violence: A Multi-country Study.* Calverton, MD: ORCMacro.

Longman C., & Bradley T. (2015). Introduction to 'harmful cultural practices'. In C. Longman, & T. Bradley (Eds.). *Interrogating Harmful Cultural Practices: Gender, Culture and Coercion* (pp. 1–10). Routledge.

Lugones, M. (2008). The coloniality of gender. Worlds & Knowledge Otherwise, 1–17. Spring 2008. https:// globalstudies.trinity.duke.edu/wp-content/ ::: /v2d2_ Lugones.pdf

Lugones, M. (2010). Toward a decolonial feminism. *Hypatia, 25*(4), 742–759. https://doi.org/10.1111/j.1527-2001.2010.01137.x

Lugones, M. (2016). The coloniality of gender. In W. Harcourt (Ed.). *The Palgrave Handbook of Gender and Development* (pp. 13–33). Palgrave MacMillan.

Mackie, G. (2000). Female genital cutting: The beginning of the end. In B. Shell-Duncan, & Y. Hernlund (Eds.). *Female "Circumcision" in Africa: Culture, Controversy and Change* (pp. 253–282). Lynne Rienner Publishers.

Mackie, G., Moneti, F., Shakaya, H., & Denny, E. (2015). *What Are Social Norms? How Are They Measured?* UNICEF. http://globalresearchandadvocacygroup.org/wp-content/uploads/2018/06/What-are-Social-Norms.pdf

Maguigan, H. (2003). Wading into Professor Schneider's Murky Middle ground between acceptance and rejection of criminal justice responses to domestic violence. *American University Journal of Gender, Social Policy & the Law, 11*(2), 427.

34 Theorising violence

Mfecane, S. (2019). *In My Opinion: Decolonise Man and Masculinity Studies to End Gender-Based Violence.* Centre for Sexualities, AIDS and Gender Blog. https://www.csagup.org/2019/09/18/in-my-opinion-decolonise-men-and-masculinity-studies-to-end-gender-based-violence/

Ministry of Health, Nepal. (2017). *Nepal Demographic and Health Survey (NDHS) 2016.* Nepal: Ministry of Health, Nepal, New ERA, & ICF. www.dhsprogram.com/pubs/pdf/fr336/fr336.pdf

Mukhopadhyay, M. (2016). Mainstreaming gender or "streaming" gender away: Feminists marooned in the development business. In W. Harcourt (Ed.). *The Palgrave Handbook of Gender and Development* (pp. 77–91). Palgrave Macmillan. https://doi.org/10.1007/978-1-137-38273-3_6

Quijano, A., & Ennis, M. (2000). Coloniality of power, eurocentrism, and Latin America. *Nepantla: Views from South, 1*(3), 533–580.

Robins, S. (2011). Towards victim-centred transitional justice: Understanding the needs of families of the disappeared in postconflict Nepal. *International Journal of Transitional Justice, 5*(1), 75–98. https://doi.org/10.1093/ijtj/ijq027

Samuels, F., Jones, N., & Abu Hamad, B. (2017). Psychosocial support for adolescent girls in post-conflict settings: Beyond a health systems approach. *Health Policy and Planning, 32*(supp 5), v40–v51. https://doi.org/10.1093/heapol/czx127

True, J. (2010). The political economy of violence against women: A feminist international relations perspective. *Australian Feminist Law Journal, 32*(1). 39–59. https://doi.org/10.1080/13200968.2010.10854436

True, J. (2012). *The Political Economy of Violence against Women.* Oxford University Press. https://doi.org/10.1093/acprof:oso/9780199755929.001.0001

Tuhiwai Smith, L. (2012). *Decolonizing Methodologies: Research and Indigenous Peoples* (2nd ed.). Zed Books.

UNDP. (2020). *Human Development Reports: Gender Inequality Index (GII).* United Nations Development Programme. http://hdr.undp.org/en/indicators/68606#

Walker, L. (1979). *The Battered Woman.* Harper & Row.

Wedgwood, N. (2009). Connell's theory of masculinity–Its origins and influences on the study of gender. *Journal of Gender Studies, 18*(4), 329–339. https://doi.org/10.1080/09589230903260001

WEF. (2019a). *Mind the 100 Year Gap.* World Economic Forum. https://www.weforum.org/reports/gender-gap-2020-report-100-years-pay-equality

WEF. (2019b). *Accelerating Gender Parity in Globalization 4.0.* World Economic Forum. https://www.weforum.org/agenda/2019/06/accelerating-gender-gap-parity-equality-globalization-4

Westoff, C. (1988). Is the KAP-gap real? *Population and Development Review, 14*(2). 225–232. https://doi.org/10.2307/1973570

2
VAWG MAINSTREAMING – A FRAMEWORK FOR ACTION[1]

Introduction

If there is finally to be an end to violence against women and girls (VAWG), then a commitment to addressing it needs to be embedded within all development programmes, regardless of sectoral focus. Women and girls are vulnerable across the board, and recognition of this reality is an essential first step. This chapter sets out a VAWG Mainstreaming Framework that addresses how to position a VAWG lens at the centre of development and humanitarian emergency programming. The framework is presented through discussion of a number of key stages. It is then applied to two programme areas, microfinance and HIV, in order to demonstrate its applicability across development issues.

Sustainable Development Goal 5 (SDG 5) aims to *Achieve gender equality and empower all women and girls*. Within SDG 5 are nine targets, the common objective of which is to end gender inequality in all its forms, including VAWG. Two targets focus specifically on VAWG: 5.2, which seeks to *Eliminate all forms of violence against all women and girls* and 5.3, which is to *Eliminate all harmful practices*. There is some debate around the potential limitations of the targets. For example, arguments have been made for the removal of any age caps, to acknowledge that violence can and does occur at all stages of a woman's life, from earliest childhood into oldest age, as well as for disaggregation of data and analysis.[2] While there are many examples of programmes, policies, and international commitments to end VAWG, we argue that without a systematic VAWG mainstreaming model, SDG 5, its targets and indicators, will not be achieved.

This chapter provides a template that might be applied at both the sectoral and the multi-sectoral level. The detail offered for each of the proposed steps towards developing the VAWG Mainstreaming Framework is intended to provide readers with sufficient information to adapt and shape the framework in ways that make

DOI: 10.4324/9780429280603-2

36 VAWG mainstreaming framework

it applicable to their own sector and sphere of work. The sector and context-specific adaptation of the framework is central to its potential efficacy.

Definitions of violence

This chapter uses the definition of VAWG from the UN Declaration on the Elimination of Violence Against Women (DEVAW) which is:

> Any act of gender-based violence that results in, or is likely to result in, physical, sexual or psychological harm or suffering to women and/or girls, including threats of such acts, coercion or arbitrary deprivations of liberty, whether occurring in public or private life.
>
> *(UN, 1993)*

However, and as already discussed in the Introduction to this volume, across the globe, definitions of violence vary considerably; as a concept, it is used to categorise certain forms of interpersonal behaviour and, as such, it is subject to socio-cultural interpretation. Some acts and structures viewed as violent by societies in the Global North may not be viewed as such elsewhere, and opinions about whether and how to challenge them will, therefore, vary. The diversity of interpretations regarding what constitutes violence also applies to academic research, which frequently operates with different definitions according to discipline (e.g. gender studies, law, or peace studies). This lack of clarity across contexts and academic fields can lead to difficulty in cross-cultural approaches to programme and policy design. As such, research on VAWG requires a broad definition of violence that recognises it as both a physical and a psychological phenomenon, and acknowledges that it operates on multiple levels, from the personal to the macro-structural.

As noted in the introductory chapter, one major global programme aimed at to tackling VAWG is the UK Department for International Development's (DFID) 'What Works'. Phase I of the programme (2016–2020) supported projects and evaluations in more than 20 countries in Africa and Asia. What Works applied a VAWG vantage point, informed by the ecological model (Heise, 1998, 2011; see also Scriver, Duvvury, Ashe, Raghavendra, & O'Donovan, 2015); the approach taken in the programme is discussed in detail below. This theoretical perspective facilitates an understanding of the multidimensional nature of violence while drawing attention to the interconnected aspects of the personal, situational, socio-cultural (structural), and global factors.

We argue that a mainstreaming framework needs to refine the social ecology perspective somewhat through the addition of intersectional analysis and a VAWG spectrum. In combination, these perspectives allow for the emergence of a more complex and nuanced understanding of *why violence happens*. Through this analysis, strategies and actions that have been effective for particular people or groups in specific contexts can be identified.

The reasons for mainstreaming VAWG prevention

Apart from specific programmes focused solely on ending VAWG, there are no models for mainstreaming a VAWG perspective within programmes that focus on other sectors. Here, we bring together the contextual research on VAWG and the literature that is focused on analysing and understanding why it happens. In doing so, we have developed a model that could lead the way in shaping how development and humanitarian emergency actors include VAWG as a central strand of their programming, regardless of sectoral focus.

As we set out our theoretical framework, we do so with the intention that we and other practitioners may test the model's appropriateness and validity when we have future opportunities to do so, and then improve it through evaluation and reapplication. Because there is no agreed, commonly applied, approach to mainstreaming VAWG prevention into sectoral and multi-sectoral programmes, such action can be aided by building partly on best practices, lessons learnt, and indeed on the failures, of gender mainstreaming.

The urgent need for a mainstreaming approach was clearly stated in a 2016 Independent Commission for Aid Impact (ICAI) review of DFID's VAWG programming (ICAI, 2016). While DFID was praised for its significant investment in world-leading innovations and research, it was also noted that, if VAWG is to be eradicated, it must become a key focus across sectors. This must happen in any programme, whether or not violence, gender, women and girls, or VAWG is the key focus. This observation will be just as valid for other development partnerships.

What is meant by VAWG and why is a mainstreaming framework necessary?

Having discussed interpretations of what constitutes violence and given reasons for mainstreaming VAWG prevention, we now explore how VAWG is conceptualised and discuss why the development of a mainstreaming framework is necessary. We present a staged approach to applying the VAWG Mainstreaming Framework, followed by two illustrative examples of how it could be applied to specific programmes in order to demonstrate its applicability across sectors. First, we look at how VAWG mainstreaming might work in one country context by applying our model to Nepal. While the nationwide and government-led Integrated Women's Development Programme (IWDP) has so far focused on promoting and supporting women in microfinance initiatives, it intends to expand its remit into building resilience to end VAWG and open access to justice. We subsequently consider how a VAWG mainstreaming lens could be applied across interventions that focus on a specific issue by considering the example of HIV prevention programmes.

We argue that, in order for the goal of ending VAWG to be embedded into a development project (regardless of sectoral focus), attempts need to be made to do the following:

- Create an enabling environment to support action against VAWG, including policy and legal change, and support services (such as health services, psychosocial support, and provision of advice over exit options). All such work requires increased spending and funding that is ringfenced, and concerted efforts towards capacity building.
- Work on changes to social norms that limit women and girls' opportunities to participate in society free from fear of VAWG. Such activities necessitate work that fosters and sustains positive changes to *male attitudes and behaviours*, as well as those of wider society. Specifically, there need to be targeted challenges to the normalisation of violence in everyday life.
- Shift social perceptions in favour of girls and women being equal partners in societies and encourage people to see the benefits and value of gender equity, thereby working to reduce the levels of social/violent control to which women and girls are subjected.

The proposed VAWG Mainstreaming Framework is based on the premise that it must include male perspectives, not solely identified as perpetrators of violence, but potentially as champions of more equal gender relations, as community members with authority and leadership potential to support social norm change, as active participants in debates about gender issues, and also as survivors of sexual violence.[3] VAWG mainstreaming provides opportunities for policymaking and legislative work to respond more effectively to the needs of all. It can support interventions to be more effective in tackling the continuation and perpetuation of inequality and social norms that enable VAWG, but that also normalise violence in general.

VAWG mainstreaming should not be taken to simply mean seeking to avoid the reinforcement of inequalities that adversely affect women and men. Rather, to be effective and sustainable, it must work from current situations, identify and tackle inequalities, support the development of evidence-based policy and practice that address the reasons for VAWG, and seek to dismantle the social norms that perpetuate and justify violence, that provide impunity to perpetrators, and that persistently fail survivors. Certainly, this approach will be grounded in gender mainstreaming – one without the other cannot work. Gender inequality contributes to the normalisation of VAWG and, for this reason, tackling gender inequality is at the core of addressing VAWG. This means bringing together all stakeholders with investment either in maintaining or in seeking to change existing systems and policies that prevent action. Moreover, to be sustainable, efforts to bring about policy change in any one sector must be reflected in and supported by similar efforts in others: a multi-sectoral approach to VAWG mainstreaming is crucial if policy is to translate into practice.

VAWG is the most widespread form of abuse worldwide, affecting 35% of all women during their lives (WHO, LSHTM, & SAMRC, 2013). Though there has been increased acknowledgement, the majority of development pro-grammes do not and are unlikely ever to prioritise spending on activities aimed at improving the lives of women and girls, including elimination of VAWG. This is why VAWG mainstreaming is essential (see also Chapter 9 on funding shortfalls).

What works to prevent VAWG? A review of the evidence so far

Despite the need for context specificity, certain broad, base-level, and cross-cultural observations can be made about what causes VAWG and what can be done to prevent it. These observations must not shape policy or programme design, as such, but instead are a useful baseline from which to formulate ques-tions and begin analytical processes in more focused, contextual research.

During Phase I, DFID's What Works conducted a global review of the VAWG literature, one output of which was a paper summarising the relative effectiveness of VAWG prevention and response mechanisms (Jewkes, 2014). The paper found that the existence of shelters and protection orders with proactive arrest policies is 'promising', as are counselling and paralegal programmes. Less convincing evidence had been found to support projects such as advocacy interventions or 'batterers' programmes. Broadly speaking, single-component programmes appear to be less effective than multi-component programmes. But the paper also notes that it paints a general picture, and it is therefore not reflective of the context specificity that is necessary and that we argue here is a critical first step for effective VAWG mainstreaming.

Further to this call for more contextual evidence, What Works also defined critical gaps in current knowledge about VAWG perpetration and prevention, including the following:

- Current evidence is biased towards individual predictors of violence (both victimhood and perpetration); more information is needed about factors operating at the relationship and community levels, including greater understanding of the range of potential male responses to VAWG in those situations (the 2015 *Lancet* series on VAWG gives an overview of the com-plexities of the issues, e.g., García-Moreno et al., 2015);
- There are few studies that consider macro-level factors in the geographic distribution of violence types, and how global, economic, and political structures affect the dynamics of VAWG (Elmusharaf et al., 2019; Remme, Michaels-Igbokwe, & Watts, 2014; Taylor Bell, Jacobson, & Pereznieto, 2014; UNAIDS, 2012a);
- More information is needed about how different levels of the social ecology (i.e. individual, household, community, broader society, national, global) interact to protect or endanger women and girls; and
- Researchers and practitioners must stop working in silos and instead must embrace comparative approaches in terms of methods, analytical angles, and research foci (e.g. multi-community, organisational, structural).

40 VAWG mainstreaming framework

Empowerment of women and girls

We argue that all development interventions should seek to empower women and girls by ensuring an enabling environment within which their rights are respected. Empowerment in a broad sense depends on improvements in women's position: alterations in patterns of control. This has often been expressed in terms of the *power quartet* (Table 2.1).

TABLE 2.1 The power quartet

Type of power relation	Implications for an understanding of empowerment
Power over: ability to influence and coerce	Changes in underlying resources and power to challenge constraints
Power to: organise and change existing hierarchies	Increased individual capacity and opportunities for access
Power with: increased power from collective action	Increased solidarity to challenge underlying assumptions
Power from within: increased individual consciousness	Increased awareness and desire for change

Women do not form a homogenous group. Rather, gender intersects with other forms of socio-economic discrimination to produce a diverse array of oppressive environments for women (intersecting issues include race, nationality, sexuality, class, religious identity). The distinction between women's practical gender needs and their strategic gender interests (Molyneux, 1985) allows for the development of generalised gender policy by distinguishing between context-specific practical requirements on one hand and a 'deductive analysis of the structures of women's subordination' on the other hand (Kabeer, 2012, p. 6).

Kabeer's contribution to this overarching feminist politics has been substantial; she offers a specific definition of empowerment, which covers women's sense of self-worth and social identity, their desire and ability to challenge their subordination, their capacity to exercise strategic control over their lives and to renegotiate relationships, and their ability to participate alongside men in the reformation of their societies in ways that lead to more fair and democratic distributions of power and opportunity (Kabeer, 2008, 2012).[4]

Box 2.1 Kabeer's empowerment definition: empowerment = agency, resources, and achievement

Agency encompasses both observable action in the exercise of choice – decision-making, protest, bargaining, and negotiation – and the meaning, motivation, and purpose that individuals bring to their actions, their sense of agency (Kabeer, 2003).

Kabeer's definition also offers an overarching agenda, while simultaneously leaving room for analyses of intersecting aspects of social discrimination that affect women differently according to context. Additionally, this definition of empowerment encompasses the need for attention to position and condition. The transformation of social and cultural power structures (i.e. improving position) must be accompanied by efforts to enable people to benefit from such changes (i.e. people must have good conditions – health, economic opportunities, etc. – in order to benefit from the possibilities available). Thus, meeting basic needs is not bypassed by the drive for empowerment, or vice versa. Addressing condition and position must go hand in hand, but while care should be taken to combine and sequence both, they should not be confused with each other.

Presenting the VAWG mainstreaming lens

Here, we set out our mainstreaming approach, which comprises a series of stages designed to guide programmers when embedding a VAWG lens in their activities.

Stage 1. *Framing knowledge collection around VAWG to guide programme design*

A VAWG lens requires actors to reflect on how and if a programme will change patterns and/or prevalence of violence in the context of their planned intervention(s). A series of critical and reflective questions that consider if and how interventions might have a positive or negative impact on levels of VAWG should be asked throughout the design stage. Figure 2.1 sets out the requisite conditions for achieving genuine

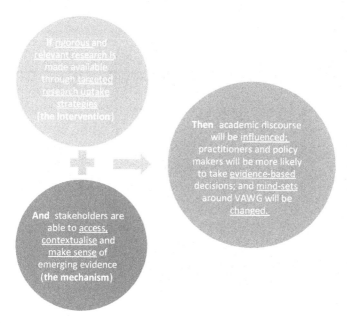

FIGURE 2.1 Intervention and mechanism process.

change in policy and practice: a research-focused intervention must be balanced by practitioners and stakeholders who make sense of the evidence and use it to work towards an evidence-based shift in action on VAWG prevention (Table 2.2).

TABLE 2.2 Critical and reflective questions to ask throughout the design stage

Design questions	*Programme reflection*
• Do we understand the types of violence most commonly experienced by women and girls programme recipients? • To what extent are these types of violence commonly talked about and acknowledged to be unjust and abusive? What level of normalisation exists? • To what extent is this normalisation of violence similarly applied by men and women, boys and girls? • Are some groups more likely to project normalised views of VAWG? • Who are the most vulnerable groups? • And what material resources and/or social/cultural capital do they have to draw on?	Understanding these types of violence should involve an understanding of the contexts in which it occurs (at home, school, work on the way to school or work, etc.) If this is not known should a piece of research be commissioned in order to gather this knowledge? Similarly, an exercise to map out what resources and forms of social and cultural capital already exist (e.g. through established community groups) is needed in advance of programme design. Projects should build wherever possible on tried and tested approaches so as to minimise the risk of triggering a backlash (and therefore potentially increasing the vulnerability of certain groups).
• What internal differences can be seen in patterns and types of violence and in the triggers for it? • In other words, are certain forms of VAWG more common in particular areas and under certain conditions?	Can a one size fits all approach to programming respond to the complex contexts of VAWG even in one country? To what extent will a more locally tailored response be necessary and if so, is this feasible?

Another way to represent this reflective and reflexive process is shown in Figure 2.2.

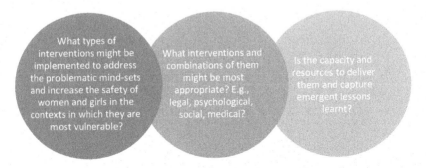

FIGURE 2.2 With this knowledge in place…

The starting point should be understanding the experiences of vulnerable groups and working outwards into the environment and contexts in which they live, and asking: what can the programme do to end the violence they suffer? Building this knowledge can be supported through the theoretical yet practically useful approach of the ecological model, which has already been discussed in Chapter 1, but bears repetition here due to its centrality to perspectives and approaches throughout this volume (Figure 2.3).

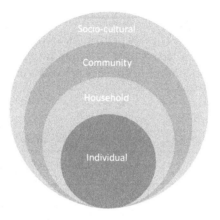

FIGURE 2.3 The ecological model.

This model supports an outward approach that begins with the experiences of individuals. It is understood that these personal experiences are triggered by dynamics – which are largely gendered – occurring at the household level, which, in turn, are shaped by community structures and then wider socio-cultural beliefs and values. Recent work has made a strong case for expanding the ecological model to include the global level. For example, Fulu and Miedema (2015, p. 1433) seek to 'move beyond static conceptualizations of globalization and connect global trends with tensions, resistance and change at the local level' by expanding empirical links of the ecological model to better frame women's experiences of VAWG, positioning them in the overarching within the context of globalisation. This, they argue, opens up 'an important analytical space to assess how global shifts interact with and influence the rest of the [ecological] model'.

The ecological model, particularly when expanded to include global dynamics, brings to the surface important questions regarding the ways in which decisions are made: who, for example, has the power to decide what they (and others) can and cannot do with their life? And who has the most access to resources such as food, but also medicines and wages? It also leads to a reflection on what happens when individuals challenge these power structures: is violence used as discipline and to maintain the status quo? Is it used to remind household members of the hierarchy of power? How are these structures and behaviours shaped by

44 VAWG mainstreaming framework

worldviews? And are these views adhering to a status quo that marginalises some and, in doing so, creates groups who are vulnerable because they have less power?

Stage 2. *Operationalising knowledge on VAWG: designing a programme*

The ecological model can be used to steer questions in ways that make them specific to the goals of programmes. Table 2.3 illustrates this with an example in relation to access to justice (A2J) programming. In the context of A2J, the creation of a genuine enabling environment must have equitable justice as a goal. This would require both the removal of harmful laws and practices, as well as ensuring that women know what are their rights and are empowered to claim them (see Nussbaum, 2001, and for further discussion in this volume, see Chapter 7 on the rule of law and VAWG).

TABLE 2.3 Using the ecological model for access to justice programming

Social ecology level	Meta-question	Factors to think about for operationalisation
Global	How does globalisation influence local and international A2J processes specific to gender and VAWG?	Where are the key gender and VAWG inflection points in both acceptance of and resistance to globalisation? (How) does the aetiology of VAWG resonate in global A2J and other structures?
Socio-cultural	What cultural practices and common views exist with regard to women and girls and specifically the use of violence against them?	Are there views emerging that need to be captured, challenged, and changed by the programme?
Community	What community mechanisms exist to mitigate VAWG or offer security and protection to victims?	How effective are the community mechanisms perceived to be and could they be built upon by the programme?
Household	What dynamics exist at household level that may support or perpetuate VAWG?	Are there certain intra-/inter-household behaviours that need to be challenged by the programme? Is there opportunity to use the programme to tap into certain change dynamics (e.g. is there evidence that young, educated women challenge their parents about the use of violence?). Can they be supported by the programme?
Individual	What room is there for individuals to challenge and change social norms surrounding VAWG?	Can individuals who may be in the minority but wish to see VAWG end tap into wider networks and support structures to mobilise the change they want to see? If the answer is yes can the programme build on them? If it is no, can the programme in fact build them?

Stage 3. *Implementing and monitoring change: embedding a VAWG lens at all stages*

Building on the knowledge gained through the first two stages as set out above, a 'three-dimensional VAWG lens' could then be used to implement, shape, monitor, and adapt such a programme. The proposed framework operationalises the ecological model used in Stage 2 to help develop detailed contextual knowledge around why and how VAWG materialises and flourishes. The model consists of three dimensions: an enabling environment; social norm change; and developing positive social perceptions of the benefits of girls and women (Heise, 1998).

These represent the spaces and areas where change most needs to happen if VAWG is to end permanently. In programme/project design, implementation, monitoring, and knowledge generation, and during any programme adjustment, questions should be asked in relation to each of the three dimensions. Below, we discuss how each of these dimensions can be addressed with continued reference to the A2J example.

Creating an enabling environment to support action against VAWG, including policy and legal change and increased spending

Programmes will need to address any lack of processes, systems, and resources (human and material) in relation to the spheres that make up this environment

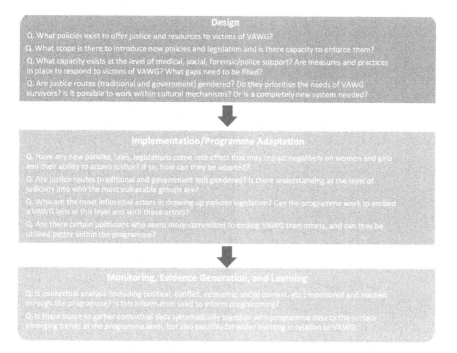

FIGURE 2.4 Questions to guide the creation of an enabling environment to support action against VAWG.

46 VAWG mainstreaming framework

(i.e. government, legal, police, social/psychological support [including safe houses], and medical [forensics and treatment]). Central to creating an enabling environment is the introduction of legal rights and A2J. Mainstreaming VAWG within development needs, therefore, should be framed in terms of the creation of a sustainable and enabling environment that takes a survivor-centric approach. In other words, one that places women and girls front and centre, while working with other key partners such as public institutions, community groups, and men and boys (Figure 2.4 – see previous page).

Changes to social norms that limit women and girls' opportunities to participate in society free from fear of VAWG

The ecological model can be used to draw out in-country differences and guide understanding of what kind of change interventions might be appropriate, particularly in relation to social norms. Testing of innovative new interventions, as well as trialling programmes that have worked elsewhere, needs to be done with caution and close monitoring: there are no quick solutions and what works in one context will not necessarily be successful in another (Figure 2.5).

Design
Q. How can normalised mind-sets that accept VAWG be challenged without triggering backlash?
Q. What possibilities exist at the level of education (schooling), community, and households? Can behaviour change programmes be woven into aspects of school curriculum?

Implementation/Programme Adaptation
Q. Are women and girls' voices being gathered during programme implementation to provide feedback on the programme in general and in relation to social norms?
Q. Are changes to social norms being identified and used (where appropriate) as evidence of success to other programme beneficiaries? Are there systems in place to reward positive change?

Monitoring, Evidence Generation, and Learning
Q. How can changes in attitudes and behaviours in relation to VAWG be monitored (e.g., a cohort study in a number of schools implementing such a programme or areas where interventions have focused on social norm change)?
Q. Are areas of potential backlash against the supported social norm changes being monitored? Is a system in place in case the situation escalates?

FIGURE 2.5 Questions to guide understanding of what kind of social norm change interventions might be appropriate.

Developing social perceptions of the benefits and value of girls and women being equal partners in societies free from VAWG

If greater opportunities exist and enhanced well-being (including a reduction in or end to VAWG) can be seen, then we can confidently suggest that the value of women and girls will have increased. Programmes need to make efforts to support the development of new opportunities for women in education and the workplace and build on networks already in existence. Ultimately, this third dimension will be able to be achieved only if the second has also been successful. At programme level, this dimension might well be supported by tapping into capacity at the level of women's social movements and civil society organisations. If there are organisations advocating for women in public spaces, this will likely help to promote the value and benefit of women's full and equal participation in life. The barriers that may prevent this (of which VAWG is a significant example) will need to be removed as part of the process (Figure 2.6).

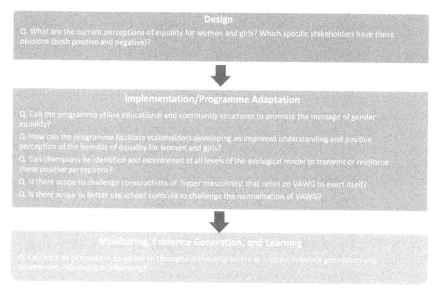

FIGURE 2.6 Questions to guide increasing social perceptions of the value and benefit of women's full and equal participation in life.

The application of the three dimensions to the proposed VAWG Mainstreaming Framework feeds into a sequence of theories of potential change, setting out the processes and pathways required to bring about such shifts (Figure 2.7).

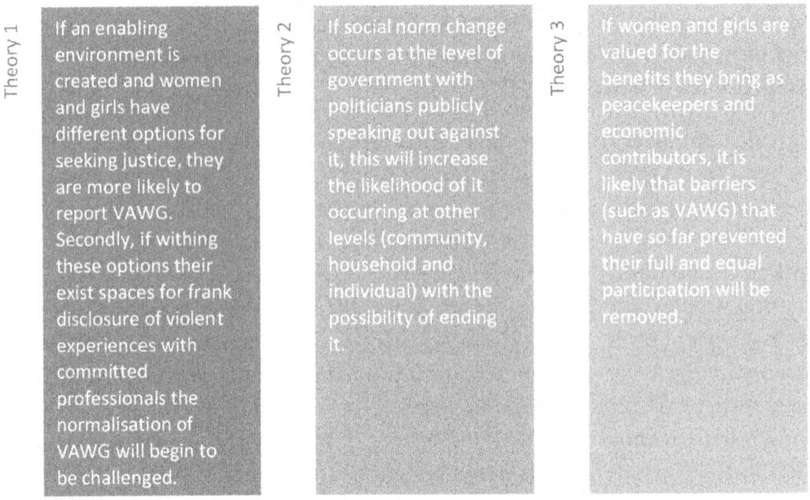

48 VAWG mainstreaming framework

Theory 1	Theory 2	Theory 3
If an enabling environment is created and women and girls have different options for seeking justice, they are more likely to report VAWG. Secondly, if withing these options their exist spaces for frank disclosure of violent experiences with committed professionals the normalisation of VAWG will begin to be challenged.	If social norm change occurs at the level of government with politicians publicly speaking out against it, this will increase the likelihood of it occurring at other levels (community, household and individual) with the possibility of ending it.	If women and girls are valued for the benefits they bring as peacekeepers and economic contributors, it is likely that barriers (such as VAWG) that have so far prevented their full and equal participation will be removed.

FIGURE 2.7 Theory sequence linked to the VAWG Mainstreaming Framework.

Applying the VAWG Mainstreaming Framework in other contexts

Here, we provide two brief illustrative examples of applying the VAWG Mainstreaming Framework using the three dimensions of the ecology model. First, we consider the framework in the context of a national level women's development programme in Nepal, and then, to show how it might be applied effectively at the sectoral level, we consider the many ways in which VAWG intersects with HIV prevention programming.

The Integrated Women's Development Programme (IWDP) Nepal

The IWDP is a long-standing women-focused development programme that the Government of Nepal has been implementing for the past 30 years. The programme covers 1 million women, who are formed into self-help groups (SHGs), some of which have also been federated into co-operatives, with 1,600 nationally. Although the programme has been ongoing, many of the SHGs had become defunct, and the government is currently reviving them. The group structures of the IWDP are widely thought to be useful for enhancing economic empowerment, but also in offering a forum where women can talk about and address other issues of concern.

There have been challenges along the way for IWDP. For instance, when paralegal workers started becoming effective at the group level, some began to take money to settle cases. The formal judicial system then objected to this informal system.

The IWDP has taken women's economic engagement as its entry point to the wider goal of women's empowerment and increased equality. However, the assumption that economic engagement will help protect women from violence may, in some cases, be misguided, or at least oversimplified. This is why, if violence is to be reduced, an explicit VAWG lens must be embedded into the programme. Income on its own is not enough to build resilience and the wider infrastructural support needed to end VAWG. In fact, it can sometimes increase women's vulnerability to violence.

Nepal's constitution 2015 enshrines gender equality as a core goal, which is now being supported by donor and government commitment to the gender equality and social inclusion (GESI) framework. In 2009, Nepal passed the Domestic Violence and Punishment Act, which defines domestic violence as physical, emotional, financial, and sexual abuse. This government-level commitment is undoubtedly positive and signals wider momentum in the movement to transform women's lives. Yet without a coherent approach, the laws and frameworks will be at risk of remaining disconnected from 'ground level' experiences of continued violence. The 2016 Nepal Demographic and Health Survey (DHS) data suggest that almost one-fifth of women had experienced some form of intimate partner violence (IPV) in the 12 months prior to the survey. Physical violence was the most cited form of IPV, followed by emotional and sexual violence (Ministry of Health, Nepal, 2017).

Among factors associated with experiencing violence, residence in specific ecological zones was significant, with women from the Terai zone reporting higher incidence violence compared to other zones. Women from the richest households in urban areas were less likely to be victims of any form of IPV when compared to women from the poorest households. Women's education significantly reduced the odds of experiencing any form of violence in both rural and urban areas, while women who had witnessed their father beating their mother were more likely to experience violence. In rural areas, the less a woman worked the more the more likely they were to agree with norms justifying wife-beating. Conversely; in urban areas this trend was reversed: a higher proportion of women who agreed with three or more statements justifying wife-beating were employed, compared to women who said there was no justification for wife-beating.

Applying the VAWG mainstreaming lens to the IWDP

Creating an enabling environment

In the context of the IWDP, where strong support networks between women involved in SHGs exist, the designation of community advocates or mobilisers with a specific remit to support survivors of violence has the potential to see positive results. This mobiliser/advocate would offer emotional support and link survivors to key provisions, including legal, medical, and psychological services. The IWDP will need to invest in building this human resource and also in building wider infrastructure so that mobilisers/advocates can refer women to specific services and support through a process of access to justice and resolution.

While the IWDP has invested in paralegals, the linking between these various levels of legal and medical support is lacking. The effectiveness of these services is also patchy, and a concerted attempt within the IWDP to build these is clearly necessary.

Social norm change

While the IWDP has made significant inroads in terms of increasing women's income, now is the time to incorporate strategies to reverse harmful attitudes that render women vulnerable to violence. A 2016 survey across the IWDP programme found that women who earn an income are 1.4 times more likely to suffer IPV (Ministry of Health, Nepal, 2017). This could be because, as women earn more, they start to challenge the traditional gender norms of men as the primary wage earner. Understanding what triggers a shift in gendered attitudes is complex. However, one study has highlighted the importance of local women's organisations that are specifically focused on ending VAWG, arguing that they are a key factor in shifting female attitudes towards violence. The study also found that women who were engaged with a women's organisation were more likely to recognise violence as abuse (challenging its normalisation) and would be more likely to take action (Htun & Weldon, 2012). Building the capacity of local women's organisation may help the IWDP to catalyse a shift in attitudes towards gender that, in turn, should reduce instances of violence.

Changing the perceived value of women and girls

VAWG is normalised because of the devaluing of women. It is hoped that by taking a holistic multidimensional approach, programmes will build women's voice through education and employment, which, in turn, will instigate a re-conceptualisation of the value that women bring to society and to the home.

Mainstreaming VAWG prevention within the IWDP requires two main adjustments. First, the introduction of designated mobilisers to work to end VAWG, and to support and advocate on behalf of survivors. These should be integrated within the pre-existing SHGs, but they should also work more widely across communities. Second, building the resourcing and capacity of local women's organisations, especially those working solely to end VAWG, will be key to bringing about the long-term structural shifts needed if VAWG in Nepal is to end.

Linking HIV focus into VAWG mainstreaming[5]

Here we briefly consider vulnerability to HIV infection linked to violence and the need for such intersections to be addressed within the proposed VAWG Mainstreaming Framework. All mainstreaming work requires the essential component of quality, disaggregated data that can support evidence-based planning, interventions, and reporting. The development of a robust and regularly updated database to support calls for investment into VAWG and HIV mainstreaming policy and programming will help to build the evidence for why such support matters, what needs to be instituted and achieved if an enabling environment is to be created and sustained.

Applying the VAWG mainstreaming lens to HIV

Addressing VAWG, especially by intimate partners, is considered an essential part of achieving treatment targets (Heise & McGrory, 2016). Globally, IPV is by far the most common type of abuse, with 30% of women experiencing physical and/or sexual violence by an intimate partner within their lifetime (WHO, LSHTM, & SA MRC, 2013). The links between IPV and possible HIV infection have been the subject of much policy and programmatic attention and work. But the extent and relative strength of the connections between IPV and vulnerability to HIV infection continue to be debated. These discussions consider many variables, including location, risk factors pertaining to different groups of women and girls, and the relative security of the local environment. Nonetheless, evidence indicates that exposure to IPV can increase women's risk of HIV infection through forced sex with an infected partner, limited or compromised negotiation of safer sex practices, or increased sexual risk-taking behaviours (Maman, Campbell, Sweat, & Gielen, 2000). A detailed study in 2015 determined that:

> Analysis of pooled DHS data from 12 surveys and ten sub-Saharan African countries confirms that reported intimate partner violence is associated with a significantly raised risk of HIV infection in women.
>
> *(Durevall & Lindskog, 2015, p. 40)*

Two prospective longitudinal cohort studies from Uganda and South Africa similarly indicate the associations between IPV and HIV infections; the Uganda study suggests that were IPV not to happen, one in five new HIV infections could be avoided (Jewkes, Dunkle, Nduna, & Shai, 2010; Kouyoumdjian et al., 2013a, 2013b).

The opportunities for women to report IPV to formal and informal (customary) justice systems may be difficult, dangerous, and fraught. In situations where vulnerability to HIV infection exists, such avenues may be even further compromised for reasons such as fear of stigmatisation, ostracism, and abandonment by spouse and/or family. In addition, there is evidence that women disclosing their positive HIV status may be even more vulnerable to IPV (UNAIDS, 2014).

Creating an enabling environment

As this chapter argues, the proposed starting point for VAWG mainstreaming is to approach it as a comprehensive, in-depth examination of a given sector as a whole, and as a tool for identifying and operationalising effective links to other sectors. Therefore, to address the many complexities of HIV within the wider context, and to do so within the wider context of mainstreaming VAWG, it is necessary to undertake a continuous process of integration of the two areas of focus throughout the functioning of an organisation or sector; it is not a time-bound and once-only goal. If a sector is to be responsive and reflexive to mainstreaming and engages with other relevant sectors, those institutions, groups, and individuals participating might be able to shape how prevention and mitigation of VAWG and HIV can jointly be addressed in a more holistic and potentially effective fashion.

Such action will certainly be challenging and will require effective engagement and cooperation across sectors that might not always be natural partners. It will also need lengthy, sometimes small-scale community action that is likely to need reinforcement in the longer term, in order to counter any resurgence of entrenched social norms.

Social norm change

The ecological model can be used to draw out in-country differences and to guide understanding of what kind of social norm change interventions are required. Testing of innovative new interventions, and trialling of programmes that have worked elsewhere need to be implemented with caution and close monitoring: there are no quick solutions and what works in one context may well not do so elsewhere.

Programmes such as SASA! (originally implemented in Uganda and now more widely), which work at the community level to address and reduce instances of IPV and minimise risk of HIV infection, indicate that long-term measures to address often deeply entrenched social norms accepted by both men and women can be effective. SASA! is a community mobilisation approach developed by the Ugandan NGOs Raising Voices and CEDOVIP. It aims to prevent violence against women and HIV by addressing a core driver of both: gender inequality. Such initiatives may be particularly effective when a commitment is made to engage for the longer term. The success of the original SASA! programme and the lessons learnt from the multi-disciplinary study into its effectiveness (conducted between 2008 and 2012) have led to the approach being adapted and rolled out in other countries across sub-Saharan Africa, as well as in Southeast Asia, Pacific Islands nations, the Caribbean, and Latin America (Abramsky et al., 2014; Kyegombe et al., 2014; LSHTM et al., 2016).

Changing the perceptual value of women and girls

One activity central to addressing the connections between VAWG, HIV, and justice is to develop gender-responsive policy frameworks at central and local government levels that are sufficiently robust to then facilitate moving the policy from the page into action. Inextricably linked to this is work with communities, first to understand current perceptions of women and girls' value, and then to identify where and how more equitable attitudes and behaviours can be developed. Deeply entrenched perceptions mean that structures of power will need to be challenged, and certain groups may resist any reduction in the value of their own place and space within society. Bridging the divide between change that happens at the structural level and seeing this reflected in shifts in the perceived value of women and girls is a major challenge.

Justice and security practitioners and officials may well be unwilling to alter statutory and customary systems to provide a foundation to support and provide guidance to achieve changes in perceptual value. This reluctance might be due to lack of knowledge regarding the level of VAWG that exists, or the risks of IPV and HIV infection; it might also be a result of individuals' own perceptions of gender relations. Thus, while formal, statutory justice mechanisms generally set out equal access under the law, women's legal rights education might be severely limited and support from households or communities to seek justice might be lacking. In practice, this could mean that, though women have equal rights under the law, they do not have equal access to them. In addition, proposed alternative mechanisms (such as restorative justice) might well be shaped through perspectives that are insufficiently gender aware and fail to understand existing socio-cultural dynamics and the extent to which social norms might need to change in order to achieve lasting, equitable access to justice.[6] Any such approach must include the meaningful participation of women living with HIV, whose rights under formal and customary laws are often even more circumscribed and whose opportunity and/or willingness to seek public redress for VAWG, including IPV, might well be minimal. Nonetheless, people living with HIV, their families, and other community members can be supported in terms of both knowing their legal and sexual and reproductive health rights, and the sanctions that exist (at least on the statute books) to prevent and punish illegal acts (Gruskin et al., 2013; UNAIDS, 2012a, 2012b).

Conclusion: beyond VAWG mainstreaming to further action

While there are no magical solutions or a single blueprint or formula to end VAWG, we believe that adopting a systematic and evidence-based approach is a good starting point. By doing so, outlined above, it is possible to produce robust and sensitive programmes that represent a positive way forward in achieving SDG 5, and, even more importantly, contributing to ending VAWG.

Notes

1 This chapter is informed by the paper by Bradley and Gruber (2018).
2 In a wide field, see Crockett, McCleary-Sills, Cooper, and Brown (2016), and Douglas (2007) on older women's experiences of VAWG, the Staszewska (2015) overview on the SDGs and VAWG, and UNFPA 2013 on the paucity of reliable and disaggregated data on VAWG, especially in situations of conflict and displacement.
3 See, e.g., Alexander-Scott, Bell, and Holden (2016), Fulu, Warner et al. (2013), Fulu, Jewkes, Roselli, and García-Moreno (2013), Jewkes, Flood, and Lang (2014), Morrell, Jewkes, and Lindegger (2012), Raising Voices (2015).
4 Kabeer's parallel attention to resources and agency (structure and culture) has been incorporated into or has informed innumerable research and policy frameworks on women's empowerment (Kabeer, 2003, 2008, 2012).

54 VAWG mainstreaming framework

5 This section on how action on HIV might be interwoven into VAWG mainstreaming is informed by Abramsky et al. (2014), Durevall & Lindskog (2015), Gruber (2005, 2006), Heise and McGrory (2016), Klot and Nguyen (2009), Klot et al. (2012), Kyegombe et al. (2014), LSHTM (2016), Maman, Campbell, Sweat, and Gielen (2000), Stone (2017), UNAIDS (2012a), WHO, LSHTM, and SA MRC (2013).
6 See Deng (2013) for a partial overview of the challenges involved in seeking to begin to address access to justice in insecure settings, for all those who require redress, including survivors of VAWG.

References

Abramsky, T., Devries, K., Kiss, L., Nakuti, J., Kyegombe, N., Starmann, E., Cundill, B., Francisco, L., Kaye, D., Musuya, T., Michau, L., & Watts, C. (2014). Findings from the SASA! Study: A cluster randomized controlled trial to assess the impact of a community mobilization intervention to prevent violence against women and reduce HIV risk in Kampala, Uganda. *BMC Medicine, 12*(1), 122. http://doi.org/10.1186/s12916-014-0122-5

Alexander-Scott, M., Bell, E., & Holden, J. (2016). *DFID Guidance Note: Shifting Social Norms to Tackle Violence Against Women and Girls (VAWG).* Department for International Development (DFID). https://www.gov.uk/government/publications/shifting-social-norms-to-tackle-violence-against-women-and-girls

Bradley, T., & Gruber, J. (2018). VAWG mainstreaming in access to justice programmes: A framework for action. *Development in Practice, 28*(1), 16–32. https://doi.org/10.1080/09614524.2018.1398716

Crockett, C., McCleary-Sills, J., Cooper, B., & Brown. B. (2016). *Brief on Violence against Older Women.* World Bank, Global Women's Institute, IDB and ICRW. https://www.un.org/esa/socdev/documents/ageing/vawg_brief_on_older_women.pdf

Deng, D. (2013). *Challenges of Accountability: An Assessment of Dispute Resolution Process in Rural South Sudan.* South Sudan Law Society. https://www.icnl.org/research/library/south-sudan_sslsdeng/

Douglas, S. (2007). Gender Equality and Justice Programming. Equitable Access to Justice for Women. *Primers in Gender and Democratic Governance, 2.* UNDP. https://iknowpolitics.org/sites/default/files/gendergovpr_justice_undp.pdf

Durevall, D., & Lindskog, A. (2015). Intimate partner violence and HIV in ten sub-Saharan African countries: What do the demographic and health surveys tell us? *The Lancet Global Health, 3*(1), e34–e43. https://doi.org/10.1016/S2214-109X(14)70343-2

Elmusharaf, K., Scriver, S., Chadha, M., Ballantine, C., Sabir, M., Raghavendra, S., Duvvury, N., Kennedy, J., Grant-Vest, S., & Edopu, P. (2019). *Economic and Social Costs of Violence against Women and Girls in South Sudan: Country Technical Report.* Galway: NUI Galway. https://doi.org/10.13025/5rjp-zw58

Fulu, E., Jewkes, R., Roselli, T., & García-Moreno, C. (2013). Prevalence of and factors associated with male perpetration of intimate partner violence: Findings from the UN Multi-country Cross-sectional Study on Men and Violence in Asia and the Pacific. *The Lancet Global Health, 1*(4), e187–e207. https://doi.org/10.1016/S2214-109X(13)70069-X

Fulu, E., & Miedema, S. (2015). Violence against women: Globalizing the integrated ecological model. *Violence against Women, 21*(12), 1431–1455. https://doi.org/10.1177/1077801215596244

Fulu, E., Warner, X., Miedema, S., Jewkes, R., Roselli, T., & Lang, J. (2013). *Why Do Some Men Use Violence against Women and How Can We Prevent It? Quantitative Findings from the United Nations Multi-Country Study on Men and Violence in Asia and the Pacific.*

UNDP, UNFPA, UN Women and UNV. https://gsdrc.org/document-library/why-do-some-men-use-violence-against-women-and-how-can-we-prevent-it-quantitative-findings-from-the-united-nations-multi-country-study-on-men-and-violence-in-asia-and-the-pacific/

García-Moreno, C., Zimmerman, C., Morris-Gehring, A., Heise, L., Amin, A., Abrahams, N., Montoya, O., Bhate-Deosthali, P., Kilonzo, N., & Watts, C. (2015). Addressing violence against women: A call to action. *The Lancet, 385*(9978), 1685–1695. https://doi.org/10.1016/S0140-6736(14)61830-4

Gruber, J. (2005). Silent survivors of sexual violence in conflict and the implications for HIV mitigation: Experiences from Eritrea. *African Journal of AIDS Research, 4*(2), 69–73. https://doi.org/10.2989/16085900509490344

Gruber, J. (2006). Does conflict increase vulnerability to HIV infection? Issues for a research agenda. *African Journal of AIDS Research, 5*(1), 41–48. https://doi.org/10.2989/16085900609490365

Gruskin, S., Safreed-Harmon, K., Ezer, T., Gathumbi, A., Cohen, J., & Kameri-Mbote, P. (2013). Access to justice: Evaluating law, health and human rights programmes in Kenya. *Journal of the International AIDS Society, 16*(3S2), 18726. https://doi.org/10.7448/IAS.16.3.18726

Heise, L. (1998). Violence against women: An integrated, ecological framework. *Violence Against Women, 4*(3), 262–290. https://doi.org/10.1177/ 1077801298004003002

Heise, L. (2011). *What Works to Prevent Partner Violence? An Evidence Overview.* DFID. http://strive.lshtm.ac.uk/resources/what-works-prevent-partner-violence-evidence-overview

Heise, L., & McGrory, E. (2016). *Violence against Women and Girls and HIV: Report on a High Level Consultation on the Evidence and its Implications, 12–14 May, 2015.* STRIVE Research Consortium, London School of Hygiene and Tropical Medicine. http://strive.lshtm.ac.uk/resources/greentree-ii-violence-against-women-and-girls-and-hiv

Htun, M., & Weldon, S. (2014). *Progressive Policy Change on Women's Economic and Social Rights.* UN Women. https://malahtun.files.wordpress.com/2015/03/2014-htun-weldon-un-paper.pdf

ICAI. (2016). *DFID's Efforts to Eliminate Violence against Women and Girls. A Learning Review.* London: Independent Commission for Aid Impact. https://icai.independent.gov.uk/wp-content/uploads/ICAI-Learning-Review-DFIDs-Efforts-to-Eliminate-Violence-Against-Wome....pdf

Jewkes, R. (2014). *What Works to Prevent Violence against Women and Girls? Evidence Review of the Effectiveness of Response Mechanisms in Preventing Violence against Women and Girls.* DFID. https://www.gov.uk/government/publications/what-works-in-preventing-violence-against-women-and-girls-review-of-the-evidence-from-the-programme

Jewkes, R., Flood, M., & Lang, J. (2015). From work with men and boys to changes of social norms and reduction of inequities in gender relations: A conceptual shift in prevention of violence against women and girls. *The Lancet, 385*(9977), 1580–1589. http://doi.org/10.1016/S0140-6736

Jewkes, R. K., Dunkle, K., Nduna, M., & Shai, N. (2010). Intimate partner violence, relationship power inequity, and incidence of HIV infection in young women in South Africa: A cohort study. *The Lancet, 376*(9734), 41–48. https://doi.org/10.1016/S0140-6736(10)60548-X

Kabeer, N. (2003). *Gender Mainstreaming in Poverty Eradication and the Millennium Development Goals.* London: The Commonwealth Secretariat.

Kabeer, N. (2008). *Mainstreaming Gender in Social Protection for the Informal Economy.* London: Commonwealth Secretariat.

Kabeer, N. (2012). *Women's Economic Empowerment and Inclusive Growth: Labour Markets and Enterprise Development*. SIG Working Paper 2012/1. www.idrc.ca/sites/default/files/sp/Documents%20EN/NK-WEE-Concept-Paper.pdf

Klot, J., & Nguyen, V. K. (Eds.) (2009). *The Fourth Wave: Violence, Gender, Culture, and HIV in the 21st Century*. UNESCO. https://www.ssrc.org/publications/view/the-fourth-wave-violence-gender-culture-hiv-in-the-21st-century/

Klot, J. F., Auerbach, J. D., Veronese, F., Brown, G., Pei, A., Wira, C. R., Hope, T. J., & M'boup, S. (on behalf of the participants in the Greentree Meeting on Sexual Violence and HIV) (2012). Greentree white paper: Sexual violence, genitoanal injury, and HIV: Priorities for research, policy, and practice. *AIDS Research and Human Retroviruses, 28*(11), 1379–1388. https://doi.org/10.1089/aid.2012.0273

Kouyoumdjian, F. G., Calzavara, L. M., Bondy, S. J., O'Campo, P., Serwadda, D., Nalugoda, F., Kagaayi, J., Kigozi, G., Wawer, M., & Gray, R. (2013a). Intimate partner violence is associated with incident HIV infection in women in Uganda. *Aids, 27*(8), 1331–1338. https://doi.org/10.1097/QAD.0b013e32835fd851

Kouyoumdjian, F. G., Findlay, N., Schwandt, M., & Calzavara, L. M. (2013b). A systematic review of the relationships between intimate partner violence and HIV/AIDS. *PLoS One, 8*(11), e81044. https://doi.org/10.1371/journal.pone.0081044

Kyegombe, N., Starmann, E., Devries, K. M., Michau, L., Nakuti, J., Musuya, T., Watts, C., & Heise, L. (2014). 'SASA! is the medicine that treats violence'. Qualitative findings on how a community mobilisation intervention to prevent violence against women created change in Kampala, Uganda. *Global Health Action, 7*(1), 25082. https://doi.org/10.3402/gha.v7.25082

LSHTM, Raising Voices, CEDOVIP & Makerere University. (2016). *Stronger Together: Engaging Both Women and Men in SASA! To Prevent Violence against Women* (Learning from Practice Series: Paper 4). London School of Hygiene and Tropical Medicine, Raising Voices, Center for Domestic Violence Prevention and Makerere University. https://raisingvoices.org/wp-content/uploads/2015/09/LP4.StrongerTogether.FINAL_.dec2015.pdf

Maman, S., Campbell, J., Sweat, M. D., & Gielen, A. C. (2000). The intersections of HIV and violence: Directions for future research and interventions. *Social Science & Medicine, 50*(4), 459–478. https://doi.org/10.1016/S0277-9536(99)00270-1

Ministry of Health, Nepal. (2017). *Nepal Demographic and Health Survey (DHS) 2016*. Nepal: Ministry of Health, Nepal, New ERA, & ICF. www.dhsprogram.com/pubs/pdf/fr336/fr336.pdf

Molyneux, M. (1985). Mobilization without emancipation? Women's interests, the state, and revolution in Nicaragua. *Feminist Studies, 11*(2), 227–254. https://doi.org/10.2307/3177922

Morrell, R., Jewkes, R., & Lindegger, G. (2012). Hegemonic masculinity/masculinities in South Africa: Culture, power, and gender politics. *Men and Masculinities, 15*(1), 11–30. https://doi.org/10.1177/1097184X12438001

Nussbaum, M. (2001). *Women and Human Development: The Capabilities Approach*. Cambridge: Cambridge University Press. https://doi.org/10.1017/CBO9780511841286

Raising Voices. (2015). *Stronger Together: Engaging Both Women and Men in SASA! To Prevent Violence against Women* (Learning from Practice Series No. 4: Research Perspectives). https://raisingvoices.org/wp-content/uploads/2015/09/LP4.StrongerTogether.FINAL_.dec2015.pdf

Remme, M., Michaels-Igbokwe, C., & Watts, C. (2014). *What Works to Prevent Violence Against Women and Girls? Evidence Review of Approaches to Scale Up VAWG Programming and Assess Intervention Cost-effectiveness and Value for Money*. South African Medical Research Council. https://www.gov.uk/research-for-development-outputs

Scriver, S., Duvvury, N., Ashe, S., Raghavendra, S., & O'Donovan, D. (2015). *Conceptualising Violence: A Holistic Approach to Understanding Violence Against Women and Girls* (Working Paper). What Works to Prevent Violence Against Women and Girls. https://www.whatworks.co.za/resources/evidence-reviews/item/85-conceptualising-violence-a-holistic-approach-to-understanding-violence-against-women-and-girls

Staszewska, K. (2015). *Promises to Keep: Using the SDGs to Stand with Fearless Women to End Violence.* Action Aid. https://www.actionaid.org.uk/sites/default/files/publications/promises_to_keep_-_using_the_sustainable_development_goals_to_stand_with_fearless_women_to_end_violence.pdf

Stone, L. (2017). A continuum of suffering: Violence against women and girls in the South Sudan conflict. *Humanitarian Exchange, 68*, 22–25. https://odihpn.org/magazine/the-crisis-in-south-sudan/

Taylor, G., Bell, E., Jacobson, J., & Pereznieto, P. (2015). *DFID Guidance Note. Part A: Addressing Violence Against Women and Girls through DFID's Economic Development and Women's Economic Empowerment Programmes.* DFID. https://www.oecd.org/dac/gender-development/DFID-Addressing%20Violence%20Against%20Women-GuidanceNote_PartA.pdf

UN. (1993). *Declaration on the Elimination of Violence Against Women* (General Assembly resolution 48/104 of 20 December 1993). United Nations. https://www.ohchr.org/EN/ProfessionalInterest/Pages/ViolenceAgainstWomen.aspx

UNAIDS. (2012a). *The User Guide for the HIV-related Human Rights Costing Tool: Costing Programmes to Reduce Stigma and Discrimination and Increase Access to Justice in the Context of HIV.* UNAIDS. https://www.unaids.org/en/media/unaids/contentassets/documents/document/2012/The_HRCT_User_Guide_FINAL_2012-07-09.pdf

UNAIDS. (2012b). *Key Programmes to Reduce Stigma and Discrimination and Increase Access to Justice in National HIV Responses* (Guidance Note). UNAIDS. https://www.unaids.org/en/resources/documents/2012/Key_Human_Rights_Programmes

UNAIDS. (2014). *Unite with Women. Unite against Violence and HIV.* UNAIDS. https://www.unaids.org/en/resources/documents/2014/20140312_JC2602_UniteWithWomen

UNFPA. (2013). *The Role of Data in Addressing Violence Against Women and Girls.* UNFPA. https://www.unfpa.org/resources/role-data-addressing-violence-against-women-and-girls

WHO, LSHTM, & SA MRC. (2013). *Global and Regional Estimates of Violence against Women: Prevalence and Health Effects of Intimate Partner Violence and Non-Partner Sexual Violence.* World Health Organization, London School of Hygiene and Tropical Medicine & South African Medical Research Council. https://www.who.int/publications/i/item/9789241564625

3

WOMEN, INTERNAL DISPLACEMENT, AND VIOLENCE IN NEPAL AND MYANMAR

Introduction

This chapter goes into granular detail about two specific, closely focused studies on VAWG in the context of internal displacement, which is an under-researched area. The findings from the research presented here reveal many similarities. Across the two contexts, the prevalence and forms of violence that exist are different to those that were observed in the humanitarian contexts covered in Chapters 4 and 5. As such, this chapter draws attention to the web of violence experienced, primarily by women, in contexts of acute stress, vulnerability, and uncertainty, and sheds light on how previous attitudes and behaviours linked to intimate partner violence (IPV) persist. This reveals that very little work has so far been with regard to experiences of VAWG among internally displaced people. The evidence shows that violence intensifies during times of stress and does so to such an extent that responses to crises ought to include actions that are specifically targeted towards mitigating the rise in cases of VAWG. This chapter will apply the mainstreaming framework presented in Chapter 2 demonstrating how useful it is a mechanism for ensuring every opportunity to end VAWG is utilised even in non-VAWG-specific programming.

This chapter focuses on internal displacement triggered by humanitarian emergencies due to naturally occurring hazards in Myanmar and Nepal. In doing so, it provides evidence to support the overarching argument of this volume – that a VAWG sensitised lens is in fact required across all development and humanitarian emergency sectors and that applying our proposed VAWG Mainstreaming Framework (see Chapter 2) provides a practical approach to addressing VAWG prevention across sectors and contexts. We begin by illustrating why such an approach is needed by setting out the evidence that VAWG, specifically IPV, spikes during times of emergency. The chapter then presents secondary data collected

DOI: 10.4324/9780429280603-3

Women, internal displacement, and violence **59**

by one of the authors as part of a funded project exploring the links between women, violence, and displacement in South Asia. The geographical focus in Nepal was Kathmandu (Middle Hill Area) and the Eastern Terai region. In Myanmar, work was conducted in outer Yangon and Magway. The primary causes of internal displacement in these research contexts were environmental: earthquake and flooding in Nepal, and hurricane and flooding in Myanmar.

The data presented here come from two quantitative sets of approximately 800 respondents in each country, 40 qualitative interviews with women and 20 stakeholder interviews in each country. In both countries, the methodology was mixed, which allowed for data to be triangulated in order to better understand and address the following questions: does VAWG increase and, if so, how much? What seem to be the key triggers of VAWG within a displacement setting specifically? And finally, what level of awareness is present among stakeholders and what level of response exists?

The chapter is organised into two sections that present the data from Nepal and Myanmar, respectively. This is then followed by a final section that offers a number of synthesised reflections and conclusions regarding the need to mainstream VAWG when planning and implementing responses to internal displacement. See also Chapters 4 and 5 for further discussion of VAWG in all humanitarian emergencies, whether caused by naturally occurring hazards, such as addressed here, or by conflict.

Women, violence, and displacement in Nepal

In Nepal, two field sites were selected. The first of these was in the earthquake-affected area of the Kathmandu district. This included the Shankharapur Municipality, which is situated in the North-East part of Kathmandu Valley, approximately 37 km from Kathmandu. This area saw massive internal displacement as a result of the April 2015 earthquake. Most of those experiencing internal displacement were from low socio-economic groups, with weak capacity to cope during the earthquake and to recover from its impact. This part of the study was conducted in two specific clusters. The first cluster was in Nangle Village (taken as the displacement site) and the second was in Palubaari Village (taken as the control site). These two sites were mixed settlements of different caste groupings, including *Tamang, Brahmin, Chhetri, Newar*, and *Dalit* communities.

The second site was the Morang villages, which are situated in the eastern Terai region of the country and about 377 km from Kathmandu and are affected yearly by flooding. Within Morang district, the sites that were selected for the study are Biratnagar Metropolitan City (BMC) and Katahari Rural Municipality (KRM), where the vast majority of households were displaced by the flooding of July and August 2017. In KRM, *Kadam Gachhiya* was selected for the study, and in BMC, *Khap Tole* was the study site. Most inhabitants of both sites in Morang were from the following castes: *Musahar* or *Rishidev* and *Sataar* (*Dalit* community) and other castes, including *Rajbanshi, Shah, Mandal*, and *Mahat*.

60 Women, internal displacement, and violence

Methods and data sets

For the quantitative research, 880 respondents were surveyed (49% from Kathmandu and 51% from Morang). The qualitative data set was gathered through in-depth interviews with 20 participants at each site and an additional 20 interviews with key stakeholders in the development sector (specifically those responding to displacement) were conducted across both sites and in total.

Respondents to the surveys were aged between 18 and 49, and were of various castes and ethnicities, and varied socio-economic status. Most were married (98%) and mainly living with their spouse. In total, 49% of the participants were living in temporary accommodation following either the earthquake or flooding.

Sampling strategy

The aim of the sampling strategy was to ensure that we selected households/ participants who were relevant to the study purpose, while also being able to draw statistically significant conclusions at the study and village/municipal level. In order to achieve this, we applied a mix of purposive and random sampling. We employed a clustered sampling strategy, where we first selected the districts, clusters (i.e. villages/municipality), and then households. Districts and villages/ municipality were selected purposively in order to locate the specific groups of interest. We attempted to achieve representativeness at the study level through random sampling.

Levels of violence

The quantitative and qualitative data revealed that instances of IPV were high across all sites, with an average of 57% emerging from the surveys. However, a much higher prevalence was recorded in Morang with 73% of female respondents reporting that violence against women is 'severe'. Male respondents across both the Morang and Kathmandu districts stated that instances of violence against women were 'low'. While women reported having been forced into sexual intercourse by partners or knowing of other women who had, all the male respondents interviewed denied that forced sexual intercourse perpetrated by the husband occurred. This reveals stark differences in perceptions and points to the presence of a more intense normalisation of violence against women in the minds of men. According to the 2016 Nepal Demographic and Health Survey (NDHS) (Ministry of Health, Nepal, 2017), 30% of women and 23% of men agree that a husband is justified in beating his wife for many reasons such as if she burns food, argues with him, goes out without telling him, neglects the children, or refuses to have sex with him. It also reveals that men do not admit to perpetrating violence against their wives (Ministry of Health, Nepal, 2017).

It is estimated that 35% women worldwide have experienced either physical and/or sexual IPV or sexual violence by a non-partner (not including sexual

Women, internal displacement, and violence **61**

harassment) at some point in their lives (WHO, LSHTM, & SA MRC, 2013). In both our quantitative and qualitative data sets, more than two-thirds of all respondents (male and female) reported that IPV was the most common form of violence (71%), while 22% described violence perpetrated by another family member. The second most common perpetrators of physical violence (after husbands) were as mothers-in-law, which were reported by 8% of the 880 respondents.

According to the 2016 NDHS (Ministry of Health, Nepal, 2017), most ever-married women who have experienced physical violence since age 15 report that their current husbands are perpetrators of that violence (84%), while 7% report mothers-in-law and 5% report other in-laws as perpetrators. These findings broadly align with the findings of the study documented in this chapter.

Knowledge and understanding of violence were found to be higher among the participants in the qualitative data collected in Morang compared with the findings of the quantitative survey. Across sites, 90% of the women interviewed in both the survey and the in-depth interviews understood what the term violence against women means, and they could list forms of violence in line with global classifications. In Morang, female respondents felt that violence was a serious daily issue, impacting on their community; this view was less apparent in Kathmandu. Of 720 female respondents to the survey in Morang and Kathmandu districts, 261 (36%) reported that they had faced or were facing physical violence perpetrated by their husband. According to NDHS survey data, 22% of women in Nepal aged 15–49 have experienced physical violence after the age of 15. Our findings document higher levels in both Kathmandu and Morang when compared against the NDHS data.

Frequency of violence

Out of 864 married respondents (male and female) from both Kathmandu and Morang districts, 36% of women and 40% of men reported that married women had been facing physical violence in their home. Out of 318 survey respondents who reported experiencing physical violence, 112 (35%) stated that they had experienced it in the last 11 months. Again, more serious or more extreme forms of physical violence were reported in Morang compared to Kathmandu. Reporting of sexual violence is notoriously under reported. We found that 14% of women surveyed disclosed experiencing it in the last 11 months, but as mentioned above, men unanimously denied it was a problem. Out of the 864 married men and women surveyed across both districts, a total of 118 respondents (16 men and 102 women), or 14%, reported that they had experienced or perpetrated (in the case of the male respondents) forced sexual intercourse. Out of those 118 respondents, 47 (40%) stated that the forced sexual intercourse they were reporting had happened in the last 11 months. The 2016 NDHS (Ministry of Health, Nepal, 2017) found that 7% of women have experienced sexual violence, and 3% have experienced sexual violence in the past year. Our research indicates that the prevalence of sexual violence is higher in the study districts than suggested by the NDHS data.

Reporting rates

Only 8% of the 736 women surveyed reported that they had attempted to seek help at the time of violence. Additional support around violence is essential, especially when due to displacement, according to 78%. In terms of perceptions as to the most effective avenue for support, 28% of the women surveyed felt female members (members of what?) were best placed. 60% of male respondents felt that the police were the best option. The 2016 NDHS data show that more than one in five women (22%) who had experienced physical or sexual violence sought help. The most common sources of help for women who have experienced physical or sexual violence are their own family (65%) and neighbours (31%), but almost two-thirds of women never sought help or told anyone (Ministry of Health, Nepal, 2017).

The main triggers for violence

Male alcohol consumption

Across the two sites, there was a general perception (noted in responses from 60% of both men and women) that male alcohol consumption was the main trigger for violence against women. For example:

> In my personal view, alcohol leads to violence and should be banned. Men consume alcohol after getting their salary and thus, are unable to provide food for their family which results in violence. Every woman wants to have a good life, wear good clothes, but men spend all of their money on alcohol which results in violence.
>
> *(Kathmandu, female, 40, married, Christian, 4 children, Pariyar caste).*

Household income and domestic labour

Interestingly, though, low income was not seen as a trigger for violence. Perceived poor performance of household chores, however, was seen by 59% of women as the trigger for violence, while a husbands' jealousy was a factor in 40% of the surveys. In the survey data from both sites, there was no relationship between physical violence and insufficient food supply.

Caste and vulnerability

The female respondents of the Terai Dalit community were found to be the most affected by violence. Out of 228 such respondents, 52% reported being affected by violence. The group reporting the second highest prevalence were the caste of *Terai Janajati*, of whom 17% (of 156 women surveyed) reported having been affected by violence. Alcohol was again seen as contributing to this:

Here, the condition of women is vulnerable... violence against women is increasing in this society. Harassment is increasing. Torture is being increased. As I feel that, there are lots of problems for women in this society. Women become victims of violence because of alcohol consumption. On a daily basis, they are being beaten. If they give a birth to a baby girl, they are being beaten. They are tortured through dowry.

(Morang, female, 36, Dalit caste)

Literacy levels

In the data collected, low literacy levels were associated with higher vulnerability to physical violence; of the 261 women surveyed who were not literate, 62% reported that they had experienced violence. This reflects the 2016 NDHS, which found that more than one in three women (34%) with no education have experienced physical violence, compared with one in ten (less than 10%) of women with the School Leaving Certificate or higher education (8%), demonstrating that the likelihood of experiencing physical violence declines with the level of education (Ministry of Health, Nepal, 2017).

Other intersectional dimensions

It was clear that discrimination against single women is present in both sites, and single women reported feeling more vulnerable post-earthquake. There was also evidence of discrimination against disabled women at both sites, with associated increases in their vulnerability post-earthquake or flooding. One interviewee, a 33-year-old disabled woman, *'They hate me. They even told me I am like a dog and elephant'* (disabled woman, Kathmandu, 33). Additionally, the movement of women is closely monitored and under scrutiny, which causes stress. Although many women reported feeling vulnerable while using public transport, lower caste women who are more dependent on cheap transport were affected disproportionately. Though there were no specific quantitative data related to the violence suffered by single women in the 2017 NDHS (Ministry of Health, Nepal, 2017) or our survey data, the NDHS revealed that women who are divorced, separated, or widowed (48%) are nearly twice as likely to have experienced IPV compared to women who were married at the time of the survey (26%).

Displacement as a trigger

The qualitative data highlighted displacement as a trigger for more intense violence than the survey data, perhaps because identifying the link needs requires time for reflection, especially given the already high levels of violence. Understanding the triggers for VAWG is also difficult due the length of time families have been living in temporary accommodation. In the survey, 51% said displacement was not a trigger, while 49% said it was. Out of the 261 women who

64 Women, internal displacement, and violence

disclosed that they had suffered from violence, 54% were living in temporary accommodation.

The qualitative research revealed that women's vulnerability to violence is widely considered to have increased as a result of the earthquake, yet participants do not make a direct link between IPV increases and the earthquake. That said, it is widely reported that the shared shelter conditions following the earthquake did increase tensions and a few reported that this tipped over into IPV.

Options for support

Across both sites, family members were reported as the first option for support (52%), followed by peer networks (35%), and the third option was local government (25%). Among the female respondents (approximately 700), 170 stated that there were no options for support and cited a lack of local organisations as a key barrier. Only 21% of those surveyed reported being aware of the presence of any specialised organisations working with women to end violence and advocate for justice, with 13% saying that they had no knowledge of any such organisations.

The importance of female peer networks in providing support against violence was highlighted by 78% of the women surveyed, and this view was expressed particularly strongly in Morang:

> The women of the village are involved in trying to prevent such cases of violence from occurring. However, the police are not very supportive in such cases. If a woman complains about her husband's behaviour with the police, they tell her to ask her husband to limit the consumption of alcohol.
> *(Woman, 32, Morang)*

Trust in local government figures to deal with instances of violence against women is high in Biratnagar Morang District. This may be down to the targeted recruitment of trusted 'social mobilisers' into government there. Since the government of Nepal moved to a more decentralised system, more women have been recruited into political positions and at all levels, which has been motivated by a country-level gender equality policy. It is perhaps not surprising that women already in local leadership roles (such as social mobilisers) have come forward for elected office and have been successful. This is testament to the level of trust they have acquired among communities.

The government response to the earthquake is largely regarded as having been poor and uncoordinated. NGOs have focused on providing basic support, such as shelter and food provision, but have not addressed VAWG. Additionally, our interviews with stakeholders suggest that interventions to provide basic needs have not considered gender, and that the construction of shelters, for example, has been insensitive to gender and other vulnerabilities.

> Nothing can be done in other's matter. The victim has to suffer on her own. Married women with children are the most vulnerable because they

are unable to leave their marital status and children, and they do not have any work for their survival.

(Woman, 43, shop owner, Kathmandu, Brahmin caste)

Role and impact of local women's organisations

The qualitative research made clear that when engagement with a women's organisation and/or network committed to ending violence has happened, the impact is always recorded as positive in terms of building the confidence to challenge violence and to support the realisation that violence should not happen. There is also evidence that 'positive deviants' have an impact at the local level. Positive deviant is a term that has emerged within social norm theories to identify individuals who go against dominant social and cultural gendered expectations. These individuals are trail blazers, in the sense that they are motivated to be different and to bring about change (see, e.g., Bradley & Sahariah, 2018).

There was a greater willingness both to talk about violence and to challenge it in Biratnagar compared to Kathmandu, which may be a reflection of the success of women's organisations in the region. There may be a stronger link between the activism and awareness raising of organisations in Biratnagar compared to Kathmandu. While conversely, fewer women's organisations seem to be active in Kathmandu Valley where women seem to be less willing to talk about violence or challenge it. This suggests that there is a link between the existence of women's organisations and more openness to discussing violence, the positive impact of which we can see in Biratnagar. Most women's organisations that do exist in Kathmandu tend to focus on micro loans and do not work to end VAWG.

> They can share their thoughts in peer groups and, since these days organisations like us have come, they can directly share their thoughts with us. However, such problems have not arisen. If such problems arise, we first try to solve their problem within the family. If the problem is not solved in that way, we go to the ward office and again if it does not work, we finally go to the police station.
>
> *(Woman, 25, married, no children, Kathmandu, Hindu)*

Findings from the stakeholder interviews

Organisations already engaged in issues surrounding women's rights and gender acknowledged and spoke of a spike in violence against women following displacement.

> Not much attention is given to violence perpetrated against women in post disaster phase, but it is definitely a problem. I think organisations working specifically for the cause of women might have campaigned about it but not much attention is given to it.
>
> *(Worker for a women's organisation in Kathmandu)*

66 Women, internal displacement, and violence

Those organisations and individuals who were not focused on or pursuing activities specifically in relation to gender tended to report that violence did not increase post internal displacement but were aware it is always a problem.

> We haven't heard of those cases here as I think people are aware of such things. They have a feeling of mutual respect and would not do such activities. The vulnerable groups like women and children and senior citizens definitely struggle during those times. As women go through menstruation and lack proper sanitation but we do not have a record of violence in any form in this area.
>
> *(Chair of the local judicial committee, Kathmandu)*

Findings from Myanmar

In Myanmar, two main sites were chosen, Magway and Minbu, both of which are affected by yearly flooding, and outer North and West Yangon, both impacted by Cyclone Nargis in 2006 (Table 3.1).

Data set

In total, 805 respondents were surveyed from five different districts. Out of the total respondents, 15% were male and 85% were female. The respondents of the age group 43+ represented 53%, followed by the age group 24–32 (31%), then 33–38 (13%), and the remaining respondents (3%) were aged 18–23. Most of the respondents (97%) were married and the vast majority (81%) were living with their spouse. Two per cent of respondents were living separately from their spouse, and 4% were divorced. One-tenth of the respondents were widows or widowers. Most participants were from the Bamar ethnic community or Kayin. In total, 61% of the respondents were living in temporary shelter due to the internal displacement. In addition to the survey data, qualitative data was collected across all sites, totalling 41 interviews, all of which were conducted with women.

TABLE 3.1 Number of participants from each site (female and male)

District	Gender		Total (N = 805)
	Male (N = 120)	Female (N = 685)	
Magway	–	63 (100)	63 (100)
Minbu	44 (16)	230 (84)	274 (100)
North Yangon	58 (17)	292 (83)	350 (100)
Pwint Phyu	16 (22)	56 (78)	72 (100)
West Yangon	2 (4)	44 (96)	46 (100)
Total	**120 (15)**	**685 (85)**	**805 (100)**

NB. The figures in parentheses indicate the percentage.

Levels of violence

Over two-thirds of the female respondents (67%) reported that there was severe violence against women in their community, and more than one in four (83%) of the male respondents supported this claim. Almost one-third of the respondents (29%) reported that violence against women occurred in 50–100% of households in their own community. Almost half the respondents (46%) reported that in their community, violence against women happened 'most of the time'.

Types of violence

IPV is the main form of violence

More than 90% of both the male and female respondents reported that the husband was the most common perpetrator of physical violence. Out of 685 female respondents, 184 (27%) reported that they had experienced physical violence perpetrated by their husbands. Among male respondents, 31 of 120 (26%) accepted that they were involved in violence against their spouse. Out of 215 respondents, 44 (20%) stated that the physical violence they reported had occurred within the past 11 months.

It was reported by 15% of the 685 female respondents that they had experienced forced sexual intercourse by the husband. As with the findings from Nepal, male respondents refused to accept that this was a problem. All male respondents reported that they were not involved in forced sexual intercourse during the past 11 months.

Forced sexual intercourse by a non-family member

One per cent of women reported that they had experienced forced sexual intercourse in their community with the perpetrator being someone other than a family member or members. All the female respondents who had faced attempted or actual rape by others (eight in total) were living in temporary accommodation when it took place.

Mother-in-law as the perpetrator

The second most frequent perpetrator of physical violence was the mother-in-law, which was reported by 0.5% of the 805 respondents. Violence perpetrated by mothers-in-law emerged as a finding in both Nepal and Myanmar. Given the high level of IPV also recorded, there is clearly a cycle of violence that needs further investigation. It is likely, given the IPV levels, that many of the mothers-in-law cited in this study as being violent had suffered IPV themselves, or violence perpetrated by their own mother-in-law. Suffering and even surviving violence are not necessarily a trigger for change in terms of motivating a person to challenge

68 Women, internal displacement, and violence

the same types of violence. In many ways, the prevalence of mother-in-law violence is an indication of how deep the normalisation of VAWG is. If violence endured as a young wife can translate into violence against a daughter-in-law later in life, there is clearly a negative process occurring whereby survivors sometimes adopt the harmful behaviours they themselves experienced.

The findings in terms of mother-in-law perpetration are particularly poignant, given the levels of awareness among women (in both contexts) of what constitutes violence. Between 10% and 20% of male respondents and between 35% and 58% of female respondents were knowledgeable regarding what constitutes VAWG. Respondents were generally found to have an awareness of both physical and sexual violence. There was also (to a lesser degree) awareness of what constitutes psychological violence, but the understanding violence related to deprivation/neglect was very limited.

The triggers for violence

As the findings from Nepal also showed, alcohol is a trigger

Over a fifth of the respondents (22%) claimed that the alcoholic behaviour of husbands was the trigger for violence. More than one-third (38%) of the respondents reported that wives faced physical violence on a weekly basis as a result of the alcohol-related behaviour of husbands.

> I was 40 years old when my husband laid his hands on me. He was always intoxicated at that moment; he arrived back home and hit me with his hands. He only hit me to an extent, so there was no appearance of blood. At the time, my children were only students; our family was experiencing financial struggles that involves their academic fees. It was not a pleasant time for us. I was abused when stress was a part of our daily lives. Thankfully, my sons acted as barriers and protected me. I believe his anguish plaguing him was due to our financial difficulties and excessive alcohol consumption.
>
> There are myriad number of women in this village who are in an abusive relationship – whether physically, mentally, or verbally. There are plenty of women who are victims of domestic abuse; women who are just like me concealing our sufferings and chose not to talk about.
>
> *(Woman, 47, married, 2 sons, 1 daughter. Lives with her daughter and her family)*

Low income is a trigger, but given the levels of poverty, perhaps not as much as we might have assumed. More than half of respondents (52%) reported that low income was a causative factor for violence occurring daily and weekly.

Another factor was the perceived responsibility for women to perform household chores. Nearly one-third of respondents (29%) reported that there

Women, internal displacement, and violence 69

was violence triggered by husbands who believed their wives to be performing household tasks to a poor standard. Also, gambling and/or misuse of household money by male family members was cited as a cause by the same number of respondents (29%). Jealousy (i.e. husbands thinking their wives were having affairs with other men) was perceived as a major trigger, with 43% of respondents stating that it played a part in increasing VAWG.

As we saw in Nepal, the impact of internal displacement on the prevalence of VAWG was evident. There was a positive correlation between physical violence by the husband and the nature of people's accommodation.

> My husband's and my problems arose after our evacuation to my mother-in-law's place. It was not necessarily the reason behind our conflicts, but it plays a role in where the behaviour of my mother-in-law interrupts my peace of mind, and that in turn creates a domino effect on other aspects of my personal life. I do not feel safe. Other than sleeping, cooking and eating, I travel to my parent's home and stay there.
>
> *(Woman, 28, married, 2 sons, Thein Gone Village)*

When applying an intersectional lens, additional factors emerge that share some similarities with those observed in Nepal. For example, taking ethnicity as an analytical category reveals that the female respondents of the Bamar community were affected by IPV more so than any other ethnic group. Conversely, taking education, specifically literacy, as an intersectional dimension reveals that 70% of the women who reported physical violence in our study were, in fact, literate. This finding challenges certain assumptions that have emerged in other studies, i.e. low levels of education make a woman or girl more vulnerable to violence. In Myanmar, women are typically educated (at least formally) to a higher level than men. There are more female graduates than male, for example. This is mainly because men start work earlier and women are expected to concentrate on their education until they marry. This inverse relationship warrants further investigation to identify if and how education of both men and women can be leveraged help to tackle VAWG.

Options for support

When asked where women and girls would first find support when suffering from violence, 43% said that local government would be the first option, followed by 12% who said they could and/or would seek support from family members. As with the findings from Nepal, peer networks and local women's organisations represent an important source of support. Almost all the female respondents, 94%, stated that female peer networks were an important part of minimising violence. In terms of organisational support, around 29% of female respondents reported that there were organisations offering support for survivors of violence, but 11% of female respondents expressed that they had no awareness of any such

70 Women, internal displacement, and violence

organisations. The qualitative interviews with non-governmental and community stakeholders in the area of the data collection revealed that, in general, there is a lack of support that is specifically focused on VAWG. While some welfare provision exists, it is generally not tailored to respond to violence. This finding again resonates clearly and strongly with the conclusions drawn from the Nepal research.

Throughout the research, it was evident that support for survivors of VAWG is severely lacking: almost all respondents, 95%, said that additional support is essential for women at the time of displacement, but only 15% of female respondents who had experienced VAWG sought out help at the time when the violence occurred. In terms of combatting the prevalence of violence, 83% of the 685 female respondents believed that telling a local community leader is the best way of countering violence, followed by telling another family member. Similarly, 72% of the 120 male respondents expressed the view that telling a local community leader is the best way of countering violence, but this was followed by reporting to the police. It is clear that the perceived importance of community leaders must be considered when understanding how to address VAWG, but there is a discrepancy across men and women regarding the perceived role of family members and trust in more formal mechanisms, such as police, which must also be taken into consideration.

Conclusion

From our research in Nepal and Myanmar, violence is clearly normalised in women's everyday lives across contexts and sites. This makes evidencing the specific impact of internal displacement in terms of triggering an increase in violence particularly difficult. That said, the data suggests that VAWG does increase at times of stress triggered, in these situations, by displacement. As the stakeholder interviews conducted in Nepal reveal, although there are significant efforts at displacement relief, there is a lack of specific, coordinated response to this increase in VAWG, either within them or alongside them. Displacement as a trigger for VAWG is compounded by additional factors. For example, alcohol consumption among men emerges as the main trigger for male violence, particularly IPV. Men across both sites acknowledged that physical violence against women occurs, but they do not generally accept that sexual violence between husbands and wives occurs. For example, while women report that they are forced into or coerced into sex by their husbands, the men do not acknowledge that this is violence.

Various other personal characteristics and individual circumstances (which include ethnicity, caste/class, marital status, ability/disability, level of education, socio-economic status, and so on) also intersect with gender to shape a person's vulnerability and/or resilience to VAWG. For example, being categorised as lower caste/class women (specifically, Dalit in Nepal and Bamar in Myanmar) are more vulnerable and greater effort and resourcing is clearly needed to support them, particularly at times of crisis. Peer networks and women's organisations are acknowledged across sites as an important source of support and, as such, increasing the level of access to and inclusion within these, especially among those who might otherwise be excluded, will be an important step.

Certain high-risk behaviours can also increase and become more visible, and can perhaps be better mitigated, during times of stress that are likely to exacerbate them, including during displacement. As mentioned earlier, male alcohol consumption is a potential route for intervention that could help to prevent or reduce the prevalence and severity of some forms of VAWG. There is also the response of mothers-in-law, which is an area that needs to be monitored and would benefit from further research in order to identify the triggers and risk factors that lead to it. It may be possible to extend the role of social mobilisers, for example, so that they can be empowered and resourced to identify families and individuals at greater risk of adopting violent behaviours. However, mobilisers will only be effective if situated within a wider enabling environment that acknowledges the realities of VAWG and that is able to take a holistic approach to challenging it.

Community leaders were identified as important actors with the potential to help build the necessary enabling environment. Particularly in the case of Nepal, the formalisation of these actors in local and national government structures has begun to take place, but in both contexts, local government needs to offer advocacy, legal support, and counselling support to women and work actively to challenge the normalisation of violence both in communities and among professionals (e.g. the judiciary). The work of local social mobilisers and organisations needs to be better resourced at times of crisis but also into the long term. And, in order to address VAWG, violence prevention and response both need to be further mainstreamed and localised in humanitarian emergency response mechanisms, especially at sub-national levels.

References

Bradley, T., & Sahariah, S. (2019). Tales of suffering and strength: Women's experiences of working in Nepal's informal entertainment industry. *International Journal of Gender Studies in Developing Societies, 3*(1), 20–36. https://doi.org/10.1504/IJGSDS.2019.096758

Ministry of Health, Nepal. (2017). *Nepal Demographic and Health Survey (NDHS) 2016.* Nepal: Ministry of Health, Nepal, New ERA, & ICF. www.dhsprogram.com/pubs/pdf/fr336/fr336.pdf

UN. (2015). *Violence against Women—Key Findings.* United Nations. https://unstats.un.org/unsd/gender/downloads/Ch6_VaW_info.pdf

WHO, LSHTM, & SA MRC. (2013). *Global and Regional Estimates of Violence against Women: Prevalence and Health Effects of Intimate Partner Violence and Non-Partner Sexual Violence.* World Health Organization, London School of Hygiene and Tropical Medicine & South African Medical Research Council. https://www.who.int/publications/i/item/9789241564625

4

FOCUS ON VAWG IN HUMANITARIAN EMERGENCIES

The scale of the problem and responses

Introduction

The subject of VAWG in humanitarian emergencies is so complex that we cover it in two chapters. This is to ensure that some of the most relevant issues and responses are addressed. Our intention is to provide a discussion of the extent to which the global community succeeds in providing support and redress to VAWG survivors. The depth of suffering in the context of a humanitarian emergency is profound, from its onset until such time as resolution, restoration of community and economy, and opportunity for refugees to return home may become possible. Acknowledgement of this suffering and the often extraordinary courage, hope, resilience, and resourcefulness of affected individuals, groups, and communities lie at the heart of both chapters.[1] Every humanitarian emergency involves insecurity, sexual, physical, psychological, and economic violence, displacement internally or across international borders, loss of home, livelihood and hope, for the people and communities who feel its effects. Such events result in critical threats to life, personal and bodily integrity, physical and mental health and well-being, livelihood and security.

The Women, Peace, and Security (WPS) Agenda is highly relevant to discussions relating to VAWG in humanitarian emergencies, and it is examined in detail in Chapter 6. In this chapter, we provide and consider definitions of 'humanitarian emergencies' in relation to identifying key triggers of VAWG, the mechanisms that underpin it, and actions that can and should be taken to address it. We describe the scale of humanitarian emergencies across the globe and what this means in terms of numbers of people affected, and we seek to draw attention to the fact that within those vast numbers are millions of individual life stories and experiences. We offer an overview of the complexities brought about by different definitions of and approaches to VAWG in emergencies, and we look

DOI: 10.4324/9780429280603-4

at current key multi-partner components and initiatives within the international humanitarian system, specifically regarding the attention paid (or not) to VAWG.

The multi-partner focus has been revitalised since the turn of the 21st century. We consider – where the evidence allows – whether increased support, focus, and action on VAWG in humanitarian emergencies have resulted in more effective prevention and response mechanisms. It is worth noting, as discussed further in Chapter 5, that it was only at the SDG meeting in Addis Ababa, held in October 2019, that a migration indicator was added. It was initially argued that the indicator would sit best in SDG 16 (*promote peaceful and inclusive societies for sustainable development, provide access to justice for all and build effective, accountable, and inclusive institutions at all levels*), and come under target 16.3 (*promote the rule of law at the national and international levels, and ensure equal access to justice for all*) and specifically address refugees through indicator 16.3.3 (*proportion of population who are refugees by country of origin*).

However, the upshot of debate before and during the Addis Ababa meeting is that there will now be a migration indicator under SDG 10 (*reduce inequality within and among countries*) and target 10.7 (*facilitate orderly, safe, regular, and responsible migration and mobility of people, including through implementation of planned and well-managed migration policies*). The new SDG indicator is 10.7.2 (*number of countries with migration policies to facilitate orderly, safe, regular, and responsible migration and mobility of people*) (UN DESA, 2019).[2]

What happens in a humanitarian emergency?

Here, we provide a snapshot of one humanitarian emergency to contextualise what it means for those who are internally displaced, who become refugees, or who act as host communities. It is important to think about each humanitarian emergency as unique, despite often sharing common triggers (such as conflict or natural disasters). Using an illustrative example allows for complexity to be drawn out while also indicating which questions might need to be considered when seeking to understand the unique context of other emergencies.

Box 4.1 Case Study: Venezuelan refugees and migrants in Colombia: VAWG in a humanitarian emergency

Context

By 2019, Colombia hosted more than 1.2 million Venezuelan refugees and economic migrants – nearly 50% of all those displaced since 2015 and, in 2019, as many as 4,000 people continued to arrive each day. The entire journey being undertaken by these refugees and migrants, including crossing the border, may present a grave risk of various forms of VAWG, including coercion, rape, enslavement, and trafficking. Transactional (survival) sex is said to be frequent and widespread. Instances of Intimate Partner Violence (IPV) appear to be high, which is aggravated by the emergency – as is often the case in such contexts.

Colombia is itself slowly recovering from decades of armed conflict, with much internal displacement and violence, including VAWG. Such experiences and visible impunity for acts of VAWG may have contributed to the violence experienced by refugees and migrants. Indigenous populations in the border region are particularly disadvantaged because they may be stateless and many have been internally displaced, losing access to ancestral lands.

Sex and age-disaggregated data are limited, making it difficult to gain an understanding of the extent to which different types of violence are perpetrated, by and against whom, and at which times during displacement. The number of female and/or child-headed households is increasing, with some mothers and children (including pregnant women) being abandoned by male partners or parents en route. Those who are alone or isolated, as well as others who are vulnerable (e.g. the disabled and the elderly), are more at risk of violence and are less likely not to have easy access to services and information relating to VAWG.

While in some border areas there are reasonable health and other services, elsewhere the arrival of Venezuelan refugees has placed extreme stress on an already weak infrastructure. For women and girls, lack of access to post-VAWG services, overall protection, sexual and reproductive health care (including contraception and HIV testing), and water, sanitation and hygiene (including menstrual hygiene) (WASH) services, is of deep concern.

Response

Beyond work undertaken by CARE International, the IRC, and their local partners, coordinated, targeted protection and support programmes that focus on VAWG prevention and response interventions (whether government, International NGO [INGO], or locally led) appear to be limited. There also seems to be limited interaction between INGOs and local Civil Society Organisations (CSOs), as well as with refugees and migrants themselves in terms of active engagement and participation.

The UNHCR Regional Refugee and Migrant Response Plan refers to protection issues linked to GBV and the need for various sectors to address prevention and response, but no over-arching, coherent GBV/VAWG strategy is discussed. While the UNHCR Plan notes that Colombia is the only host country in the region to have humanitarian assistance structures, including a UN Cluster system, it does not mention, let alone advocate for, activating the Protection Cluster with its GBV sub-cluster.

Relevant here is that training, which applied the Cluster approach, on the 2015 Inter-Agency Standing Committee (IASC) GBV Guidelines was provided to Colombian humanitarian actors in 2016/17, including on GBV. (Sources: CARE International, 2019; IASC, 2017c; IRC, 2018b; UNHCR, 2019a; Wirtz et al., 2014.)

Definitions of a humanitarian emergency

Our definitions of 'humanitarian emergency' are based on a review of United Nations High Commissioner for Refugees (UNHCR), International Organisation for Migration (IOM), UN IASC and other documentation (see DFID, 2013; IASC, 2015a, 2017a, 2017b, 2018a, 2019b; IDMC, 2019; UNHCR, 2002, 2018a, 2018b, 2019b; UN OCHA, 2016b, 2019a).

Typically, a humanitarian emergency is understood to have been caused by one or more of the following: a 'man-made' emergency or hazard, a 'naturally occurring' hazard, a 'natural disaster'.

A 'man-made' emergency or hazard generally refers to conflict, whether involving state and/or non-state armed forces, militias, and aggressor civilian groupings. These can be international (occurring in and affecting or involving actors from multiple states) or internal conflicts (affecting all or part of one country).

Naturally occurring hazards

- Meteorological – e.g. cyclones and hurricanes;
- Climatological – e.g. drought;
- Hydrological – e.g. flooding;
- Geophysical – such as tsunamis and earthquakes;
- Biological – such as epidemics (e.g. Covid-19).

Taken together, natural and man-made hazards are often referred to as 'humanitarian emergencies', which is also the way in which we use the term in this chapter.

It is worth noting, however, that other terms or definitions are frequently used in the academic and grey literature. For example, 'natural disasters' is still sometimes used, though less frequently as it is now generally acknowledged that many so-called 'natural' hazards, such as drought or an epidemic, can be brought about or amplified by human action or inaction (see, e.g., Maskrey et al., 1993). At times, particular terms are used either to generalise across or to distinguish between types of contexts, including 'Humanitarian setting', 'conflict setting', 'sudden onset humanitarian crisis', and 'complex emergency', which may refer to either a naturally occurring hazard or conflict, or indeed to a combination of both.

Rarely is there a sharp division between one type of crisis and another. Conflict, for example, can exacerbate existing or emerging natural hazards (and vice versa), and disputes over natural resources can lead to conflict. An example of the latter can be found in attempts by various groups to control valuable mineral supplies in Eastern Democratic Republic of the Congo (DRC), which has fuelled the complex conflict in that region, has contributed to natural resource depletion, and resulted in hazards such as landslides occurring.

Many humanitarian emergencies are protracted, with longer term impacts lasting for years or even decades. Examples of the protracted impact can be seen in the ongoing exodus of Syrian refugees and in the continued existence of the Dadaab camp in Northern Kenya, which was first set up for Somalian refugees in 1991 and for many years the largest settlement of its kind in the world (IRC, 2018a).

How many people are affected by humanitarian emergencies?[3]

According to the UN Office for the Co-ordination of Humanitarian Affairs (UN OCHA, 2019a, p. 4), almost '168 million people will need humanitarian assistance and protection in 2020. This represents **1 in about 45 people in the world** and is the highest figure in decades'. This figure covers both man-made and naturally occurring hazards. The people who are affected by a humanitarian emergency may remain in their homes or move a short distance to stay with family, or they may be displaced internally or internationally, becoming refugees (depending on whether they cross an internationally recognised border).[4] When this happens, they might become members of host communities, or be categorised as asylum seekers or 'stateless' (e.g. the Rohingya).

As of June 2019, UNHCR calculates that 70.8 million people globally were experiencing forced displacement due to conflict. Of these, 25.9 million were refugees (i.e. were outside their country of origin), of whom more than half were under the age of 18. Internally displaced persons (IDPs) numbered some 41.3 million, while 3.5 million people were formally recognised as asylum seekers. The best estimate by UNHCR is that there were 3.9 million stateless people in 2019 (UNHCR, 2019b; see also IDMC, 2019 and 2020). These figures do not include members of host communities, people into whose locality IDPs or refugees have moved.

It has been estimated that each day, 37,000 people are being forced to flee their homes due to conflict and/or fear of persecution – these are the highest numbers ever recorded (UNHCR, 2019b).

Estimates on the total global number of IDPs (as of late 2019) are that perhaps as many as 33.4 million people were newly displaced in 2019 alone, of whom 24.9 million were displaced due to disasters, and of those, 23.9 million IDPs were affected by 'weather-related' events (IDMC, 2019) (Figure 4.1).

The estimated number of people who were internally displaced in 2018 due to 'sudden onset' naturally occurring hazards was 17.2 million, but figures for

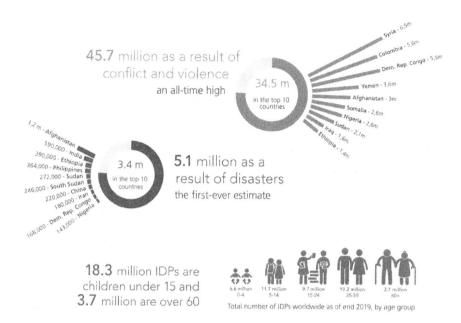

FIGURE 4.1 IDPs in 2019.
Source: (IDMC & NRC, 2020, p. 2; reprinted with permission)

those internally displaced due to 'slow onset' naturally occurring hazards, such as drought, are unavailable (IDMC, 2019).

Overall, in 2018, there appeared to be equal numbers (globally aggregated) of males and females in the populations of concern to UNHCR. Of the 31.5 million people for whom age-disaggregated data were available, 52% were younger than 18 years. Gender and age (i.e. being children and/or being female) are understood to increase vulnerability, meaning that within this already at-risk population, approximately three-quarters (women and children) are in need of enhanced and specific support during humanitarian emergencies.[5]

VAWG (and GBV) in the context of humanitarian emergencies

In its *Handbook for coordinating GBV interventions in emergencies* (GBV AoR – GPC, 2019), the UN-managed GBV Area of Responsibility (the 'AoR': under the Global Protection Cluster [GPC]) defines the gender inequalities that are at the heart of VAWG. The AoR represents an important focal point for the UN and wider work on VAWG/GBV in humanitarian emergencies. Importantly, the *Handbook* highlights three stubborn 'GBV myths':

1   *If you prioritise women and girls in GBV programming, men and boys will be excluded and not have equal access to services;*
2   *Prioritising women and girls for GBV programming means you are not involving men and boys in finding solutions, which is essential to addressing the root causes of GBV;*
3   *LGBTQI+ (lesbian, gay, bisexual, transsexual, queer, and intersex) concerns will be left out if you prioritise women and girls in GBV programming*

(GBV AoR – GPC, 2019, pp. 24–25)

On the ground, most humanitarian emergency policy makers and practitioners do continue to prioritise VAWG when responding to the risks of violence that emerge, primarily because the majority of acts of violence affect females. Such prioritisation is also advocated for in the IASC (2015a) *Guidelines for Integrating Gender-Based Violence Interventions in Humanitarian Action* advocates. Nonetheless, deep concerns and expressions of urgency have been raised about what many see as a dilution of focus away from VAWG and the marginalisation of women and girls in humanitarian emergency actions addressing 'GBV' (see, e.g., GBV AoR – GPC, 2019).

One theme with current traction is that male survivors of GBV may be more stigmatised and face graver repercussions than women. Men are sometimes described as an 'under-served' population, and COFEM notes that the UNHCR 2011–2016 SGBV Strategy omitted specific action on women and girls, while addressing children, men, and boys and LGBTQI+ populations. Moreover, the section on children did not specify girls, although practices noted, (e.g. child marriage, and not least FGM) affect them almost exclusively (see COFEM, 2017; also, COFEM, 2018a, 2018b). A review of the document entitled *Sexual and Gender-based Violence: prevention, risk mitigation and response* (UNHCR, 2019c) also did not reveal any targeted focus on women and girls.

Practitioners have brought attention to the challenges involved in working with men on GBV, which includes the dilution of focus due to male needs, views, and positions taking priority, women not having equal voice, and men 'advising' women what to do (see, e.g., Holmes & Bhuvanendra, 2014a).

However, others have different views, with some arguing that all those who experience gendered violence require equal attention and that equal focus on men and boys will not have negative repercussions for women and girls (for balanced views of such matters, see, e.g., Chynoweth, Freccero, & Touquet, 2017; Small Arms Survey, 2016).[6]

How are women and girls affected by VAWG in humanitarian emergencies?

Each humanitarian emergency will have its own unique triggers and challenges. However, far too many women and girls will experience times of extreme vulnerability to violence, and too little is known about the extent and nature of VAWG during all types of humanitarian emergencies. Available data suggest that VAWG, particularly IPV, is a major problem during humanitarian emergencies. This is not dissimilar to VAWG in non-emergency settings, where IPV is often the most common form of violence (GWI & IRC, 2016; GWI, 2019; What Works, 2019). Yet, targeted programming to address IPV in the wider context of VAWG in humanitarian settings is limited (Jewkes, Stein, & Ramsoomar, 2019; UNICEF, 2016). For instance, the UN Secretary General's 2019 report on 'conflict-related sexual violence' does not discuss IPV in any detail (OSRUNSG, 2019). Primary attention has been given to rape by armed groups, with little attention to what can grimly be described as 'everyday violence' against women and girls, or the social norms that perpetuate both gender inequality and VAWG (see Heise, 1998 and 2011; Meger, 2016; Read-Hamilton & March, 2016; What Works, 2019).

VAWG can occur at any stage of an emergency, including during displacement, upon return and once the emergency itself is over, but particular contexts appear to pose extremely high risks. For example, refugees in increasing numbers are now held in 'transit countries' (such as Syrians in Turkey), and in these settings there is growing evidence of sometimes extreme vulnerability to VAWG (MSF, 2015; UNHCR, UNFPA, & WRC, 2015).

UN OCHA has calculated that approximately one in five women living in a humanitarian emergency environment will have experienced sexual violence (UN OCHA, 2019), and in these contexts it is more likely that the potential consequences of this violence will be more severe. For example, when a woman is raped, she has a maximum of 120 hours to address an unwanted pregnancy, 72 hours to prevent HIV transmission, and only a few hours (sometimes less) to ensure that life-threatening injuries do not become fatal (IRC, 2015). The necessary services to ensure these immediate and time-sensitive needs of survivors are met are all too often entirely absent in a humanitarian emergency.

In 2019, upwards of 25% of women in an emergency situation, approximately 35 million women and girls aged 15–49 worldwide, were of reproductive age, and around 20% were thought to be pregnant (all data from UNHCR, 2019a; see also CARE International, 2017). This is significant because approximately 60% of preventable maternal deaths occur in humanitarian emergencies; every day in 2016, an estimated 507 women and adolescent girls died in humanitarian emergency settings as a result of complications relating to pregnancy and childbirth (UN OCHA, 2016b).

Women and children in female and/or child-headed households are among the most vulnerable to VAWG in humanitarian situations. It has been estimated that 39% of Syrian households in Jordan were female headed in 2015/16 (CARE International, 2016b). This is partly because economic opportunities are limited, resulting in increased vulnerability to coerced labour, enslavement and unsafe working practices. Damage and loss assessments are seldom disaggregated by sex and are usually recorded in terms of productive resources, which tend to be owned by men. This can lead to a substantial undervaluation of the repercussions for women.

The impacts of humanitarian emergencies on children's education are extreme; in 2014/15 36% of the world's out-of-school children lived in conflict-affected countries (UNESCO, 2015). Adolescent girls face particular barriers to education in conflict situations: they are 90% more likely to be unable to get to school, or to be kept away, often due to concerns about safety (Plan International, 2016). Non-attendance at school can increase rates of early marriage and transactional sex in a humanitarian emergency. This means that, in certain circumstances, avoiding the risk of violence (i.e. not travelling to school) can result in increased vulnerability to other forms of violence or abuse (such as sexual exploitation or forced marriage). Understanding how these risks and vulnerabilities interact is a critical part of tackling VAWG effectively.

Key multi-partner initiatives to address VAWG in humanitarian emergencies

Multi-partner initiatives have the greatest potential *globally* to make a difference – in terms of access to resources, capacity to roll out support at (relative) speed, and to advocate for increased focus on VAWG in humanitarian emergencies.

> The world has never seen a stronger expression of commitment than… today from key donors, UN agencies and practitioners to prevent and respond to GBV in emergencies, including through increased funding and strengthened accountability. [Initiatives] have brought international attention to GBV in emergencies and secured high-level commitments from donors, UN agencies and non-governmental organisations (NGOs) in various areas, including to prioritise GBV as a life-saving intervention and to work with all humanitarian sectors on GBV risk reduction, with a focus on sector-wide accountability.
>
> *(IRC, 2015, p. 2)*

An example of the growing movement to end violence was the first conference to 'combat sexual and gender-based violence in humanitarian crises', hosted by Norway in May 2019 (UNFPA, 2019). Commitment to address VAWG is stated by national governments, multilateral organisations, and civil society, as well as by practitioners. However, local CSOs (including those working on VAWG), and especially survivors and other community members, have been less involved. Engagement in the so-called 'localisation' activities represents, at best, work in progress (see also Chapter 5). To a significant extent, the calls to action made prior to the 2019 conference (again, see Chapter 5) echo those made before and after the 2016 World Humanitarian Summit (ABAAD et al., 2015; WHO, 2016).

The greater awareness in recent years of the severe shortfalls in funding, along with the creation of a number of major initiatives, has revitalised international attention on VAWG in humanitarian emergencies. Countries, agencies, and organisations have pledged funds and other support, and there has been more consideration of the need for coherent, concerted, and effective effort. Partnerships, structures, and groupings have been set up and essential guidelines and manuals have been developed (see also Chapter 9 for detailed consideration of funding for VAWG prevention and response in both humanitarian emergencies and development contexts).

To a modest extent, there is also a growing focus on holding all actors to account. This is seen not only in terms of structures, such as funding mechanisms, but also making perpetrators accountable. An example of this is the UN *Prevention of Sexual Exploitation and Abuse* mechanism (PSEA) (for PSEA actions, see UNHCR, 2018b; UNSC, 2016; UN SG, 2019; Whalan, 2017).

VAWG in humanitarian emergencies: actions over time

Here, we consider seven milestones of action, all of which are multi-partner initiatives and concentrate on improving responses to VAWG in humanitarian emergencies. International standards, policies, and manuals have been developed, and the international community continues to be galvanised to support VAWG/GBV prevention and response interventions. These seven initiatives are among the most significant and influential at a global level in the last three decades in terms of clarity of purpose (however diffuse on occasion), funding (however limited), and capacity (however constrained) to put policy into practice (however restricted that practice might be).

1991 and beyond: the IASC, the Cluster system, and the AoR

The Inter-Agency Standing Committee (IASC) was established in 1991. It is envisaged as the primary global strategic coordination mechanism for inter-agency humanitarian response. Ten UN agencies are IASC members; 'standing invitees' include other non-member UN agencies, non-UN agencies (such as the Red Cross/Crescent movement) and NGO networks. The IASC defines joint policy, sets standards, and oversees development of guidelines for humanitarian action across the board, i.e. not solely for VAWG and gender.

Where is the IASC positioned within the current humanitarian emergency landscape?

The over-arching structure is the Cluster system, established after the 2005 UN humanitarian reform agenda. Each of the eleven Clusters comprises a group of humanitarian organisations, both the UN and non-UN, and each has its own responsibilities for coordination. The Cluster approach is the primary mechanism for response in humanitarian emergencies and, as such, acts as the pivot point for global action.

In 2011, the IASC adopted the 'Transformative Agenda', which addresses effective collective response (IASC, 2015b). The Transformative Agenda has had positive impacts, including in terms of defining and developing a humanitarian programme cycle, but little improvement has so far been seen in other areas, such as capacity development at country level beyond IASC members, or increasing accountability to affected populations. The Transformative Agenda is fairly quiet on VAWG and gender aspects of humanitarian emergency response structures, actions, and accountability. For example, the 'review of [IASC Transformative Agenda] reviews' makes no direct reference to either (GPPI, 2016). That said, the IASC does have a Reference Group on Gender in Humanitarian Action, co-chaired by UN Women, which 'specifically works to ensure that humanitarian action delivered by the UN and other actors responds to gender-differentiated needs and realities on the ground' (IASC, 2017a, 2017c).

The **GBV Area of Responsibility** (the GBV AoR) was founded in 2006 and has been led by the UN Population Fund (UNFPA) since 2016. It sits within the IASC Global Protection Cluster, and its remit is to strengthen system-wide preparedness and technical capacity. To do so, it brings together relevant actors under the shared objective of ensuring life-saving, predictable, and accountable GBV prevention, risk mitigation, and response in emergencies. There are also GBV 'sub-clusters' at national level.

1995: the Beijing conference

At the Beijing Conference (the Fourth World Conference on Women), widely considered to have been ground-breaking for its range and focus, 189 UN member states unanimously adopted the Beijing Declaration and Platform for Action (the POA), which set out a detailed, wide-ranging, global agenda to bring about greater gender equality and human rights for women and girls. Twelve areas of critical concern were identified in the POA. Two of these twelve *strategic objectives and actions* are of particular relevance here, as they home in on violence against women (Objective D) and women in conflict (Objective E). Much has been achieved since Beijing, and yet its objectives still remain elusive goals (see UN Women, 2014).

2000: UN Security Council Resolution 1325, and subsequent UNSCRs addressing VAWG

One major action that has resulted in increased global attention being focused on VAWG in humanitarian emergencies is the UN Security Council Resolution 1325 (SCR 1325) on women, peace, and security, adopted on 3rd October 2000. It represents the culmination of decades of work by actors, including CSOs and advocacy groups to bring issues of VAWG in humanitarian emergencies to wider attention (UNSC, 2000) (see Chapter 6 for further discussion with reference to the WPS Agenda).

Resolution 1325 marks a step change in attention to VAWG in conflict situations. Specifically, it asks '*all parties to conflict to take special measures to protect women and girls from gender-based violence, particularly rape and other forms of sexual abuse, in situations of armed conflict*' (UNSC, 2000, p. 3).

Since 1325 further UNSCRs have highlighted or expanded the focus to include accountability, and awareness of the roles that female survivors and other community members and civil society can play in working to reduce VAWG (see Chapter 6 for a discussion of the WPS Agenda).

2013: the Call to Action on protection from gender-based violence in emergencies

The Call to Action is a multi-stakeholder initiative, set up in 2013, and by 2018 had brought together some eighty partners. At its core is a commitment to bring global attention to a 'long-neglected' issue. Its goal is to transform how GBV is addressed in emergencies, to mitigate the risk of it happening, and to support survivors – especially women and girls. Call to Action is considered to have the potential to achieve high-level commitment and for its platform to highlight how much of a threat GBV (especially VAWG) is in a humanitarian emergency (see, e.g., IRC, 2017). *The 2016–2020 Road Map* provided an operational framework, outlined concrete actions, and focused on pledges by partners translating into action, and this focus has been continued in the recently launched *2020+ Roadmap*. Partners are expected to ensure that their commitments will contribute to achieving the ambitious, far-reaching objectives (see Call to Action, 2015, 2018, 2019).

2015: The Real-Time Accountability Partnership (RTAP)

RTAP was launched in January 2015 and is a global, multi-agency initiative addressing GBV in emergencies (RTAP, 2017a, 2017b; see also UN OCHA, 2016a). It represents a shared commitment between Call to Action partners and the wider humanitarian community and, as such, is intended to build upon (not duplicate or divert) Call to Action objectives. It also builds on the GBV *Guidelines* (IASC, 2015) and later IASC and AoR documentation, including the IASC *Guideline on Gender* (IASC, 2018a), the *Handbook on people with disabilities* (IASC, 2018c), and the *AoR Handbook* (GBV AoR - GPC 2019).

In 2016, baseline assessments were conducted for the RTAP in Nigeria, South Sudan, Myanmar, Iraq, and Turkey. Key conclusions (none of which were new) were that coordination is crucial for more effective responses, specific funding for coordination is necessary to achieve better GBV programming, specialised technical support is required to ensure programmes achieve their objectives, and capacity development at a local level is essential for responsive and supportive GBV interventions (ISG, 2017; RTAP, 2017a, 2017b). The baseline led to the development of the RTAP *GBV Accountability Framework*, adopted in 2018 by Call to Action in order to support the operationalisation of its Road Map. The framework is intended to support and strengthen field implementation and to facilitate fulfilment of the Call to Action goal, which is to ensure that every humanitarian response provides safe and comprehensive life-saving services for GBV survivors and mitigates the risks of GBV.

The RTAP *Baseline Report* also reviews much of the research and advocacy around GBV prevention and response in emergencies, noting that there has been 'little success' in terms of prioritisation and accountability (ISG, 2017). This statement could be read as something of an indictment of earlier initiatives to address GBV/VAWG in humanitarian emergencies. RTAP is apparently intended address this lack of success through a focus on strategic actions under the mandate

84 Focus on VAWG in humanitarian emergencies

of its partners during each stage of a humanitarian emergency. The *GBV Accountability Framework* was piloted through collective actions by humanitarian actors (purposely not solely those addressing GBV prevention and response) in South Sudan and Iraq from 2017 to 2018.[7]

Now, the focus must be on assessing the coherence and compatibility of the framework, Road Map and Call to Action, identifying how much space there is for localisation, and better understanding what is happening to support survivors and those at risk of VAWG.

2015 and onwards: the IASC GBV Guidelines and the AoR GBV Handbook[8]

These are highly comprehensive initiatives that are reflective of the increasing stated commitment to improvements in overall response to GBV/VAWG, which is to be achieved through enhanced efficiency, coordination, evidence (although this is articulated less often and less clearly), and greater funding.

The extensive (366 pages) document *Guidelines for Integrating Gender-Based Violence Interventions in Humanitarian Action. Reducing risk, promoting resilience and aiding recovery* was published in 2015. The need to revise the earlier (2005) guidelines is well illustrated by the case study of the impact of Typhoon Haiyan, which struck the Philippines in November 2013. In Haiyan's aftermath, there was a great deal of attention, support, and funding provided to VAWG prevention and response, as well as evaluation of how effective the support had been.

Box 4.2 Case Study: The Typhoon Haiyan humanitarian emergency and efforts to prevent and respond to VAWG

Haiyan struck the Philippines on 8th November 2013, bringing widespread devastation. To date, it is the most powerful naturally occurring hazard to strike the country. Haiyan killed 6,000 Filipinos, displaced 4 million people, and affected upwards of 16 million. Communities and local, national, and international humanitarian actors were entirely unprepared for disaster of this scale. Flooding and destruction of infrastructure led to major delays in reaching people in great need, and the UN declared an IASC Level 3 humanitarian emergency – a classification reserved for the most challenging and complex situations. The 2005 IASC *GBV Guidelines* served as the key tool for initiating and implementing interventions to address VAWG.

To what extent did the response meet the needs of women and girls?

Limited disaggregated data are available for VAWG that is specifically linked to Haiyan. It is known that sexual violence against children intensified, that the desire for safe and sex separate spaces was not met, and that there was inadequate coordination of VAWG survivor services. The 2013 Demographic and Health Survey indicated high levels of IPV, rape, coercion, and exploitation in the Philippines, and such violence was exacerbated after Haiyan (IRC, 2015b; IRC & GWI, 2015).

ITAD, IRC, and GWI research indicates that VAWG prevention needs were not adequately and coherently addressed and coordination was limited. DFID was the largest bilateral donor during Haiyan, providing £77M, yet even the weight of DFID's significant global role on VAWG 'failed to translate into commensurately improved quality or quantity of [VAWG] programming at field level in the Haiyan response' (ITAD, 2015, p. 7).

Despite the steps set out in the 2005 IASC Guidelines, women and girls and local women's groups were insufficiently consulted and engaged at all stages of the humanitarian response. Neither sex disaggregated data nor VAWG-specific information was collected during the first wave of the Multi Cluster/Sector Initial Rapid Assessment (MIRA I). Although the second wave, MIRA II, was an improvement, attention to VAWG and GBV remained modest, and where there was attention gender and GBV were too often conflated. Moreover, when the Guidelines and the linked GBV Minimum Standards were ignored or inadequately applied, there was little accountability of local or international actors. The most notable successes in VAWG prevention and response came from local NGOs, women's groups, and GBV experts (see DFID, 2015; IASC, 2005; IFRC, 2018; IRC, 2015; IRC & GWI, 2015; ITAD, 2015).

The 2015 *GBV Guidelines* are intended to provide practical guidance and effective tools for non-GBV specialist humanitarian actors and communities. These guidelines support coordination, planning, implementation, and monitoring and evaluation of essential actions for the prevention and mitigation of GBV at all stages of a humanitarian response, providing thematic area guides and sector-specific recommendations for GBV risk mitigation strategies.

The revised 2019 *AoR GBV Handbook* forms part of the 2018–2020 GBV AoR strategy, the objective of which is to coordinate global activities to combat GBV in emergencies (GBV AoR – GPC, 2019; see also IASC, 2017c, 2017d). *The GBV Handbook* sets out core GBV principles, grounded in the principle of 'do no harm' (see also the 2018 SPHERE *Handbook* and its *Humanitarian Charter and Minimum Standards*).[9] Core principles for GBV coordination and programming are safety, respect, confidentiality, and non-discrimination, for a survivor-centred approach.

The target audience and perceived primary applications of the 324-page AoR *GBV Handbook* are described as follows:

> This Handbook is designed primarily for GBV coordinators, which may include UN, international or local NGO or national government coordinators at the national and sub-national levels. It will also be a useful tool for sub-cluster

members... [It] is a quick-reference tool that provides practical, field-level guidance to establish and maintain a GBV sub-cluster in a humanitarian emergency... [Its] focus is on GBV coordination...to promote and ensure best practices and standards across an integrated humanitarian response.

(GBV AoR – GPC, 2019, p. 1)

The two documents were revised by the GBV AoR under the IASC Global Protection Cluster. No information is available on why two such major undertakings were necessary. It is perhaps based on a perceived requirement for separate and tailored support to be given to non-technical GBV actors (i.e. the 2015 IASC *GBV Guidelines*) and technical specialists (i.e. the 2019 *AoR GBV Handbook*).

Have the IASC GBV Guidelines and the AoR GBV Handbook been applied?

No independent assessment appears to have been carried out to establish the effectiveness of using the 2015 *GBV Guidelines* in a humanitarian emergency, nor has there been any appraisal of the views or opinions of national governments or local and international NGOs as members of Clusters. Nonetheless, several UN agencies have 'institutionalised' the IASC *GBV Guidelines* (see, e.g., UNICEF, 2016, 2017; WFP, 2016). Thus, UNFPA has worked on alignment and integration of the *GBV Guidelines* into its activities (UNFPA, 2015, 2017) and has used them for training (IASC, 2017b; however, see also the Colombia and Venezuela case study above for a counter example). For the more recent AoR *GBV Handbook*, published in 2019, no information is yet available on the extent or effectiveness of its use.

Is there effective co-working? The *GBV AoR Handbook* describes the relationship between the AoR and the Call to Action. The 2018–2020 GBV AoR Strategy is aligned with both the Global Protection Cluster (GPC) *Strategic Framework* and the Call to Action *Road Map*; the GBV AoR has made commitments to the Call to Action, including supporting GBV sub-clusters to engage and enhancing work with local CSOs. Regional Emergency GBV Advisor (REGA) support has been promised and indeed provided.[10] The intention throughout is for improved coordination and action.

The 2015 IASC *GBV Guidelines* seem to have since been retrofitted to become more aligned with the Call to Action and RTAP:

Core to achieving the implementation goals is to link the GBV Guidelines' roll-out with ongoing initiatives related to GBV in emergencies, such as the Call to Action on Protection from GBV in Emergencies [and] the Real Time Accountability Partnership on GBV in Emergencies.

(IASC, 2017b, p. 1)

Two-year Call to Action Road Maps were created in 2018 for North-eastern Nigeria and the DRC in order to develop and field test operationalisation of the Call to Action. In both locations, the core objective was effective integration of efforts addressing GBV challenges into humanitarian response, thereby improving services for survivors and those at risk. The ambition was to achieve results through actions such as greater localisation, increased funding, and more stringent accountability measures. Support was provided by REGA, through the GBV AoR (Call to Action, 2019), but no reports on impact or outcomes appear to be available.

2016: the world humanitarian summit

The World Humanitarian Summit (the WHS) in May 2016 is said to have ushered in a 'new way of working' to address the nexus between humanitarian emergencies, vulnerability, security, and peacebuilding, under the umbrella of achieving the SDGs. Perhaps the weightiest of the initiatives emerging from the 2016 WHS is the Grand Bargain (Chapter 9 looks at this and other funding streams in greater detail).

In advance of the WHS, a grouping of 20 NGOs and networks working on VAWG prevention and response and gender equality set forward six priority objectives to combat VAWG in humanitarian emergencies in order to expand genuine WPS engagement and to strengthen coordination of existing mechanisms and international instruments (ABAAD et al., 2015). To date, its six priorities have not been adequately addressed in any of the Grand Bargain work streams.

Concluding remarks

Work on this chapter has revealed the urgent need for a comprehensive, independent review of (i) the extent to which duplication, confusion, and hurdles act as a barrier for the effective funding and participation of national and local actors, and (ii) the extent to which survivors truly have a voice. Such a review should also investigate whether the mechanisms that are (or are not) in place ensure that those who hold the purse strings, as well those managing and administering interventions, can be held accountable. At the very centre of any such review should be the needs and voices survivors and those who remain most at risk of VAWG.

There needs to be a concerted, global, and frank look at the extent and severity of VAWG vs. other forms of GBV, particularly those suffered by men and boys. Such an assessment would have to gain an understanding of scale, gather robust disaggregated data, clarify types of violence suffered, and identify who is most at risk. There are many voices urging that attention be paid to potential or actual dilution of focus away from VAWG and the dangers inherent in such shifts. Despite the important recognition that men and boys may also be at risk of particular forms of violence, it stands true that women and girls represent the overwhelming majority of those most vulnerable to sexual, physical, emotional, economic, and other forms of violence. This is true in most local and national contexts and at the global level.

88 Focus on VAWG in humanitarian emergencies

Notes

1 This chapter has been informed by interventions and literature from all parts of the globe. See Bradley and Gruber, (2018); CARE International (2016b, 2017); Glass et al. (2018); Gruber (2005); IAWG (2018); OHCHR (2019); Tappis, Freeman, Glass, and Doocy (2016); UNFPA (2017); UNHCR (2018c); UNICEF (2016); UNISDR (2017); What Works (2019). The literature addresses, e.g., shifts in focus on VAWG/GBV, attention to social norm change, the need not to lose sight of other vulnerable groups, including the elderly, the disabled, people identifying as LGBTQI, and how best to provide mental health and psychosocial support.

2 See Chapters 5, 6, and 9 for further discussion of SDG 5 and 16 Targets and Goals.

3 All displacement figures are estimates: the variation indicates the extreme challenge of accurate counting, as well as the ramifications, e.g., matching resources to actual need.

4 Refugees are protected under international law. The 1951 Refugee (Geneva) Convention defines a refugee as someone who is unable or unwilling to return to their country of origin owing to a well-founded fear of being persecuted for reasons of race, religion, nationality, membership of a particular social group, or political opinion. The 1951 Convention was updated in 1967 (the Protocol); a widely held opinion is that there is insufficient attention to sex/gender. '[The Convention and its Protocol] inadequately address gender-related persecution and, in particular, the asylum claims of refugee women' (Smith, 2016, p. 65; also, Niżynska, 2015 and UNHCR, 2002). Insufficient gender focus in the Convention and Protocol may have considerable implications, e.g., lack of robust support and justice mechanisms that enable refugees fearing gender-specific persecution, including VAWG, to seek asylum. The CEDAW Committee requests states to recognise gender-related forms of persecution and to interpret the 'membership of a particular social group' ground of the 1951 Convention to apply to women. Gender-sensitive registration, reception, interview, and adjudication processes need to be in place to ensure women's equal rights to asylum (CEDAW, 2011).

5 The 2020 UN OCHA report contains a section entitled *Zero tolerance for sexual exploitation and abuse.* However, the section is gender-blind and does not flag up any female-specific issues.

6 For further focus on men and boys in humanitarian emergencies, see CARE International UK and Promundo (2018); Edström and Shahrokh (2016); IASC (2005); Wirtz et al. (2018), etc. Conversely, for extensive literature highlighting the need to prioritise VAWG prevention and response in humanitarian emergencies, see, e.g., Badshaw and Fordham (2013); Birchall (2016); CARE International (2016a, 2016b, 2019); Casey and Hawrylyshyn (2014); Fletcher-Wood and Mutandwa (2019); GWI & IRC (2016); Holmes and Bhuvanendra (2014a, 2014b); Hossain et al. (2014); Hossain, Zimmerman, and Watts (2018); IASC (2015a, 2017d, 2018a, 2018c); IFRC (2018); IRC (2012), MHPSN (2017); Perrin et al. (2019); Plan International (2016); Read-Hamilton (2014); Read-Hamilton and Marsh (2016); UNHCR (2018a); UN OCHA (2016b, 2019); UN Women (2013); UN Women & IDS (2015); Vu et al. (2014); WHO, LSHTM, & SA MRC (2013). This chapter has also been enhanced by a close review of the 2015 *Lancet* series on VAWG – see also Chapters 2 and 9.

7 Reports were expected for late 2019, but may not yet be in the public domain.

8 The 2018 IASC *Gender Handbook* (p. 401) acknowledges that VAWG/GBV is a manifestation of gender inequality and power imbalance; there needs to be optimal dovetailing and effective integration on both issues. The target audience for the *Gender Handbook* is defined as front-line humanitarian actors across all sectors, as well as gender specialists. The Handbook is intended to be integrated across the humanitarian programme cycle, for use alongside, e.g., the IASC *GBV Guidelines* and the *SPHERE Handbook*.

9 The SPHERE project was launched in 1997; it has global membership. Its goal is improving the quality of assistance provided in humanitarian emergencies, while ensuring maximum accountability (SPHERE, 2018; UN Women, 2013). SPHERE was the first organisation to establish minimum standards for humanitarian assistance. The Handbook contains the Humanitarian Charter, which states that all people affected by a humanitarian emergency have a right to receive protection and assistance. The Code of Conduct is a further integral part. The Handbook does not mainstream VAWG/GBV or gender. There are some references to GBV, but not presented in a strategic or operationalising way. The ten Code of Conduct core principles do not refer to gender.

10 Since 2014, GBV AoR REGA have provided regional and country-level support by deploying to Level 3 emergencies. It has not been possible to find any independent REGA evaluations.

References

ABAAD, et al. (2015). *Joint Position: Calling for a Pledge to Empower Women at the World Humanitarian Summit*. Grouping of 20 NGOs and Networks, including Arab Organisation for Human Rights, Feminist Dalit Organisation, Gregoria Apaza Center for the Promotion of Women, ActionAid, CARE International, GADN, Oxfam, Somaliland NAGAAD Network and the Women's International League for Peace and Freedom (Peace Women). https://wilpf.org/wp-content/uploads/2015/08/Joint-Agency-Position-WHS-gender-120815.pdf

Badshaw, S., & Fordham, M. (2013). *Women, Girls and Disasters: A Review for DFID*. Department for International Development. https://gsdrc.org/document-library/women-girls-and-disasters-a-review-for-dfid/

Birchall, J. (2016). *Gender, Age and Migration: An Extended Briefing*. Institute of Development Studies, University of Sussex. https://opendocs.ids.ac.uk/opendocs/handle/20.500.12413/10410

Bradley, T., & Gruber, J. (2018). VAWG mainstreaming in access to justice programmes: A framework for action. *Development in Practice, 28*(1), 16–32. https://doi.org/10.1080/09614524.2018.1398716

Call to Action. (2015). *Road Map 2016–2020*. Call to Action on Protection from Gender-Based Violence in Emergencies. https://www.calltoactiongbv.com/what-we-do

Call to Action. (2018). *Road Map 2016–2020: Progress Report 2017*. Call to Action on Protection from Gender-Based Violence in Emergencies. https://1ac32146-ecc0-406e-be7d-301d317d8317.filesusr.com/ugd/c7d675_1efeaf676cfb4ba48a44176b6051fd6e.pdf

Call to Action. (2019). *Road Map 2016–2020; 2018 Progress Report*. Call to Action on Protection from Gender-Based Violence in Emergencies. https://1ac32146-ecc0-406e-be7d-301d317d8317.filesusr.com/ugd/1b9009_f8a3940dca8d45c992d8378ad941d161.pdf

CARE International. (2016a). *Empowering Women and Girls Affected by Crisis: CARE's Progress towards Achieving Gender Equality in Humanitarian Programming*. https://reliefweb.int/report/world/empowering-women-and-girls-affected-crisis-cares-progress-towards-achieving-gender

CARE International. (2016b). *New CARE Study: Four in Five Syrian Refugees Struggle Below the Poverty Line, Face Increasing Challenges*. https://www.careinternational.org.uk/new-care-study-four-five-syrian-refugees-struggle-below-poverty-line-face-increasing-challenges

Care International. (2017). *Suffering in Silence: The 10 Most Under-Reported Humanitarian Crises of 2016*. https://reliefweb.int/report/world/suffering-silence-10-most-under-reported-humanitarian-crises-2016

CARE International. (2019). *CARE Rapid Gender Analysis. Latin America and Caribbean: Venezuelan Migrants & Refugees in Colombia*. https://reliefweb.int/report/colombia/care-rapid-gender-analysis-latin-america-caribbean-venezuelan-migrants-refugees

CARE International UK & Promundo. (2018). *Men and Boys in Displacement. Assistance and Protection Challenges for Unaccompanied Boys and Men in Refugee Contexts*. CARE International UK. https://reliefweb.int/report/world/men-and-boys-displacement-assistance-and-protection-challenges-unaccompanied-boys-and

Casey, J., & Hawrylyshyn, K. (2014). Adolescent Girls in Emergencies: A Neglected Priority. *Humanitarian Exchange, 60*, 33–36. https://odihpn.org/wp-content/uploads/2014/02/HE_60_web_1.pdf

CEDAW. (2011). *Statement on the Anniversaries of the 1951 Convention Relating to the Status of Refugees and the 1961 Convention on the Reduction of Statelessness* (Adopted, 19 October 2011 during the 50th session: A call for Gender Equality for Refugees and Stateless Persons). OHCHR. https://www.ohchr.org/documents/HRBodies/CEDAW/Statements/StatementAnniversaries1951Convention.pdf

Chynoweth, S. K., Freccero, J., & Touquet, H. (2017). Sexual violence against men and boys in conflict and forced displacement: Implications for the health sector. *Reproductive Health Matters, 25*(51), 90–94. https://doi.org/10.1080/09688080.2017.1401895

COFEM. (2017). *Funding: Whose Priorities? Feminist Perspectives on Addressing Violence against Women and Girls Series* (Paper No. 4). Coalition of Feminists for Social Change. https://raisingvoices.org/wp-content/uploads/2013/03/Paper-4-COFEM.final_.sept2017.pdf

COFEM. (2018a). *Why Does GBV Programming Focus on Women and Girls? Feminist Pocketbook* (Tip Sheet 2). COFEM. https://cofemsocialchange.org/wp-content/uploads/2018/11/TS2-Why-does-GBV-programming-focus-on-women-and-girls.pdf

COFEM. (2018b). *Violence against Men and Boys. Feminist Pocketbook* (Tip Sheet 7). COFEM. https://cofemsocialchange.org/wp-content/uploads/2018/11/TS7-Violence-against-men-and-boys.pdf

DFID. (2013). *Violence against Women and Girls in Humanitarian Emergencies*. CHASE Briefing Paper. Department for International Development. https://assets.publishing.service.gov.uk/government/uploads/system/uploads/attachment_data/file/271932/VAWG-humanitarian-emergencies.pdf

DFID. (2015). *DFID Management Response to ITAD Evaluation of the UK's Humanitarian Response to Typhoon Haiyan (Yolanda)*. UK Department for International Development. https://assets.publishing.service.gov.uk/government/uploads/system/uploads/attachment_data/file/520693/Man-resp-UK_s-humanitarian-response-typhoon-Haiyan.pdf

Edström, J., & Shahrokh, T. (2016). *Reframing Men and Boys in Policy for Gender Equality: Conceptual Guidance and an Agenda for Change* (EMERGE Framing Paper). Institute of Development Studies, Promundo US and Sonke Gender Justice. http://opendocs.ids.ac.uk/opendocs/bitstream/handle/123456789/10037/EMERGE%20Reframing%20Men%20and%20Boys.pdf

Fletcher-Wood, E., & Mutandwa, R. (2019). *Funding a Localised, Women-Led Approach to Protection from Gender Based Violence: What Is the Data Telling Us?* Action Aid. https://actionaid.org/publications/2019/funding-localised-women-led-approach-protection-gender-based-violence

GBV AoR – GPC. (2019). *Handbook for Coordinating Gender-Based Violence Interventions in Emergencies.* Gender-Based Violence Area of Responsibility - Global Protection Cluster. https://gbvaor.net/sites/default/files/2019-07/Handbook%20for%20 Coordinating%20GBV%20in%20Emergencies_fin.pdf

Glass, N., Perrin, N., Clough, A., Desgroppes, A., Kaburu, F. N., Melton, J., Rink, A., Read-Hamilton, S., & Marsh, M. (2018). Evaluating the communities care program: Best practice for rigorous research to evaluate gender-based violence prevention and response programs in humanitarian settings. *Conflict and Health, 1*(1), 1–10. https:// doi.org/10.1186/s13031-018-0138-0

GPPI. (2016). *IASC Transformative Agenda: A Review of Reviews and Their Follow-Up.* Global Public Policy Institute on behalf of the INSPIRE Consortium. https://www. gppi.net/2016/02/05/iasc-transformative-agenda-a-review-of-reviews-and-their-follow-up

Gruber, J. (2005). Silent survivors of sexual violence in conflict and the implications for HIV mitigation: Experiences from Eritrea. *African Journal of AIDS Research, 4*(2), 69–73. https://doi.org/10.2989/16085900509490344

GWI. (2019). *What Works to Prevent Violence against Women and Girls in Conflict and Humanitarian Crisis: Synthesis Brief.* DFID (UK Aid) and the George Washington University, Global Women's Institute. https://www.rescue-uk.org/sites/default/files/ document/2051/p868ircsynthesisbriefreportlr.pdf

GWI & IRC. (2016). *Evidence Brief: What Works to Prevent and Respond to Violence against Women and Girls in Conflict and Humanitarian Settings?* Global Women's Institute and The International Rescue Committee. https://www.whatworks.co.za/documents/publications/66-maureen-murphy-diana-arango-amber-hill-manuel-contreras-mairi-macrae-mary-ellsberg/file

Heise, L. (1998). Violence against women: An integrated, ecological framework. *Violence against Women, 4*(3), 262–290. https://doi.org/10.1177/ 1077801298004003002

Heise, L. (2011). *What Works to Prevent Partner Violence? An Evidence Overview.* DFID. http://strive.lshtm.ac.uk/resources/what-works-prevent-partner-violence-evidence-overview

Holmes, R., & Bhuvanendra, D. (2014a). *Preventing and Responding to Gender-Based Violence in Humanitarian Contexts* (Network Paper 77). UK Overseas Development Institute & Humanitarian Practice Network. https://assets.publishing.service.gov.uk/ media/57a089b2ed915d3cfd0003a8/GBV_in_emergencies_NP_77_web.pdf

Holmes, R., & Bhuvanendra, D. (2014b). *Preventing and Responding to Gender-Based Violence in Humanitarian Contexts: Mapping and Analysing the Evidence and Identifying the Gaps.* UK Department for International Development (DFID). http://r4d.dfid.gov. uk/Output/195127/

Hossain, M., Izugbara, C., McAlpine, A., Muthuri, S., Bacchus, L., Muuo, S., Kohli, A., Egesa, C., Pearson, R., Franchi, G., & MacRae, M. (2018). *Violence, Uncertainty, and Resilience among Refugee Women and Community Workers: An Evaluation of Gender-Based Violence Case Management Services in the Dadaab Refugee Camps.* UK Department for International Development (DFID). https://www.rescue-uk.org/report/violence-uncertainty-and-resilience-among-refugee-women-and-community-workers-evaluation

Hossain, M., Zimmerman, C., & Watts, C. (2014). Preventing violence against women and girls in conflict. *Lancet, 383*(9934), 2021–2022. https://doi.org/10.1016/ s0140-6736(14)60964-8

IASC. (2005). *Women, Girls, Boys and Men. Different Needs—Equal Opportunities: Gender Handbook in Humanitarian Action.* Inter-Agency Standing Committee. https:// interagencystandingcommittee.org/gender-and-humanitarian-action-0/documents-public/women-girls-boys-men-different-needs-equal-5

92 Focus on VAWG in humanitarian emergencies

IASC. (2015a). *Guidelines for Integrating Gender-Based Violence Interventions in Humanitarian Action. Reducing Risk, Promoting Resilience and Aiding Recovery.* Inter-Agency Standing Committee. https://gbvguidelines.org/en/

IASC. (2015b). *The IASC Transformative Agenda; What Does the IASC Humanitarian System-Wide Level 3 Emergency Response Mean in Practice?* Inter-Agency Standing Committee. https://interagencystandingcommittee.org/iasc-transformative-agenda/documents-public/iasc-transformative-agenda-what-does-iasc-humanitarian

IASC. (2017a). *Addressing Gender-Based Violence: Practical Steps for Humanitarian Coordinators and Humanitarian Country Teams. IASC: Peer2Peer Support - Guidance Note.* Inter-Agency Standing Committee. https://reliefweb.int/report/world/addressing-gender-based-violence-practical-steps-humanitarian-coordinators-and

IASC. (2017b). *IASC GBV Guidelines: Reflecting on Two Years of Implementation 2016–2017.* Inter-Agency Standing Committee. https://gbvguidelines.org/en/iasc-gbv-guidelines-reflecting-on-two-years-of-implementation-2016-2017/

IASC. (2017c). *Policy: Gender Equality and the Empowerment of Women and Girls in Humanitarian Action.* Inter-Agency Standing Committee: Reference Group on Gender and Humanitarian Action. https://interagencystandingcommittee.org/system/files/iasc_policy_on_gender_equality_and_the_empowerment_of_women_and_girls_in_humanitarian_action.pdf

IASC. (2017d). *Accountability Framework for the Inter-Agency Standing Committee Policy on Gender Equality and the Empowerment of Women and Girls in Humanitarian Action 2018–2022.* Inter-Agency Standing Committee: Reference Group on Gender and Humanitarian Action. https://reliefweb.int/report/world/accountability-framework-inter-agency-standing-committee-policy-gender-equality-and

IASC. (2018a). *Guideline: The Gender Handbook for Humanitarian Action.* Inter-Agency Standing Committee Gender Reference Group. https://interagencystandingcommittee.org/system/files/2018-iasc_gender_handbook_for_humanitarian_action_eng_0.pdf

IASC. (2018b). *Protocol 1. Humanitarian System-Wide Scale-Up Activation; Definition and Procedures.* Inter-Agency Standing Committee. https://interagencystandingcommittee.org/system/files/2020-11/Protocol%201.%20Humanitarian%20System-Wide%20Scale-Up%20Activation-%20Definition%20and%20Procedures%2C%202018.pdf

IASC. (2018c). *ASC Guidelines on Inclusion of Persons with Disabilities in Humanitarian Action: Asia Regional Consultation with GBV & Gender Actors Workshop Report, May 2018.* Inter-Agency Standing Committee. https://reliefweb.int/report/world/iasc-guidelines-inclusion-persons-disabilities-humanitarian-action-asia-regional

IASC. (2019a). *IASC Structure and Working Method.* Inter-Agency Standing Committee. https://interagencystandingcommittee.org/system/files/iasc_structure-and-working-method_2019-2020_web.pdf

IASC. (2019b). *Fact Sheet 2019–2020.* Inter-Agency Standing Committee. https://interagencystandingcommittee.org/system/files/iasc_fact_sheet_2019.pdf

IAWG. (2018). *Inter-Agency Field Manual on Reproductive Health in Humanitarian Settings.* Inter-Agency Working Group on Reproductive Health in Crisis. https://www.who.int/hac/global_health_cluster/newsletter/2/fiels_manual_rh/en/

IDMC. (2019). *GRID 2019: Global Report on Internal Displacement.* Internal Displacement Monitoring Centre and the Norwegian Refugee Council. https://www.internal-displacement.org/global-report/grid2019/

IDMC. (2020). *GRID 2020: Global Report on Internal Displacement.* Internal Displacement Monitoring Centre and the Norwegian Refugee Council. https://www.internal-displacement.org/global-report/grid2020/

IFRC. (2018). *The Responsibility to Prevent and Respond to Sexual and Gender-Based Violence in Disasters and Crises. Research Results of SGBV Prevention and Response Before, During and After Disasters in Indonesia, Lao PDR and the Philippines.* International Federation of Red Cross and Red Crescent Societies. https://media.ifrc.org/ifrc/wp-content/uploads/sites/5/2018/07/17072018-SGBV-Report_Final pdf.pdf

IRC. (2012). *Lifesaving, Not Optional: Protecting Women and Girls from Violence in Emergencies.* International Rescue Committee. https://themimu.info/sites/themimu.info/files/documents/Ref_Doc_Lifesaving_Not_Optional_-_Discussion_Paper_Feb2013.pdf

IRC. (2015). *Are We There Yet? Progress and Challenges in Ensuring Lifesaving Services and Reducing Risks to Violence for Women and Girls in Emergencies.* International Rescue Committee.https://www.rescue.org/report/are-we-there-yet-progress-and-challenges-ensuring-life-saving-services-and-reducing-risks

IRC. (2017). *The Impact of the Call to Action on Protection from Gender-Based Violence in Emergencies.* International Rescue Committee. https://gbvresponders.org/wp-content/uploads/2017/07/The-Impact-of-the-CTA-on-protection-from-GBV-in-emergencies-FULL-WEB.pdf

IRC. (2018a). *2018 Annual Review: Kenya Program.* International Rescue Committee. https://www.rescue.org/sites/default/files/document/3868/ircinkenya2018annualreview.pdf

IRC. (2018b). *Needs Assessment Report. Venezuelan Migrants in Colombia: Expansion.* International Rescue Committee. https://reliefweb.int/report/colombia/needs-assessment-report-venezuelan-migrants-colombia-expansion-november-6-2018

IRC & GWI. (2015). *Responding to Typhoon Haiyan: Women and Girls Left Behind. A Study on Violence against Women and Girls Prevention and Mitigation in the Response to Typhoon Haiyan.* International Rescue Committee and Global Women's Institute. https://www.whatworks.co.za/documents/publications/18-policy-brief-responding-to-typhoon-haiyan/file

ISG. (2017). *Real Time Accountability Partnership—Baseline Assessment Final Report.* International Solutions Group. https://data2.unhcr.org/en/documents/download/54506

ITAD. (2015). *Evaluation of DFID's Humanitarian Response to Typhoon Haiyan (Yolanda).* ITAD. https://assets.publishing.service.gov.uk/government/uploads/system/uploads/attachment_data/file/501225/Eval-Humanitarian-Response-Typhoon-Haiyan.pdf

Jewkes, R., Stern, E., & Ramsoomar, L. (2019). *Preventing Violence against Women and Girls: Community Activism Approaches to Shift Harmful Gender Attitudes, Roles and Social Norms.* What Works programme. https://www.whatworks.co.za/documents/publications/357-social-norms-briefweb-28092019/file

Maskrey, A., Cardona, O., García, V., Lavell, A., Macías, J. M., Romero, G., & Chaux, G. W. (1993). *Los desastres no son naturales.* Red de Estudios Sociales en Prevención de Desastres en América Latina (La RED).

Meger, S. (2016). The fetishization of sexual violence in international security. *International Studies Quarterly, 60*(1), 149–159. https://doi.org/10.1093/isq/sqw003

MHPSN. (2017). *Interim Mental Health and Psychosocial Support Emergency Toolkit.* Mental Health and Psychosocial Support Network. https://www.humanitarianlibrary.org/resource/interim-mental-health-psychosocial-support-emergency-toolkit

MSF. (2015). *Turning a Blind Eye: How Europe Ignores the Consequences of Outsourced Migration Management.* Barcelona: Médecins sans Frontières Operational Centre. https://arhp.msf.es/sites/default/files/Turning-a-blind-eye-ENG-091115.pdf

Niżynska, A. (2015). *Gender-Based Persecution? Gender as a Criterion for Granting Refugee Status.* Institute of Public Affairs. https://www.isp.org.pl/uploads/drive/oldfiles/pdf/migrationreportengfinal18janFINAL.pdf

OHCHR. (2019). *Protection of Victims of Sexual Violence: Lessons Learned. Workshop Report.* United Nations Office of the High Commissioner for Human Rights; Women's Human Rights and Gender Section. https://www.ohchr.org/Documents/Issues/Women/WRGS/ReportLessonsLearned.pdf

Perrin, N., Marsh, M., Clough, A., Desgroppes, A., Phanuel, C. Y., Abdi, A., Kaburu, F., Heitmann, S., Yamashina, M., Ross, B., & Read-Hamilton, S. (2019). Social norms and beliefs about gender-based violence scale: A measure for use with gender based violence prevention programs in low-resource and humanitarian settings. *Conflict and Health, 13*(1), 6. https://doi.org/10.1186/s13031-019-0189-x

Plan International. (2016). *A Time of Transition: Plan International's Work With and For Adolescents in Humanitarian Settings.* Plan International. https://plan-international.org/publications/time-transition-adolescents-humanitarian-settings

Read-Hamilton, S. (2014). Gender-based violence: A confused and contested term. *Humanitarian Exchange, 60,* 5–8. https://odihpn.org/magazine/gender-based-violence-a-confused-and-contested-term/

Read-Hamilton, S., & Marsh, M. (2016). The Communities Care programme: Changing social norms to end violence against women and girls in conflict-affected communities. *Gender & Development, 24*(2), 261–276. https://doi.org/10.1080/13552074.2016.1195579

RTAP. (2017a). *Real Time Accountability Partnership Action Framework; Tackling Gender-Based Violence in Emergencies.* Real Time Accountability Partnership. https://reliefweb.int/sites/reliefweb.int/files/resources/RTAP_mockup_FINAL.7Sept2017.pdf

RTAP. (2017b). *The GBV Accountability Framework; All Humanitarian Actors Have a Role to Play.* Real Time Accountability Partnership. https://reliefweb.int/sites/reliefweb.int/files/resources/GBV%20Accountability%20Framework.pdf

Small Arms Survey. (2016). *Gender Based Violence Interventions: Opportunities for Innovation.* Humanitarian Innovation Fund Gap Analysis. Elrha. https://www.elrha.org/researchdatabase/gender-based-violence-interventions-opportunities-innovation/

Smith, M. D. (2016). Rethinking gender in the international refugee regime. *Forced Migration Review, 53,* 65–66. https://www.researchgate.net/publication/340731428_Rethinking_gender_in_the_international_refugee_regime

SPHERE. (2018). *The SPHERE Handbook: Humanitarian Charter and Minimum Standards in Humanitarian Response.* SPHERE Association (4th Edition). https://spherestandards.org/handbook-2018/

Tappis, H., Freeman, J., Glass, N., & Doocy, S. (2016). Effectiveness of interventions, programs and strategies for gender-based violence prevention in refugee populations: An integrative review. *PLoS Currents 8- Disasters,* 1–21. https://doi.org/10.1371/currents.dis.3a465b66f9327676d61eb8120eaa5499

UN DESA. (2019). *SDG Indicator 10.7.2.* (Policy Brief 1, October 2019_. UN Department for Economic and Social Affairs. https://www.un.org/en/development/desa/population/publications/pdf/technical/Policy%20Brief_10.7.2.pdf

UN OCHA. (2016a). *Real Time Accountability Partnership on GBV in Emergencies.* United Nations Office for the Co-ordination of Humanitarian Affairs. https://interagencystandingcommittee.org/system/files/rtap_announcement_-_june_2016.pdf

UN OCHA. (2016b). *World Humanitarian Data and Trends 2016. United Nations Office for the Co-Ordination of Humanitarian Affairs.* United Nations Office for the Co-Ordination of Humanitarian Affairs. https://reliefweb.int/report/world/world-humanitarian-data-and-trends-2016

UN OCHA. (2019a). *Global Humanitarian Overview 2020.* United Nations Office for the Co-ordination of Humanitarian Affairs. https://www.unocha.org/publication/global-humanitarian-overview/global-humanitarian-overview-2020

Focus on VAWG in humanitarian emergencies **95**

UN OCHA. (2019b). *OCHA on Message: Gender in Humanitarian Action*. United Nations Office for the Co-ordination of Humanitarian Affairs. https://www.unocha.org/sites/unocha/files/OOM_gender_22May2019_0.pdf

UN SG. (2019). *Conflict-Related Sexual Violence. Report of the UN Secretary General. S/2019/280 (29 March 2019). 2018 Annual Report*. Office of the Special Representative of the Secretary-General https://www.un.org/sexualviolenceinconflict/wp-content/uploads/2019/04/report/s-2019-280/Annual-report-2018.pdf

UNSC. (2000). United Nations Security Council Resolution 1325, *Women, Peace and Security*, S/RES/1325 (31 October 2000). http://unscr.com/en/resolutions/doc/1325

UNSC. (2016, March 11). *United Nations Security Council Resolution 2272: UN Peacekeeping Operations* (S/RES/2272). http://unscr.com/en/resolutions/2272

UN Women. (2013). *Violence against Women in Conflict, Post-Conflict and Emergency Settings*. The UN Entity for Gender Equality and the Empowerment of Women. https://www.endvawnow.org/uploads/modules/pdf/1405612658.pdf

UN Women. (2014). *Beijing Declaration and Platform for Action and Beijing+5 Political Declaration and Outcome* (First published in 1995). The UN Entity for Gender Equality and the Empowerment of Women. https://www.unwomen.org/en/digital-library/publications/2015/01/beijing-declaration

UN Women & IDS. (2015). *The Effect of Gender Equality Programming on Humanitarian Outcomes* (Report for the IASC Reference Group on Gender in Humanitarian Action). The UN Entity for Gender Equality and the Empowerment of Women and the Institute of Development Studies. https://www.unwomen.org/en/digital-library/publications/2015/7/the-effect-of-gender-equality-programming-on-humanitarian-outcomes

UNESCO. (2015). *Humanitarian Aid for Education: Why It Matters and Why More Is Needed*. United Nations Educational, Scientific and Cultural Organisation. https://en.unesco.org/gem-report/humanitarian-aid-education-why-it-matters-and-why-more-needed

UNFPA. (2015). *Minimum Standards for Prevention and Response to Gender-Based Violence in Emergencies*. United Nations Population Fund. https://www.unfpa.org/featured-publication/gbvie-standards

UNFPA. (2017). *Evaluation of UNFPA Support to the Prevention, Response to and Elimination of Gender-Based Violence and Harmful Practices 2012–2017*. Final inception report. United Nations Population Fund Evaluation Office (report written by ITAD and Impact Ready). https://www.unfpa.org/admin-resource/corporate-evaluation-unfpa-support-prevention-response-and-elimination-gender-based

UNFPA. (2019). *Acting Together to End Sexual and Gender-Based Violence in Humanitarian Crises*. Joint Press Release from the Governments of Norway, Iraq, Somalia, the United Arab Emirates together with United Nations Population Fund, United Nations Office for the Coordination of Humanitarian Affairs, and the International Committee of the Red Cross. https://www.unfpa.org/press/acting-together-end-sexual-and-gender-based-violence-humanitarian-crises

UNHCR. (2002). *Guidelines on International Protection. Gender-Related Persecution Within the Context of Article 1A (2) of the 1951 Convention and/or Its 1967 Protocol Relating to the Status of Refugees*. United Nations High Commissioner for Refugees. https://www.unhcr.org/publications/legal/3d58ddef4/guidelines-international-protection-1-gender-related-persecution-context.html

UNHCR. (2018a). *Reducing Risks: Sexual and Gender-Based Violence in Emergencies* (Review of the US-Funded Safe from the Start Project). United Nations High Commissioner for Refugees.

UNHCR. (2018b). *Our Fight against Sexual Misconduct: 2018 in Review*. United Nations High Commissioner for Refugees. https://www.unhcr.org/5c51a5d34.pdf

UNHCR. (2018c). *Addressing Sexual Exploitation and Abuse and Sexual Harassment. Strategy, Structure and Key Actions.* United Nations High Commissioner for Refugees. https://www.unhcr.org/uk/our-fight-against-sexual-exploitation-abuse-and-harassment.html

UNHCR. (2019a). *Regional Refugee and Migrant Response Plan for Refugees and Migrants from Venezuela January-December 2019.* United Nations High Commissioner for Refugees. https://reliefweb.int/report/colombia/rmrp-2020-regional-refugee-and-migrant-response-plan-refugees-and-migrants-venezuela

UNHCR. (2019b). *Global Trends: Forced Displacement in 2018.* United Nations High Commissioner for Refugees. https://www.unhcr.org/globaltrends2018/

UNHCR. (2019c). *Sexual and Gender-Based Violence: Prevention, Risk Mitigation and Response.* United Nations High Commissioner for Refugees. https://www.unhcr.org/uk/protection/women/5ce7d6784/sexual-gender-based-violence-prevention-risk-mitigation-response.html

UNHCR, UNFPA, & WRC. (2015). *Initial Assessment Report: Protection Risks for Women and Girls in the European Refugee and Migrant Crisis.* United Nations High Commissioner for Refugees, UNFPA and the Women's Refugee Commission. https://www.unhcr.org/uk/protection/operations/569f8f419/initial-assessment-report-protection-risks-women-girls-european-refugee.html

UNICEF. (2016). *The UNICEF Multi-Country Gender-Based Violence in Emergencies Programme Evaluation: Final Synthesis Report.* United Nations Children's Fund. https://www.unicef.org/evaldatabase/files/Full_report_with_cover_UNICEF_Multi-country_GBViE_Evaluation(1).pdf

UNICEF. (2017). *Institutionalizing the IASC GBV Guidelines: Highlights from UNICEF in 2017. Integrating the Inter-Agency Standing Committee (IASC) Guidelines for Addressing Gender-Based Violence in Humanitarian Action.* United Nations Children's Fund. http://www.unicefinemergencies.com/downloads/eresource/docs/GBV/GBV%20GL%20Highlights%20final%20print.pdf

UNISDR. (2017). *Build Back Better in Recovery, Rehabilitation and Reconstruction: In support of the Sendai Framework for Disaster Risk Reduction 2015–2030.* United Nations Office for Disaster Risk Reduction. https://www.unisdr.org/files/53213_bbb.pdf

Vu, A., Adam, A., Wirtz, A., Pham, K., Rubenstein, L., Glass, N., Beyrer, C., & Singh, S. (2014). The prevalence of sexual violence among female refugees in complex humanitarian emergencies: A systematic review and meta-analysis. *PLoS Currents, 6*, https://doi.org/10.1371/currents.dis.835f10778fd80ae031aac12d3b533ca7

WFP. (2016). *Gender-Based Violence Manual.* United Nations World Food Programme; Emergencies and Transitions Unit (OSZPH), Programme and Policy Division. https://gbvguidelines.org/en/documents/world-food-programme-gender-based-violence-manual/

Whalan, J. (2017). *Dealing with Disgrace: Addressing Sexual Exploitation and Abuse in UN Peacekeeping* (Providing for Peacekeeping 15). The International Peace Institute. https://www.ipinst.org/wp-content/uploads/2017/08/IPI-Rpt-Dealing-with-Disgrace2.pdf

What Works. (2019). *What Works to Prevent Violence against Women and Girls in Conflict and Humanitarian Crises.* What Works to Prevent VAWG Programme (Presentation Written by N. Behnam & K. Falb of the International Rescue Committee, as Part of the What Works Consortium). https://reliefweb.int/report/world/what-works-prevent-violence-against-women-and-girls-conflict-and-humanitarian-crisis

WHO. (2016). *The Grand Bargain—A Shared Commitment to Better Serve People in Need* (World Humanitarian Summit Declaration Dated 23rd May 2016). World Health Organization. https://reliefweb.int/report/world/grand-bargain-shared-commitment-better-serve-people-need

WHO, LSHTM, & SA MRC. (2013). *Global and Regional Estimates of Violence against Women: Prevalence and Health Effects of Intimate Partner Violence and Non-Partner Sexual Violence.* World Health Organization, London School of Hygiene and Tropical Medicine & South African Medical Research Council. https://www.who.int/publications/i/item/9789241564625

Wirtz, A. L., Perrin, N. A., Desgroppes, A., Phipps, V., Abdi, A. A., Ross, B., Kaburu, F., Kajue, I., Kutto, E., Taniguchi, E., & Glass, N. (2018). Lifetime prevalence, correlates and health consequences of gender-based violence victimisation and perpetration among men and women in Somalia. *BMJ Global Health, 3*(4). http://doi.org/10.1136/bmjgh-2018-000773

Wirtz, A. L., Pham, K., Glass, N., Loochkartt, S., Kidane, T., Cuspoca, D., Rubenstein, L. S., Singh, S., & Vu, A. (2014). Gender-based violence in conflict and displacement: Qualitative findings from displaced women in Colombia. *Conflict and Health, 8*(10), 1–14. https://doi.org/10.1186/1752-1505-8-10

5

VAWG PREVENTION AND RESPONSE IN HUMANITARIAN EMERGENCIES

An overview of current approaches and gaps in knowledge

Introduction

As noted in the previous chapter, the scale of both the situation and the response means that two chapters are needed to begin to do justice to current international humanitarian assistance mechanisms that prioritise VAWG prevention and response initiatives. In this second chapter on the subject, we offer a brief overview of some of the current discussions around how to support women and girls in humanitarian emergencies, gaps in provision that have been identified, a number of key overarching issues, and current priorities in policy and practice. These include:

- Humanitarian aid architecture and the extent to which it focuses on VAWG prevention and response.
- Why so much of the literature is gender blind.
- An examination of current theoretical priorities in humanitarian emergency policy and practice, such as localisation, intersectionality, and social norm change.
- The availability or not of data on VAWG, the gaps that exist in knowledge and what is being done to fill them.

We finish this chapter by applying the VAWG Mainstreaming Framework into the context of humanitarian emergencies, considering how our proposed approach might be useful.

Humanitarian emergency assistance: aid architecture

Here, we look at humanitarian aid architecture and consider the extent to which existing structures and partnerships address VAWG and gender issues. Taking stock of the trends, patterns, and current themes and priorities in humanitarian

DOI: 10.4324/9780429280603-5

and development assistance helps to highlight gaps in both theory and practice. Much of what is written here resonates across the development landscape, as many of the topics raised, such as implementation structures, overall assistance, and funding, are not unique to humanitarian emergency policy. Just one example is the 'squeezing out' of local NGOs, which are often small and under-funded when compared to the much larger INGOs.

The question of a 'new humanitarian aid architecture' arises: that there is scope, as well as an evident need, to reframe the systems and structures of power in funding, to improve the partnership and engagement of local populations, to optimise co-ordination, and to develop coherent working practices. Yet, funding and capacity to act effectively continue to fall short of the needs of people who are experiencing a humanitarian emergency. Critiques of the 'stark vertical asymmetry' that analyse the channels and hierarchies of funding observe that smaller/more local organisations seldom have equal opportunity of access to funding, have less capacity to develop proposals, and, therefore, seldom play an equal role in delivery of humanitarian assistance. This is the case both specifically for VAWG prevention and response interventions and indeed more widely. Critics have noted that the approaches of the humanitarian sector approaches are disconnected from the lives of people it intends to help or work with, or whose governments it supports (Collinson, 2016). Another criticism is the failure of aid architecture and humanitarian response to have adapted adequately, efficiently, and equitably to the realities of the 21st century (Konyndyk, 2018).

All too common elements of the new approaches to humanitarianism are gender blindness, essentialism, and lack of attention to the different roles, capacities, and needs of different groups of people.[1]

The very real and urgent need to institutionalise a gender and VAWG mainstreaming approach is at the core of seeking to remove gender blindness and to move towards a genuinely transformative agenda and more equitable humanitarian aid architecture (we discuss this chiefly in Chapter 2; see also Bradley & Gruber, 2018; CARE International, 2019; Oxfam, ECHO, & CGFPG, 2017; UN OCHA, 2019; UN Women & IDS, 2015).

It is crucial to acknowledge that all those who experience a humanitarian emergency cannot and will not be the same type of person for a multitude of reasons; yet all too often, there are aggregate references to 'people' or 'vulnerable populations'. In much of the current literature on humanitarian aid architecture, limited attention is given to understanding the experiences or needs of disaggregated separate groups, or to social norm change as a process for bringing about a shift in entrenched practices at community and societal levels. This gap is in marked contrast to much of the work being undertaken to develop a robust and evidence-based understanding of what we know and what we still need to find out about VAWG across the board, including in humanitarian emergencies.

> To assume all humans are the same, and thus equal, simultaneously assumes no difference and essentializes people to their "bare" and biological

100 VAWG prevention and response

lives. Saving lives involves counting lives, which reduces individual human beings to a dichotomous and minimalist state of living or dead. In practice, this often means that some lives are valued over others: those affected by natural disaster over those enmeshed in violent conflict, refugees over internally displaced, or international over national aid workers.

(Fast, 2015, p. 119)

If the response to a humanitarian emergency applies 'hierarchies of humanity' (see Fassin, 2012), where then is the point at which difference emerges and becomes a key pivot point in terms of action? If many of those writing on humanitarian emergencies and developing policies apply gender blind approaches and an overall deafness to difference, as well as to intersectionality, hierarchies of power, control over resources and action, what might that mean in terms of effective use of scarce resources to address VAWG prevention and response? Where is the space to be found for dedicated, expert attention to the many and varied specific issues of VAWG?

As described in Chapter 9, VAWG prevention and response in humanitarian emergencies severely under resourced: there is a profound gap between the funding needed and what is available in reality, as is evidenced by the inadequate amounts dedicated to such work.

Localisation

Much attention is currently focused on 'localisation' – again, not solely in the context of humanitarian emergencies. Localisation seeks to embed responses and actions in the lived reality of national and sub-national societies, and to work with genuinely local women's rights, gender, and other organisations. A frequently voiced phrase is for support and partnership to be '*as local as possible, as international as necessary*'. This is an area where will and urgency to reform and make humanitarian emergency actions more inclusive continue to bump into long-standing, harsh realities of power, resource control, and access to information.

Might more targeted capacity development support be possible, rather than what might too often be a speedy embracing of 'humanitarian business as usual', where international non-governmental organisations (INGOs) and elite local CSOs take centre stage and the lion's share of funding, implementation and praise? There is scepticism that previous primarily transactional relationships between funders and organisations providing inputs on the ground will change significantly now that localisation is being highlighted. And there is also concern that lack of genuine local capacity will thwart attempts for greater localisation (Barbelet, 2018). Again, significant parts of the literature on this subject are gender blind and give limited attention to the different needs and capacities of different groups of people. There is seldom consideration of the ways in which people experiencing a humanitarian emergency are positioned as part of local society, or that they might conceivably have something to offer a localisation agenda.[2]

VAWG prevention and response 101

So, what does localisation mean for work on VAWG prevention and response in humanitarian emergencies? Considerable attention has been given to potential for harnessing the efforts of the GBV Area of Responsibility (GBV AoR), the Call to Action, and the Real-Time Accountability Partnership (RTAP), to aid greater and more effective localisation. Objectives within these include:

> To facilitate a space in which local civil society organisations can share their perspectives on how the GBV AoR and other relevant processes... can meaningfully engage with them, be influenced by them, and support their work... [To] Move away from the "blessed few" approach, where a carefully chosen small group of local actors receive the lion's share of funds.
> *(GBV AoR – GPC, 2018, pp. 1 and 3)*

Nonetheless, much work remains to be done simply to inform and debate with local actors. This would mean not only having discussions about localisation *per se*, but also debating the structure and reach of global initiatives such as the Call to Action in local contexts, as well as the potential for more aligned partnerships between it, the GBV AoR, and RTAP. Bringing the Call to Action 'to the field', i.e. informing local actors of its existence, as well as their potential roles in localising its work in a humanitarian emergency, is long and slow work; many organisations do not have any access to such information (see ECHO, 2018).

Local humanitarian actors' access to funding is difficult, even when it is specifically dedicated to such purposes, as in the case of country-based pooled funds, for example (see further Bennett, 2019; Murray, 2019). If many local actors continue not to have easy access to information about multi-partner/global initiatives, their capacity to seek and receive funding will remain limited. Unsurprisingly, there is frustration at the fact that INGOs (and private-public partnerships, PPPs) are increasingly occupying the space previously inhabited primarily by local, often small NGOs – while pre-dating current focus on localisation, it remains another facet of this already thorny issue. As Mwanahamisi Salimu Singano, programme manager at FEMNET, a pan-African network of women's rights organisations based in Nairobi, forcefully notes:

> Because INGOs have never really had a shortage of praise, it is time to redress the balance with some criticism... Most INGOs are now registered as national or local NGOs in the countries [in which] they operate. By so doing, they are earning legitimacy to operate in local spaces - and therein lies the manifestation of the bigger problem!... INGOs are consciously and unconsciously taking over the space that used to be occupied by women's rights organisations. The only time they will desperately look for what they call 'local' organisations is when politics hit hard and decisions are made in favour of the unjust. Then, when things get difficult with the government, we hear calls of 'local CSOs need to take a lead'. This is the sad truth; we have to call it out, or live with it. Well, I have decided to call it out.
> *(GADN, 2019, p. 2)*

Other challenges include lack of agreed clarity on terms – localisation for one organisation may not fit another's definition; there is no central, globally agreed set of standards for measuring and monitoring capacities and skill gaps. A further concern is that even when INGOs genuinely partner with local actors, it is all too often the INGOs that design the interventions, define roles, and set implementation and monitoring procedures and standards.

Intersectionality in the context of humanitarian emergencies

Throughout this book, we refer to intersectionality, as it has relevance across the field of VAWG prevention and response. Here, we just briefly mention that attention to intersectionality is increasingly seen as necessary in humanitarian emergency situations. Such focus is important, not least because greater understanding may lead to more nuanced, tailored VAWG interventions.

Critically assessing intersectionality requires attention to how systems and structures work to perpetuate either privilege or powerlessness, and how any one label, such as 'VAWG survivor', cannot ever properly and fully identify any one individual and her or his capacities, needs, opportunities, constraints, and so on. Hierarchies, social stratification, and patriarchy can limit an individual's opportunities, as well as shape their social identity (Edström & Shahrokh, 2016).

Action on social norm change – even in a humanitarian emergency?

When so much is to be done in order to ensure even the most basic human needs, such as food, water, and shelter, are being met, what place might actions to address social norm change have a humanitarian emergency? Are they even feasible in such a context? The same question could also be asked of our proposed VAWG Mainstreaming Framework, and there are certainly logistical obstacles that need to be overcome. Vulnerable people are often on the move, both in conflict situations and during and after naturally occurring hazards. Those providing humanitarian assistance face difficult decisions as to where to use scarce human and financial resources to provide support to IDPs, refugees, and host community members. How, then, might a community-wide, immersive violence reduction programme be envisaged, planned, implemented, and evaluated in such volatile, challenging environments?

The short answer is that no solution could ever be quick and easy, because any genuine and sustainable social norm change requires immersive work on societal and community hierarchies, power structures, perceptions of individuals' value, and how such perceptions are played out, as well as many more entrenched attitudes and behaviours. All such matters may be exacerbated and become more extreme in a humanitarian emergency.

At issue is the core question about VAWG prevention and response: however slow and faltering action may be, is there not a fundamental ethical requirement

VAWG prevention and response **103**

to address social norms that enable such behaviour? Even in a humanitarian emergency, there can and should be planning and action, with the genuine participation of as many local actors as possible (from various perspectives, see, e.g., Asgary, Emery, & Wong, 2013; Freedman, 2016; Gibbs, Duvvury, & Scriver, 2017; Jewkes, Stern, & Ramsoomar, 2019; McAlpine, Hossain, & Zimmerman, 2016).[3]

To facilitate this, we should give greater attention to innovation. Innovation does not imply dismissal of all the work that has gone before, but more an imaginative engagement with new practice, or review of existing models from other disciplines and sectors. Having the courage (and the opportunity, and the funds) to innovate in the context of a humanitarian emergency is a subject that has been given considerable attention in the past decade. The focus has often been on an iterative process (with as wide a partnership as possible, so linking into localisation) to improve a sector or system-wide response, and to generate robust evidence of the benefits of any such innovation (e.g. Small Arms Survey, 2016). An example of this might be the true integration of gender equality and VAWG perspectives in humanitarian aid architecture/policy theorisation and development, perspectives that put different people and groups (i.e. not just aggregate 'people') at the centre.

Evidence: what don't we know?

We look now at the gaps in evidence relating to VAWG prevention and response in humanitarian emergencies, what does or does not work, the research undertaken, and whether findings have informed planning and delivery of VAWG prevention and response services. We concentrate on existing knowledge and identify evidence gaps specific to humanitarian emergencies. However, many of the points raised and much of the discussion again have relevance in the wider sphere of VAWG prevention and response across the development landscape. Thus, the challenges in collecting, disaggregating, and tracking data on funding allocations for VAWG actions are always considerable. As such, inadequate funding will inevitably limit space for collection of data and the opportunity to build an evidence base.

Much work has been devoted to the development of comprehensive manuals and guidance documents to support the highest quality research being done in a humanitarian emergency (GWI, 2017; Hossain & McAlpine, 2017; WHO, 2007). All these resource documents emphasise the make or break criterion of ensuring safety for everyone – respondents most importantly, but also researchers and facilitators, as well as the wider community – and of assuring confidentiality and informed choice to participate or not. All discuss how research design and objectives must be guided by the realities of an emergency setting, while always seeking to achieve the best possible data collection, analysis, and dissemination of findings and recommendations. The ethical validity of seeking to collect data in what will often be extremely unsafe situations has always to be the primary consideration.

104 VAWG prevention and response

In light of the above, there continue to be widespread and significant gaps in VAWG data and in the capacity to analyse, not least using gender analytical approaches. These gaps have negative impacts on systematic, mainstreamed focus on VAWG, hindering optimal effectiveness and efficiency of VAWG prevention and response service delivery (see, e.g., GBV AoR – GPC, 2017; Murphy, Hess, Casey, & Minchew, 2019; What Works, 2019[4]).

Building an evidence base on VAWG prevention and response in a humanitarian emergency is still seen as 'a relatively new and constantly evolving field of practice' (Read-Hamilton & Marsh, 2016, p. 264). Nonetheless, evidence on the scale of VAWG in humanitarian emergencies is slowly growing, with phase 1 of the DFID-funded *What Works to prevent VAWG research and innovation* programme (2016–2020) a major contributor. Its component 2 on conflict and crises has identified gaps and lessons learned and provided research to inform emerging best practice (Kerr-Wilson et al., 2020). At the same time, there is acceptance that expecting detailed, high-quality data sets in an emergency is often futile, due to insecurity, absence of researchers, etc. In other words, while building an evidence base is essential, when a humanitarian emergency happens, speedy action is imperative. One often cited example is the '[VAWG] prevalence red herring' (Bain & Guimond, 2014; also, IASC, 2015). Experts argue that the approach must be to assume VAWG is occurring and to provide support and services from the outset, not to wait for survey findings.[5]

Despite the many policies, guidelines, and initiatives such as Call to Action and the Prevention of Sexual Violence in Conflict Initiative (PSVI) (see Chapter 6), reviews of VAWG prevention and response actions in humanitarian settings consistently highlight the lack of evidence on effective implementation of programmes. An easily accessible knowledge base of lessons learned and best practice is still work in progress: a 2013 review identified only 40 studies between 1990 and 2011 that had addressed the impacts of initiatives in humanitarian emergencies seeking to prevent and respond to sexual violence (Spangaro et al., 2013; see also Holmes & Bhuvanendra, 2014; What Works phase I website).

In public health terms there is, in fact, evidence on what needs to be done to support survivors of VAWG and how to make such services accessible. Yet far too many survivors delay seeking help. This will only be exacerbated in a humanitarian emergency where health and other services may be distant, the journey might be fraught with danger, and social norms create barriers (Bernard & Durham, 2014; Gruber, 2005). What is lacking is clear evidence of the best mechanisms to deliver truly survivor-centred health and psychosocial services. The absence of credible evidence of what does and does not work in terms of delivery of VAWG prevention and response services and support has surely hampered evidence-based planning and response to VAWG.

Without robust evidence, how can high-quality planning and implementation be achieved, and appropriate indicators and targets be developed for assessing the relative efficacy of VAWG prevention and response interventions in humanitarian emergencies?

As mentioned in Chapter 4, **The Sustainable Development Goals** (SDGs) did not initially include an indicator or target measuring any aspect of forced migration (including VAWG).[6] Since 2015, this omission has been identified as a significant lost opportunity for greater evidence gathering and for linking such evidence to other SDG targets and indicators, most notably SDG 5: *Achieve gender equality and empower all women and girls.*[7] VAWG indicators under SDG 5 (and indeed also SDG 16) do not refer to refugees or IDPs. The implications of such a gap cannot be overstated (see, e.g., IRC, 2019).

> SDG 16 claims to seek to reduce 'the horrors which are a result of armed conflict or other forms of violence with societies'. However, there are no indicators monitoring the number of populations being forcibly displaced outside the country of origin at a global level. The omission of indicators on refugees and internally displaced people is inconsistent with the specific importance accorded to them in the 2030 Agenda for Sustainable Development and weakens the indicator framework as a key mechanism for fulfilling the pledge that 'no-one will be left behind'.
>
> *(UNHCR, 2019b, p. 1; also, UNHCR, 2018c)*

Why there was initially no indicator is unclear, especially as the 2030 *Agenda for Sustainable Development* does (briefly and generally) review forced migration issues.

The decision taken in 2019 to include a migration indicator under SDG 10 enables evidence gathering and is important. As previously noted, the new SDG indicator is 10.7.2: *Number of countries with migration policies to facilitate orderly, safe, regular, and responsible migration and mobility of people.* The fact that it does not address VAWG at all is cause for considerable concern.

Two multilateral data collection systems are the Gender-based Violence Information Management System (GBVIMS) and the Monitoring, Analysis and Reporting Arrangements (MARA).

GBVIMS is an inter-agency initiative, founded in 2007, whose members include UN agencies and INGOs; its purpose is to collect data on incidents of GBV in humanitarian emergencies. Since 2012, funding has been through UN Action's Multi Partner Trust Fund. As of 2016, GBVIMS had been applied in South Sudan, Dadaab refugee camp in Kenya, in Colombia, Iraq, Nepal, and Thailand.

A 2014 independent evaluation of the GBVIMS found that there was evidence of the system collecting and analysing data subsequently used in programme planning, implementation, and advocacy and that joint working on GBVIMS data had enhanced inter-agency co-operation and co-ordination (ISG, 2014).[8]

MARA was set up in 2010 under UNSCR 1960, to strengthen collection and use of conflict-related data on sexual violence, primarily to support UN Security Council action. The chief reporting channel for data collected and/or verified through MARA support is the annual report on sexual violence in conflict, published under the aegis of the UN Secretary General (see UNSG, 2019). This

106 VAWG prevention and response

relative narrowness of focus and use means that MARA cannot 'solve the problem' of collecting and using data on VAWG in conflict (see O'Gorman, 2013).

Relevant across the field of VAWG evidence building is the fact that there continue to be relatively few independent evaluations of humanitarian emergency VAWG interventions. This means that discussions about robustness of data, application of ethical standards, lesson learning, and sharing of recommendations will also be limited and hampered. VAWG policymakers and practitioners, including those working in humanitarian emergencies, know that a larger body of more robust and credible evidence would provide better data to underpin the design, implementation, and assessment of more context-specific, robust, and tailored interventions. Even where evidence exists, methodological inexactitude, i.e. the absence of a commonly agreed set of definitions to be used in either research or interventions (hence, the sometimes interchangeable use and/or conflation of terms, including GBV, SVC, CRSV, VAWG, Violence Against Children, etc.), does not promote easy comparison of data.

The collection and use of sex and age-disaggregated data, linked to gender analysis wherever feasible, is among the most effective ways to promote attention to VAWG prevention and response, and to wider gender equality interventions, in humanitarian emergencies. However, sex and age-disaggregated data are patchy. For example, only 131 countries provided such data in 2018, compared to 147 countries in 2017, but no reasons have been provided for the drop in reporting (UNHCR, 2019a).

Progress and key evidence gaps

One key finding in the past decade is that while sexual violence in conflict (SVC) is widespread and all too frequently perpetrated with impunity, rates of IPV are extraordinarily high and more prevalent in a humanitarian emergency. While there has been much attention given to SVC, less work has been done not only on IPV, but also on other forms of VAWG, including child marriage, sexual exploitation and abuse, abduction, and trafficking in conflict and non-conflict settings. A start has been made on gathering evidence (e.g. by the What Works and Spotlight programmes, see Murphy, Hess, Casey, & Minchew, 2019), but evidence remains sparse for actions that will effectively prevent and respond to VAWG in conflict (for studies that seek to provide an overview, see, e.g., Hossain, Zimmerman, & Watts, e2014; Murphy et al., 2016; Read-Hamilton & Marsh, 2016; Spangaro et al., 2013; Spangaro, Adogu, Zwi, Ranmuthugala, & Davies, 2015; Tappis Freeman, Glass, & Doocy, 2016; UN OIOS, 2018; UN Women, 2013; What Works, 2017).

While much of the evidence available relates to the lived experience of refugees (Vu et al., 2014, 2017; Wachter et al., 2018) there is also documentation on conflict IDPs (Ager, Bancroft, Berger, & Stark, 2018), on people displaced by natural disasters (UNESC 2014), on refugees living in urban settings (Koizumi & Hoffstaedter, 2015) as well as in Protection of Civilian camps (PoCs) (as in South Sudan), and work addressing perpetrators of conflict VAWG includes a study on UN peacekeepers (Whalan, 2017; also UNHCR, 2018a, 2018b).

While disaggregated data are all too often lacking or minimal, women and girls can nonetheless be identified as disproportionately exposed to risk, to VAWG, to increased loss of livelihoods, security, and loss of life, both during and in the aftermath of naturally occurring hazards. One stark example is that, during the monsoon season in Bangladesh, women and girls are especially affected by flooding as many cannot swim or are unable to leave their homes due to social norms and cultural barriers (CARE International, 2017). Data gaps impede proper understanding of, and prevention and response to, the impacts of naturally occurring hazards on women and girls compared to the experiences of men and boys.

One major evidence gap is the lack of attention until recently to adolescent girls' needs, engagement, roles, etc., in humanitarian emergencies. This is the case in terms of availability of disaggregated data and robust evidence, and also for evidence of which initiatives that work with girls and young women are providing appropriate and desired interventions (Casey & Hawrylyshyn, 2014; Le Masson, Lim, Budimir, & Selih Podboj, 2018; Murphy, Bingenheimer, Ovince, Ellsberg, & Contreras-Urbina, 2019; Murphy, Hess, Casey, & Minchew, 2019; Rubenstein & Stark, 2017; Swaine, Spearing, Murphy, & Contreras, 2018; What Works, 2019). Reports on the experiences of child and adolescent girls frequently refer to the opportunities for their active participation in shaping their own futures, from however much of a difficult situation of conflict and displacement. One such study seeks not only to describe often extremely grim and violent living conditions, but also the resilience and potential of the young and adolescent girls experiencing a humanitarian emergency (Tanner & O'Connor, 2017).

A major factor that limits development of an evidence base is that many VAWG survivors, whether it is perpetrated by a non-partner or is IPV, or whether it is in the form of coercion, exploitation, early marriage or other types of violence, will be immensely reluctant to speak about their experiences (Bradley & Gruber, 2018; IASC, 2015 and 2018a). One reason is the frequent unavailability of sexual and reproductive health interventions, mental health and psychosocial care, and other support services such as reliable police and justice systems. The obvious question that arises is why risk speaking out if no help or redress is available? Where services do exist, survivors will face many barriers, including stigma (and self-stigma), fear of being named, shamed, and blamed for the possible physical sequelae of VAWG such as sexually transmitted infections and pregnancy, opportunity costs, and overall lack of information on the existence of such care and support (García-Moreno et al., 2015; IAWG, 2018; IRC, 2015; LSE CWPS, GAPS & WWI, 2016; Magone, 2014; Murphy, Hess, Casey, & Minchew, 2019).

Reluctance to come forward as a survivor inevitably results in patchy, incomplete, and all too often unreliable data. These gaps in knowledge mean that it is seldom easy to gain a detailed overview of the individuals involved or their sex, age, disability, whether they are accompanied or unaccompanied, etc. Such gaps in data are likely to result in less than optimally tailored initiatives; focus on preventing and responding to vulnerabilities (including VAWG) might not speak to people's differing needs, and emerging lessons learned, and best practices might not always be effectively discussed and disseminated.

In conclusion: applying the ecological model to humanitarian emergencies

Here we provide an example of how our mainstreaming VAWG Mainstreaming Framework could be used to inform humanitarian emergency programming by adapting the ecological model (see Chapter 2 for the detailed, step by step discussion of how we propose adapting the **ecological model**, with flexibility across all sectors). Table 5.1 provides questions that support humanitarian emergency programming by providing insights into the relationship between VAWG and humanitarian emergencies at each level of the social ecology.

Any design process should seek to understand the experiences of vulnerable groups and work outwards into the environment and contexts in which they live, asking: what can the programme do to prevent and end VAWG? Using the ecological model can support the development of such knowledge; its fundamental contribution lies in its focus on the embedded nature of VAWG, demonstrating that everything – from the individual to the community level and beyond – is located within (and thus shaped by) culture. This highlights the fact that structural changes (such as new ways of implementing humanitarian assistance) and interventions will not meet their full potential unless efforts are made to address the broader cultural system in which they are located, interpreted, and enacted.

The ecological model considers individual as well as environmental determinants of attitudes and behaviours and does so at different levels where people negotiate relationships, roles, power structures, and interpersonal connections. Context is key, as are the constructions developed, applied, and sustained by individuals and groups at all levels, from the household to the global. The model acknowledges that individuals are embedded within their social system and society, and that there are many and various connections between those individuals and with wider groupings. People will all have 'different stories to tell' (see, e.g., Rubenstein & Stark, 2017). Thus, while culture is clearly influential in all aspects of life, it should not be seen as a rigid meta-narrative. Culture is mobile and permeable; it does not simply govern community, household, individual, and other levels, but is also influenced by them in a two-way process.

TABLE 5.1 Using the ecological model in humanitarian emergencies

Social ecology level	Meta-question	Factors to think about for operationalisation
Global	How does globalisation influence local and international humanitarian emergency processes specific to gender and VAWG?	Where are the key gender and VAWG inflection points in both acceptance of and resistance to, globalisation? (How) does the aetiology of VAWG resonate in global humanitarian emergency planning and response systems and structures and other relevant work?
Socio-cultural	What cultural practices and common views exist in regard to women and girls and specifically the use of violence against them?	Are there existing or emerging views that should be captured, challenged and changed through humanitarian emergency response?
Community	Do community mechanisms exist to mitigate VAWG or offer security and protection to victims? What are these? What changes have been seen due to the humanitarian emergency?	How effective are the community mechanisms perceived to be and could they be built upon by programme response? Might there be evolving community mechanisms that could serve as pivot points to challenge VAWG?
Household	What dynamics exist at household level that may support or perpetuate VAWG?	Are there certain intra-/inter-household behaviours that need to be challenged by the programme? Is there opportunity to use the programme to tap into certain change dynamics: e.g. is there evidence that young educated women challenge their parents and the wider community about VAWG? Might female-headed households be supported specifically to challenge VAWG? Might such potential points of change be supported by programme response?
Individual	What room is there for individuals to challenge and change social norms surrounding VAWG?	Can individuals (probably in a small minority) seeking to end VAWG be supported to link with wider systems and structures, even in a humanitarian emergency? Is there space for such mobilisation? If there is, how can this be supported? if no, how might the response develop, build and support such actions?

110 VAWG prevention and response

Further to this, in recent years, it has been acknowledged that the ecological model can be expanded (see Fulu & Miedema, 2015 for an extension of the approach to global level). Work has also been done on configuring and/or applying the ecological model in the context of a humanitarian emergency. Much of this has centred around provision of primary and mental health services to adults and children (De Jong et al., 2015; Golden & Earp, 2012; UNICEF, 2018). GWI has published a synthesis paper on findings and lessons learned on VAWG perpetration, prevention, and response in the context of humanitarian emergencies (Murphy, Hess, Casey, & Minchew, 2019), which includes an informative 'socio-ecological model of potential risk factors for VAWG in conflict and post-conflict settings' and resonates on a number of levels with the framework we propose.

Notes

1 For examples of blindness, see, e.g., Barbelet (2018), Collinson (2016), Development Initiatives (2019), DuBois (2018), and Konyndyk (2018, 2019). See Chapter 1 for how political economy/political analyses (PEA/PA) are applied in development (less so in humanitarian contexts), and gender-focused, as well as feminist, responses to and critiques of these approaches. The gender blindness of much PEA/PA contributes to inattention to gender dimensions of power and politics and overall matters of gender inequality (Hudson & Leftwich, 2014; Hudson & Marquette, 2015). For critiques of gender blindness in PEA/PA, etc., see, e.g., Haines and O'Neil (2018), WILPF (2019), True (2010, 2012), and COFEM (2017, 2019).

2 Work considering the potential roles of women and women's groups in the context of VAWG in humanitarian emergencies and beyond includes ECHO (2018), Swaine, Spearing, Murphy, and Contreras (2018), Murphy, Hess, Casey, and Minchew (2019), Raud (2017), What Works (2019), and WRC (2016).

3 See Chapter 2 for a discussion of SASA! and its achievements on VAWG social norm change. To the best of our knowledge, while SASA! is being implemented in fragile situations, e.g., in Karamoja, Uganda, it has not yet been applied in a humanitarian emergency.

4 Component 2 of *What Works* (phase I) addressed 'VAWG in conflict and humanitarian crises'. See the programme website (https://www.whatworks.co.za/) for information about component 2s scope and research. Use of the website and its resources is recommended.

5 One core resource for provision of services to all affected by a humanitarian emergency is the *Minimum Initial Service Package* (MISP) for Sexual and Reproductive Health (SRH), first developed in 1996. It is part of the current IAWG SRH Field Manual (IAWG, 2018). The MISP contains a set of life-saving activities to be implemented at the onset of every humanitarian emergency. Implementation of the MISP is not an optional extra, but a minimum international standard of care. International law supports the rapid and unobstructed implementation of the MISP.

6 For a discussion of why an SDG indicator (at least one) on internal and cross-border forced migration (and one that includes focus on VAWG) is essential, see IRC (2019).

7 For the full relevant text from SDGs 5 and 16 (all targets and indicators), see, e.g., UN DESA (2020); also United Nations (2015).

8 Our review of the GBVIMS notes that it is a blunt instrument, with several questions asked of the survivor about the perpetrator – these are potentially extremely intrusive and will run the risk of lack of response or evasive/untrue answers. Gauging the actual extent to which the use of the GBVIMS has made a difference is difficult.

References

Ager, A., Bancroft, C., Berger, E., & Stark, L. (2018). Local constructions of gender-based violence amongst IDPs in northern Uganda: Analysis of archival data collected using a gender-and age-segmented participatory ranking methodology. *Conflict and Health, 12*(1), 1 10. https.//doi.org/10.1186/s13031-018-0140-6

Asgary, R., Emery, E., & Wong, M. (2013). Systematic review of prevention and management strategies for the consequences of gender-based violence in refugee settings. *International Health, 5*(2), 85–91. https://doi.org/10.1093/inthealth/iht009

Bain, A., & Guimond, M. (2014). Impacting the lives of survivors: Using service-based data in GBV programmes. *Humanitarian Practice Network, 60*, 15–18.

Barbelet, V. (2018). *As Local as Possible, as International as Necessary. Understanding Capacity and Complementarity in Humanitarian Action* (Humanitarian Policy Group Working Paper). Overseas Development Institute. https://www.odi.org/sites/odi.org.uk/files/resource-documents/12527.pdf

Bennett, K. (2019, 11–22 March 2019). *Presentation on the Global Study on Localisation in GBV Sub-Clusters* [Unpublished presentation]. Commission on the Status of Women Annual Meeting 63. New York.

Bernard, V., & Durham, H. (2014). Sexual violence in armed conflict: From breaking the silence to breaking the cycle. *International Review of the Red Cross, 96*(894), 427–434. https://doi.org/10.1017/S1816383115000442

Bradley, T., & Gruber, J. (2018). VAWG mainstreaming in access to justice programmes: A framework for action. *Development in Practice, 28*(1), 16–32. https://doi.org/10.1080/09614524.2018.1398716

CARE International. (2017). *Suffering in Silence: The 10 Most Under-Reported Humanitarian Crises of 2016.* https://reliefweb.int/report/world/suffering-silence-10-most-under-reported-humanitarian-crises-2016

CARE International. (2019). *A Framework for Addressing Gender Based Violence in Emergencies.* https://insights.careinternational.org.uk/images/in-practice/GBV/GBV_CARE-Framework-and-ToC-for-Addressing-GBViE_final_10042019.pdf

Casey, J., & Hawrylyshyn, K. (2014). Adolescent girls in emergencies: A neglected priority. *Humanitarian Exchange 60,* 33–36. https://odihpn.org/wp-content/uploads/2014/02/HE_60_web_1.pdf

COFEM. (2017). *Funding: Whose Priorities? Feminist Perspectives on Addressing Violence against Women and Girls Series* (Paper No. 4.). Coalition of Feminists for Social Change. https://raisingvoices.org/wp-content/uploads/2013/03/Paper-4-COFEM.final_.sept2017.pdf

COFEM. (2019). *Feminist Movement Building: Taking a Long-Term View. Feminist Pocketbook* (Tip Sheet 10). Coalition of Feminists for Social Change. https://cofemsocialchange.org/wp-content/uploads/2018/11/TS10-Feminist-movement-building-Taking-a-long-term-view.pdf

Collinson, S. (2016). *Constructive Deconstruction: Making Sense of the International Humanitarian System* (Humanitarian Policy Group Working Paper). Overseas Development Institute. https://www.odi.org/publications/10503-constructive-deconstruction-making-sense-international-humanitarian-system

de Jong, J. T., Berckmoes, L. H., Kohrt, B. A., Song, S. J., Tol, W. A., & Reis, R. (2015). A public health approach to address the mental health burden of youth in situations of political violence and humanitarian emergencies. *Current Psychiatry Reports, 17*(7), 60. https://doi.org/10.1007/s11920-015-0590-0

112 VAWG prevention and response

Development Initiatives. (2019). *Global Humanitarian Assistance Report 2019*. DI Ltd. https://devinit.org/resources/global-humanitarian-assistance-report-2019/

DuBois, M. (2018). *The New Humanitarian Basics* (Humanitarian Policy Group Working Paper). Overseas Development Institute. https://www.odi.org/sites/odi.org.uk/files/resource-documents/12201.pdf

ECHO. (2018). *EU Leadership of the Call to Action on Protection from Gender-Based Violence in Emergencies June 2017 – December 2018*. Directorate-General for European Civil Protection and Humanitarian Aid Operations (ECHO).

Edström, J., & Shahrokh, T. (2016). *Reframing Men and Boys in Policy for Gender Equality: Conceptual Guidance and an Agenda for Change* (EMERGE Framing Paper). Institute of Development Studies, Promundo US and Sonke Gender Justice. http://opendocs.ids.ac.uk/opendocs/bitstream/handle/123456789/10037/EMERGE%20Reframing%20Men%20and%20Boys.pdf

Fassin, D. (2012). *Humanitarian Reason: A Moral History of the Present*. University of California Press. https://doi.org/10.1525/california/9780520271166.001.0001

Fast, L. (2015). Unpacking the principle of humanity: Tensions and implications. *International Review of the Red Cross, 97*(897–898), 111–131. https://doi.org/10.1017/S1816383115000545

Freedman, J. (2016). Sexual and gender-based violence against refugee women: A hidden aspect of the refugee "crisis". *Reproductive Health Matters, 24*(47), 18–26. https://doi.org/10.1016/j.rhm.2016.05.003

Fulu, E., & Miedema, S. (2015). Violence against women: Globalizing the integrated ecological model. *Violence Against Women, 21*(12), 1431–1455. https://doi.org/10.1177/1077801215596244

GADN. (2019). *Solution - Or Part of the Problem? Reflections on the Role of INGOs in Women's Rights Work* (GADN Briefings). Gender and Development Network. https://gadnetwork.org/gadn-resources/solution-or-part-of-the-problem

García-Moreno, C., Zimmerman, C., Morris-Gehring, A., Heise, L., Amin, A., Abrahams, N., Montoya, O., Bhate-Deosthali, P., Kilonzo, N., & Watts, C. (2015). Addressing violence against women: A call to action. *The Lancet, 385*(9978), 1685–1695. https://doi.org/10.1016/S0140-6736(14)61830-4

GBV AoR – GPC. (2017). *Strategy 2018–2020*. Gender-Based Violence Area of Responsibility - Global Protection Cluster. https://www.refworld.org/docid/5c3702267.html

GBV AoR – GPC. (2018). *Report on Workshop to Consult on the GBV AoR Task Team on Localisation, July 2018* (Global Protection Cluster Annual Meeting). Gender-Based Violence Area of Responsibility - Global Protection Cluster. http://media.ifrc.org/grand_bargain_localisation/wp-content/uploads/sites/12/2018/08/Global-Protection-Cluster-annual-meeting-_Localisation.pdf

Gibbs, A., Duvvury, N., & Scriver, S. (2017). *What Works Evidence Review: The Relationship between Poverty and Intimate Partner Violence*. What Works to Prevent Violence Programme. https://www.whatworks.co.za/documents/publications/115-poverty-ipv-evidence-brief-new-crop/file

Golden, S. D., & Earp, J. A. L. (2012). Social ecological approaches to individuals and their contexts: Twenty years of health education & behavior health promotion interventions. *Health Education & Behavior, 39*(3), 364–372. https://doi.org/10.1177/1090198111418634

Gruber, J. (2005). Silent survivors of sexual violence in conflict and the implications for HIV mitigation: Experiences from Eritrea. *African Journal of AIDS Research, 4*(2), 69–73. https://doi.org/10.2989/16085900509490344

GWI. (2017). *Gender-Based Violence Research, Monitoring, and Evaluation with Refugee and Conflict-Affected Populations: A Manual and Toolkit for Researchers and Practitioners.* [Field Testing Version]. Global Women's Institute and the George Washington University. https://globalwomensinstitute.gwu.edu/sites/g/files/zaxdzs1356/f/downloads/Manual%20and%20Toolkit%20-%20Website.pdf

Haines, R., & O'Neil, T. (2018). *Putting Gender in Political Economy Analysis. Why It Matters and How To Do It* (Practitioners Guidance Note). Gender and Development Network & the Women's Participation and Leadership Working Group. https://gadnetwork.org/gadn-news/2018/5/9/putting-gender-in-political-economy-analysis-why-it-matters-and-how-to-do-it

Holmes, R., & Bhuvanendra, D. (2014). *Preventing and Responding to Gender-Based Violence in Humanitarian Contexts: Mapping and Analysing the Evidence and Identifying the Gaps.* UK Department for International Development (DFID). http://r4d.dfid.gov.uk/Output/195127/

Hossain, M., & McAlpine, A. (2017). *Gender-Based Violence Research Methodologies in Humanitarian Settings: An Evidence Review and Recommendations.* Elrha. https://www.elrha.org/wp-content/uploads/2017/06/ElrhaR2HC-Gender-Based-Violence-Research-Methodologies-in-Humanitarian-Settings_2017.pdf

Hossain, M., Zimmerman, C., & Watts, C. (2014). Preventing violence against women and girls in conflict. *Lancet, 383*(9934), 2021–2022. https://doi.org/10.1016/S0140-6736(14)60964-8

Hudson, D. & Marquette, H. (2015). Mind the gaps: What's missing in political economy analysis and why it matters. In A. Whaites, E. Gonzalez, S. Fyson, & G. Teskey (2015) (Eds.). *A Governance Practitioner's Notebook: Alternative Ideas and Approaches* (pp. 67–82). OECD. https://www.oecd.org/dac/accountable-effective-institutions/Governance%20Notebook.pdf

Hudson, D., & Leftwich, A. (2014). *From Political Economy to Political Analysis* (DLP Research Paper 25). University of Birmingham College of Social Sciences Developmental Leadership Program. https://www.dlprog.org/publications/research-papers/from-political-economy-to-political-analysis

IASC. (2015). *Guidelines for Integrating Gender-Based Violence Interventions in Humanitarian Action. Reducing Risk, Promoting Resilience and Aiding Recovery.* Inter-Agency Standing Committee. https://gbvguidelines.org/en/

IASC. (2018a). *Guideline: The Gender Handbook for Humanitarian Action.* Inter-Agency Standing Committee Gender Reference Group. https://interagencystandingcommittee.org/system/files/2018-iasc_gender_handbook_for_humanitarian_action_eng_0.pdf

IASC. (GenCap). (2018b). *Gender with Age Marker: Overview.* Inter-Agency Standing Committee Gender Standby Capacity Project, Norwegian Refugee Council and UN OCHA. https://interagencystandingcommittee.org/system/files/iasc-gam-information-sheet.pdf

IAWG. (2018). *Inter-Agency Field Manual on Reproductive Health in Humanitarian Settings.* Inter-Agency Working Group on Reproductive Health in Crisis. https://www.who.int/hac/global_health_cluster/newsletter/2/fiels_manual_rh/en/

IRC. (2015). *Are We There Yet? Progress and Challenges in Ensuring Life Saving Services and Reducing Risks to Violence for Women and Girls in Emergencies.* International Rescue Committee. https://www.rescue.org/report/are-we-there-yet-progress-and-challenges-ensuring-life-saving-services-and-reducing-risks

IRC. (2019). *Missing Persons: Refugees Left Out and Left Behind in the Sustainable Development Goals.* International Rescue Committee. https://reliefweb.int/report/world/missing-persons-refugees-left-out-and-left-behind-sustainable-development-goals

ISG. (2014). *Evaluation of the Gender-Based Violence Information Management System (GB-VIMS): Final Report* (Report Prepared for UNFPA). International Solutions Group.

Jewkes, R., Stern, E., & Ramsoomar, L. (2019). *Community Activism Approaches to Shift Harmful Gender Attitudes, Roles and Social Norms*. What Works Programme. https://prevention-collaborative.org/wp-content/uploads/2019/11/social-norms-briefWEB-28092019.pdf

Kerr-Wilson, A., Gibbs, A., McAslan Fraser, E., Ramsoomar, L., Parke, A., Khuwaja, H. M. A., & Jewkes, R. (2020). *A Rigorous Global Evidence Review of Interventions to Prevent Violence against Women and Girls*. What Works Programme. https://www.whatworks.co.za/documents/publications/374-evidence-reviewfweb/file

Koizumi, K., & Hoffstaedter, G. (Eds.) (2015). *Urban Refugees. Challenges, Services and Protection*. London: Routledge. https://doi.org/10.4324/9781315733258

Konyndyk, J. (2018). *Fit for the Future: Envisioning New Approaches to Humanitarian Response*. Center for Global Development. https://www.cgdev.org/publication/fit-future-envisioning-new-approaches-humanitarian-response

Konyndyk, J. (2019). *Five Takeaways on the Future of Humanitarian Reform*. Washington DC: Center for Global Development. https://www.cgdev.org/sites/default/files/five-takeaways-future-humanitarian-reform.pdf

Le Masson, V., Lim, S., Budimir, M., & Selih Podboj, J. (2018). *Disasters and Violence against Women and Girls. Can Disasters Shake Social Norms and Power Relations?* (ODI Working Paper). Overseas Development Institute. https://www.odi.org/sites/odi.org.uk/files/resource-documents/11113.pdf

LSE CWPS, GAPS & WWI. (2016). *Experts' Meeting: Sexual Violence in Conflict and the UK's Women, Peace and Security Agenda* (Chairs' Summary). London School of Economics Centre for Women, Peace and Security, Gender Action for Peace and Security and Women for Women International. https://gaps-uk.org/wp-content/uploads/2017/01/LSE-WFWI-GAPS-Experts-Meeting-SVC-and-WPS-Chairs-Summary-FINAL.pdf

Magone, C. (2014). Collecting data on sexual violence: What do we need to know? The case of MSF in the Democratic Republic of Congo. *Humanitarian Exchange, 60*, 18–20. https://odihpn.org/magazine/collecting-data-on-sexual-violence-what-do-we-need-to-know-the-case-of-msf-in-the-democratic-republic-of-congo/

McAlpine, A., Hossain, M., & Zimmerman, C. (2016). Sex trafficking and sexual exploitation in settings affected by armed conflicts in Africa, Asia and the Middle East: Systematic review. *BMC International Health and Human Rights, 16*(1), 34. https://doi.org/10.1186/s12914-016-0107-x

Murphy, M., Arango, D., Hill, A., Contreras, M., MacRae, M., & Ellsberg, M. (2016). *Evidence Brief: What Works to Prevent and Respond to Violence against Women and Girls in Conflict and Humanitarian Settings?* Global Women's Institute and the International Rescue Committee. https://www.whatworks.co.za/documents/publications/66-maureen-murphy-diana-arango-amber-hill-manuel-contreras-mairi-macrae-mary-ellsberg/file

Murphy, M., Bingenheimer, J. B., Ovince, J., Ellsberg, M., & Contreras-Urbina, M. (2019). The effects of conflict and displacement on violence against adolescent girls in South Sudan: The case of adolescent girls in the Protection of Civilian sites in Juba. *Sexual and Reproductive Health Matters, 27*(1), 1–11. https://doi.org/10.1080/26410397.2019.1601965

Murphy, M., Hess, T., Casey, J., & Minchew, H. (2019). *What Works to Prevent Violence against Women and Girls in Conflict and Humanitarian Crisis: Synthesis Brief*. DFID (UK Aid) and the George Washington University, GWI. https://www.rescue-uk.org/sites/default/files/document/2051/p868ircsynthesisbriefreportlr.pdf

Murray, S. (2019). *GBV AoR Help Desk: Research Query* [Promising Practices for Partnerships Supporting National and Local Women's Organisations and Groups Undertaking Gender-Based Violence (GBV) Prevention and Response Programming in Emergencies]. Gender-based VIOLENCE Area of Responsibility. https://www.sddirect.org.uk/media/1770/gbvie-ngo-partnerships-query-fv.pdf

O'Gorman, E. (2013). *Review of UN Action against Sexual Violence in Conflict 2007–2012. Final Report.* http://stoprapenow.org/uploads/advocacyresources/1401281502.pdf

Oxfam, ECHO, & CGFPG. (2017). *Institutionalizing Gender in Emergencies: Case Study of South Sudan.* Oxfam, ECHO Enhanced Response Capacity and Members of the Cluster Gender Focal Point Group. https://policy-practice.oxfam.org.uk/publications/institutionalizing-gender-in-emergencies-case-study-of-south-sudan-620237

Raud, W. (2017). *Gender and Localising Aid: The Potential of Partnerships to Deliver.* New York and CARE International. https://www.care-international.org/files/files/publications/Gender_and_Localizing_Aid_high_res.pdf

Read-Hamilton, S., & Marsh, M. (2016). The communities care programme: Changing social norms to end violence against women and girls in conflict-affected communities. *Gender & Development, 24*(2), 261–276. https://doi.org/10.1080/13552074.2016.1195579

Rubenstein, B. L., & Stark, L. (2017). The impact of humanitarian emergencies on the prevalence of violence against children: An evidence-based ecological framework. *Psychology, Health & Medicine, 22*(sup1), 58–66. https://doi.org/10.1080/13548506.2016.1271949

Small Arms Survey. (2016). *Gender Based Violence Interventions: Opportunities for Innovation.* Humanitarian Innovation Fund Gap Analysis. Elrha. https://www.elrha.org/researchdatabase/gender-based-violence-interventions-opportunities-innovation/

Spangaro, J., Adogu, C., Ranmuthugala, G., Davies, G. P., Steinacker, L., & Zwi, A. (2013). What evidence exists for initiatives to reduce risk and incidence of sexual violence in armed conflict and other humanitarian crises? A systematic review. *PLoS One, 8*(5), e62600. https://doi.org/10.1371/journal.pone.0062600

Spangaro, J., Adogu, C., Zwi, A. B., Ranmuthugala, G., & Davies, G. P. (2015). Mechanisms underpinning interventions to reduce sexual violence in armed conflict: A realist-informed systematic review. *Conflict and Health, 9*(1), 19. https://doi.org/10.1186/s13031-015-0047-4

Swaine, A., Spearing, M., Murphy, M., & Contreras, M. (2018). *Intersections of Violence against Women and Girls with State-Building and Peace-Building: Lessons from Nepal, Sierra Leone and South Sudan.* George Washington University, Global Women's Institute, CARE International, and the International Rescue Committee. https://insights.careinternational.org.uk/publications/intersections-of-violence-against-women-and-girls-with-state-building-and-peace-building-lessons-from-nepal-sierra-leone-and-south-sudan

Tanner, S., & O'Connor, M. (2017). *A Safe Place to Shine. Creating Opportunities and Raising Voices of Adolescent Girls in Humanitarian Settings.* International Rescue Committee and Columbia University, Mailman School of Public Health. https://www.rescue.org/sites/default/files/document/2248/irccompassglobalreport.pdf

Tappis, H., Freeman, J., Glass, N., & Doocy, S. (2016). Effectiveness of interventions, programs and strategies for gender-based violence prevention in refugee populations: An integrative review. *PLoS Currents 8- Disasters,* 1–21. https://doi.org/10.1371/currents.dis.3a465b66f9327676d61eb8120eaa5499

True, J. (2010). The political economy of violence against women: A feminist international relations perspective. *Australian Feminist Law Journal, 32*(1), 39–59. https://doi.org/10.1080/13200968.2010.10854436

116 VAWG prevention and response

True, J. (2012). *The Political Economy of Violence against Women.* Oxford University Press. https://doi.org/10.1093/acprof:oso/9780199755929.001.0001

UN DESA. (2020). *SDG Indicators: Metadata Repository.* UN Department of Economic and Social Affairs Statistics Division. https://unstats.un.org/sdgs/metadata/

UN OCHA. (2019). *OCHA on Message: Gender in Humanitarian Action.* United Nations Office for the Co-Ordination of Humanitarian Affairs. https://www.unocha.org/sites/unocha/files/OOM_gender_22May2019_0.pdf

UN OIOS. (2018). *Evaluation of the Offices of the Special Representatives of the Secretary General for Children and Armed Conflict, for Sexual Violence in Conflict and on Violence against Children.* UN Office of Internal Oversight Services Inspection and Evaluation Division.

UN Women. (2013). *Violence against Women in Conflict, Post-Conflict and Emergency Settings.* The UN Entity for Gender Equality and the Empowerment of Women. https://www.endvawnow.org/uploads/modules/pdf/1405612658.pdf

UN Women & IDS. (2015). *The Effect of Gender Equality Programming on Humanitarian Outcomes* (Report for the IASC Reference Group on Gender in Humanitarian Action). The UN Entity for Gender Equality and the Empowerment of Women and the Institute of Development Studies. https://www.unwomen.org/en/digital-library/publications/2015/7/the-effect-of-gender-equality-programming-on-humanitarian-outcomes

UNESC. (2014). *Gender Equality and the Empowerment of Women in Natural Disasters. Report of the Secretary-General.* United Nations Economic and Social Council. https://digitallibrary.un.org/record/764450?ln=en

UNHCR. (2018a). *Reducing Risks: Sexual and Gender-Based Violence in Emergencies* (Review of the US-Funded Safe from the Start Project). United Nations High Commissioner for Refugees.

UNHCR. (2018b). *Our Fight against Sexual Misconduct: 2018 in Review.* United Nations High Commissioner for Refugees. https://www.unhcr.org/5c51a5d34.pdf

UNHCR. (2018c). *Reference Metadata Template for Data Reported on the Sustainable Development Goals (SDGs).* United Nations High Commissioner for Refugees.

UNHCR. (2019a). *Global Trends: Forced Displacement in 2018.* United Nations High Commissioner for Refugees. https://www.unhcr.org/globaltrends2018/

UNHCR. (2019b). *Indicator Proposal Summary Template.* United Nations High Commissioner for Refugees. https://movendi.ngo/wp-content/uploads/2020/06/Indicator-Narrative-Replacement-for-3.5.2.pdf

UNICEF. (2018). *Child Protection Advocacy Brief. Mental Health and Psychosocial Support in Emergencies.* United Nations Children's Fund. https://www.mhinnovation.net/resources/unicef-2018-mhpss-emergencies-advocacy-brief

United Nations. (2015). *Transforming Our World: The 2030 Agenda for Sustainable Development* (A/RES/70/1). SDG Knowledge Platform. https://sustainabledevelopment.un.org/index.php?page=view&type=111&nr=8496&menu=35

UNSG. (2019, March 29). *Conflict-Related Sexual Violence. Report of the UN Secretary General* (S/2019/280). United Nations Secretary General Annual Report, 2018. https://www.un.org/sexualviolenceinconflict/wp-content/uploads/2019/04/report/s-2019-280/Annual-report-2018.pdf

Vu, A., Adam, A., Wirtz, A., Pham, K., Rubenstein, L., Glass, N., Beyrer, C., & Singh, S., (2014). The prevalence of sexual violence among female refugees in complex humanitarian emergencies: A systematic review and meta-analysis. *PLoS Currents, 6.* https://doi.org/10.1371/currents.dis.835f10778fd80ae031aac12d3b533ca7

Vu, A., Wirtz, A. L., Bundgaard, S., Nair, A., Luttah, G., Ngugi, S., & Glass, N. (2017). Feasibility and acceptability of a universal screening and referral protocol for gender-based violence with women seeking care in health clinics in Dadaab refugee camps in Kenya. *Global Mental Health, 4,* e21. https://doi.org/10.1017/gmh.2017.18

Wachter, K., Horn, R., Friis, E., Falb, K., Ward, L., Apio, C., Wanjiku, S., & Puffer, E. (2018). Drivers of intimate partner violence against women in three refugee camps. *Violence Against Women, 24*(3), 286–306. https://doi.org/10.1177/ 1077801216689163

Whalan, J. (2017). *Dealing with Disgrace: Addressing Sexual Exploitation and Abuse in UN Peacekeeping* (Providing for Peacekeeping 15). The International Peace Institute. https://www.ipinst.org/wp-content/uploads/2017/08/IPI-Rpt-Dealing-with-Disgrace2.pdf

What Works. (2017). *No Safe Place: A Lifetime of Violence for Conflict-Affected Women and Girls in South Sudan. Main Results Report.* What Works to Prevent VAWG Programme. https://www.rescue-uk.org/sites/default/files/document/1580/southsudanlgsummary reportonline.pdf

What Works. (2019). *What Works to Prevent Violence against Women and Girls in Conflict and Humanitarian Crises.* What Works to Prevent VAWG Programme (Presentation Written by N. Behnam & K. Falb of the International Rescue Committee, as part of the What Works Consortium). https://reliefweb.int/report/world/what-works-prevent-violence-against-women-and-girls-conflict-and-humanitarian-crisis

WHO. (2007). *WHO Ethical and Safety Recommendations for Researching, Documenting and Monitoring Sexual Violence in Emergencies.* World Health Organization. https://www.who.int/reproductivehealth/publications/violence/9789241595681/en/

WILPF. (2019). *Five Key Issues.* Women's International League for Peace and Freedom (Peace Women).

WRC. (2016). *The Call to Action on Protection from Gender-Based Violence in Emergencies: Field Level Implementation Urgently Required.* Women's Refugee Commission. https://www.womensrefugeecommission.org/research-resources/call-to-action-gbv-protection-in-emergencies/

6

VAWG AND CONFLICT

Focus on women, peace, and security

Introduction

This chapter focuses on responses to VAWG in conflict and post-conflict situations, looking first at the efforts of the global community, informed by UN Security Council Resolutions on **Women, Peace, and Security** (WPS). **UN Security Council Resolution 1325** (SCR 1325) and other WPS Resolutions are discussed and their impacts reviewed, and we also review WPS National Action Plans (NAPs). Two specific conflict-related sexual violence (CRSV) initiatives are examined: UN Action and the UK-funded Prevention of Sexual Violence in Conflict Initiative (PSVI). Throughout this chapter, the pivotal advocacy and activism of civil society are acknowledged. Without such commitment, the WPS Agenda would not have come about. It is a complex and wide-ranging field and, as such, not all aspects of VAWG and conflict are discussed.

The women, peace, and security agenda

The momentum and urgency from a century of peace activism and advocacy undertaken by supporters of women's rights, including in conflict-affected settings, achieved a true milestone with the adoption of **UN Security Council Resolution 1325** (SCR 1325) in October 2000.

The four pillars of the WPS agenda are:
Prevention: Prevention of conflict and all forms of violence against women and girls in conflict and postconflict situations
Participation: Women participate equally with men and gender equality is promoted in peace and security decision-making processes at national, local, regional and international levels

DOI: 10.4324/9780429280603-6

Protection: Women's and girls' rights are protected and promoted in conflict-affected situations

Relief and Recovery: Women and girls' specific relief needs are met and women's capacities to act as agents in relief and recovery are reinforced in conflict and post-conflict situations.

(UK Gov, 2018, p. 4)

The WPS Agenda has articulated issues of women's rights and roles in an international context and in efforts to build and keep peace. Protecting the legal status of women, working to strengthen respect for their rights, and endeavouring to make more space for women's engagement in peacebuilding and the political sphere are essential goals and indicators of the relative equality, resilience, and strength of communities and nations.

Definitions: In the context of WPS, the term 'conflict-related sexual violence' is most used. What is and what is not covered by CRSV goes (as always) beyond mere semantics. CRSV refers primarily to rape perpetrated by parties to a conflict. It can encompass some or all of the following: sexual exploitation and abuse (SEA), transactional sex, trafficking, sexual enslavement, and increased rates of IPV (FCO, 2017; OSCE & LSE, 2020).

The pivotal role of civil society in developing and maintaining WPS

The entirety of the WPS Agenda, from advocacy to achieve 1325 to the present day, would have been impossible without the global commitment from women's rights organisations and civil society organisations (WROs and CSOs).

For decades, and increasingly during the 1990s, WROs and CSOs advocated for action on VAWG in conflict, influenced by events in Rwanda, the former Yugoslavia, and other conflicts. Advocacy focused on the almost total absence of women from peace-making and peacebuilding bodies, both during and after conflict. Pressure continued after 1995, with Beijing+5 providing crucial evidence of the dangers of inaction. A key global advocacy group was the NGO Working Group on Women, Peace, and Security, assisted by UNIFEM (now absorbed into UN Women).

Civil society, particularly WROs, continues to play a key role in advocating for and implementing WPS Agenda objectives. SCR 1325 was ground-breaking in that it explicitly made the connection between women's rights in conflict to freedom from VAWG, and their rights to participate in peace-making, within a framework of security. Women's rights and gender equality now have at least a place in discussions on conflict, security, and peace, and women's voices are increasingly (although still very much insufficiently) heard in such fora.

Yet despite such advocacy, drive, and policy developments, women's engagement in WPS processes does not match often lofty commitments: between 1990 and 2017, women globally made up 2% of mediators, 5% of witnesses and signatories, and 8% of negotiators (Taylor, 2018). Moreover, in certain situations, there is limited space given to genuine focus on the WPS Agenda. Negative social norms, conflict, high prevalence of VAWG, extreme humanitarian need, and other such factors contribute to a narrowing of opportunities for women's participation.

CASE STUDY: is there space for the WPS Agenda in Yemen?

Yemen ranks lowest in the world in terms of gender equality. The current conflict, which began in 2014, has exponentially increased the vulnerability of women and girls throughout the country, compounding existing gender inequalities that contribute to VAWG. In late 2017, UN OCHA estimated that instances of VAWG had increased by 63% during the conflict. 'Negative coping mechanisms', such as child marriage, have increased. Some 16,000 households are headed by girls under 18. Proliferation of weapons and continuing arms sales have added to insecurity and all forms of violence.

There are perhaps some small grounds for optimism: evidence indicates that in some tribal governorates where women's organisations have historically played a part in peace negotiations, space for this remains, though in other governorates where women did not have such opportunities, their role is limited. To some small extent, the conflict has challenged a number of social norms regarding what women should and should not do; here too some space has developed for women to participate in peace and security debates. Yemeni CSOs and diaspora networks, e.g. the Women Solidarity Network, strive to contribute to peace dialogue.

Yet, the humanitarian situation remains desperate for the great majority of Yemenis. Space is limited for a genuine, inclusive, and robust engagement of women's rights and WPS-focused organisations in peace-making and peacebuilding.

> *Research on WPS in Yemen tends to depict women as passive...[not] as political actors and...potential influencers...The space for women's participation has shrunk rapidly since the National Dialogue concluded in January 2014, with all actors currently seeing women's rights and participation as of secondary importance... [There] has been a negative backlash against women's rights activists, with violence and intimidation reported across Yemen.*
>
> *(Kangas & Stevens, 2018, p. 2)*

> *Women are part of the solution – The UN and donors must ensure the meaningful participation of women's organisations in Yemen's peace talks.*
>
> *(IRC, 2019, p. 3)*
> *(See further Awadh & Shuja'adeen, 2019; IRC, 2019;*
> *Kangas & Stevens, 2018)*

The UN Security Council Resolutions on women, peace, and security[1]

The UN Security Council (the UNSC) has to date adopted ten WPS Resolutions. All are intended to guide work to promote gender equality and strengthen women's participation, protection, and rights throughout the conflict cycle, from conflict prevention to post-conflict reconstruction and beyond to peacetime governance.

These Security Council Resolutions (UNSCRs) are 1325 (2000); 1820 (2008); 1888 (2009); 1889 (2010); 1960 (2011); 2106 (2013); 2122 (2013); 2242 (2015), and 2467 (2019); 2493 (2019). The tally rises to 11 when 2272 (March 2016) on addressing SEA by UN peacekeepers is included.

UNSCRs address how CRSV is used as a weapon of war, how perpetrators act with impunity and are unlikely ever to face prosecution, and the need for evidence-based solutions. The WPS UNSCRs recognise VAWG as a threat to international stability and as a crime under international law. Central to prosecution of such crimes (as well as effective delivery of services) is collection of evidence – UNSCRs 1820 and 2016 especially emphasise the necessity for data (see Magone, 2014).

UNSCR 1325

UNSCR 1325 demonstrates how women's participation and a gender perspective are essential to negotiating peace agreements, establishing peacekeeping operations, and reconstructing war-torn societies for sustainable peace. This was the first time that violence against women in conflict settings and its impacts were properly addressed by the UNSC.

UNSCR 1325 recognised how little women's voices had been heard and how under-valued their contributions had been. There was long overdue acknowledgement of the central role played by WROs and CSOs across the globe, of which many members work in situations of danger.

Crucially, UNSCR 1325 called for 'all parties to conflict to take special measures to protect women and girls from gender-based violence, particularly rape and other forms of sexual abuse, in situations of armed conflict'. Gender and security were recognised as inextricably connected (see Jia, Gebhard, & Cham, 2019).

WPS National Action Plans

A core component of UNSCR 1325 is that it seeks to bring about normative change (as do subsequent WPS UNSCRs).[2] One key aspect is development of **NAPs on WPS**, the first of which were launched in 2006. A NAP can be for a country in conflict, post-conflict, or a state of fragility, or for countries such as the UK, which has a primary focus of integrating the WPS Agenda into its official development assistance portfolio.

122 VAWG, conflict and WPS

Among the many positive elements of NAP development are, bringing together actors who might otherwise not meet, such as security forces and gender practitioners, engaging civil society more in specific security issues, and more women working in the security sector (using a broad definition to include police, military, UN peacekeepers, and other security personnel). The focus on NAPs has enabled civil society and governments to collaborate to build a framework for WPS policies. NAPs have been used in advocacy on VAWG prevention and response in conflict (for a positive review of NAPs, see Jacevic, 2019; also, Inclusive Security, 2017; OSCE & LSE, 2020).

Progress on actual development and implementation of NAPs has been patchy

As of late 2019, 83 countries (43% of all UN member states and territories) had developed and adopted WPS NAPs. Only 28 of those 83 NAPs include an earmarked budget for implementation, 65 specify a role for civil society, and just 25 discuss disarmament. Concerns have been raised over NAPs being funded while under development, but not for implementation, or there being no budget allocation to monitoring, evaluation and building an evidence base (GAPS UK, 2019b).

Below we provide a snapshot of work in 2019 and early 2020 on WPS NAPs; the Covid-19 pandemic will doubtless have delayed activities.[3] The range of different areas of focus and thus (presumably) national/UN agency prioritisation is clear. There is remarkably little explicit reference to VAWG, however defined (CRSV, GBV or VAWG), or for civil society participation in WPS processes.

Overview of work in 2019–2020 on WPS NAPs in selected countries and UN agencies:

- **Guatemala**: links 1325 and the need for disarmament. Reference to NAP funding challenges.
- **Jamaica**: security sector focus – maximising female participation and effectiveness in the Jamaica Defence Force.
- **Latvia**: commitment to developing its 1st NAP. Working with Sweden, Namibia, and the NGO Control Arms to understand GBV as part of arms transfers and to support [WPS] engagement with the Arms Trade Treaty.
- **Palestine**: the NAP 2020–2022 will seek to hold Israel to account, e.g., at the ICC; attention also to women's role in reconciliation.
- **Sierra Leone**: its 2nd NAP is work in progress; it addresses UNSCRs 1325 and 1820. Focus too on CEDAW reporting and integration of WPS into national development plan. President to declare SGBV a national emergency.
- **Sri Lanka**: committed to its first 1325 NAP by October 2020.
- **The UK**: the 2018–2022 NAP advocates closer integration of the PSVI into the NAP, with widened focus on other aspects of VAWG, beyond CRSV (LSE CWPS, GAPS and WWI, 2016). The NAP prioritises nine countries, including DRC and South Sudan.

- **UN Special Representative to the Secretary General for Children and Armed Conflict**: gender disaggregated data to be included in all reports. There will be special attention to girls in work on the ACT to Protect Children Affected by Conflict Campaign.
- **UN Women**: a detailed overview is provided of its work – with Women Human Rights Defenders (including documentation of GBV perpetrated against them in Syria, for example), with women's CSOs, women peacemakers and peacekeepers, and on mainstreaming gender-responsive conflict analysis into all relevant UN strategic planning. A new 'rapid response window' for the Women's Peace and Humanitarian Fund is mentioned.

Further normative priorities for WPS activists and practitioners include improvements at the **International Criminal Court**. The CEDAW Committee has called for change at international and national levels to define, legislate for, and, crucially, implement safeguards against VAWG in all humanitarian emergencies and to provide remedies for such violations; and to empower women by ensuring their equal participation in WPS activities, in accordance with the CEDAW Convention and UNSCR 1325. CEDAW General Recommendation 35 (2017) states that prohibition of GBV has evolved into a principle of customary international law (CEDAW, 2017).

But although this scaffolding exists, achievement of objectives continues to falter. The gap between abundant normative instruments, protocols, guidelines and actual action, evaluation and lesson learning remains for the WPS Agenda.

Other UNSCRs addressing VAWG and the WPS Agenda

1820 (2008): recognises sexual violence as a weapon and tactic of war, and that rape and other forms of sexual violence can constitute war crimes, crimes against humanity, or a constitutive act with respect to genocide. It calls for training of troops on preventing and responding to sexual violence and for more deployment of female peacekeepers.

1888 (2009): reiterates that CRSV exacerbates armed conflict and impedes international peace and security. It urges leadership to address CRSV. This UNSCR led to the creation and deployment of a UN **Team of Experts** (ToE) on the Rule of Law and Sexual Violence in Conflict. The ToE is authorised to assist national authorities, with the aim of ensuring criminal accountability for perpetrators of CRSV. See later in this chapter for further discussion of the ToE.

1960 (2010): re-emphasises the need for an end to sexual violence in armed conflict. Its focus is on ending impunity through a 'naming and shaming' mechanism, and referral of cases to the International Criminal Court, for example. It also calls for reparations for survivors (see e.g. Ferro Ribeiro & van der Straten Ponthoz, 2017).

2467 (2019): recognises that CRSV occurs on a continuum of VAWG and acknowledges national ownership and responsibility to deal with the root causes of sexual violence. A survivor-centred approach to VAWG is urged. The needs and rights of children born as a result of CRSV are addressed. Countries should tackle male impunity. As a corollary to the last point, 2467 encourages states to strengthen legal instruments and access to justice mechanisms for survivors.

2493 (2019): this has the apparent aim to rebuild consensus around the WPS Agenda and focus attention on accountability. It re-affirms *continuing and full implementation, in a mutually reinforcing manner* of all previous WPS Resolutions. It also introduces substantive references to women's *full, equal, and meaningful participation*, and contains an indirect reference to human rights defenders, as well as recognition of the importance of a broader legislative and political environment to allow them to carry out their work.

Prevention of sexual exploitation and abuse

UNSCR 2272 (2016): addresses SEA by UN peacekeepers. Advocates had spent several decades calling for action, with mounting evidence (e.g. from Sierra Leone and Haiti) where SEA was perpetrated against refugee children by UN peacekeepers, INGO, and national NGO staff members (GADN, 2019; ICSMACC, 2019).[4]

The intention is to stop people abusing positions of power, and to ensure that individuals or armed groups committing SEA can no longer assume they can act with impunity or enjoy immunity from prosecution. Accountability refers to implementation and reporting and ensuring that all engaged in humanitarian emergency activities adhere to ethical standards and legal principles (see Whalan, 2017).

Many challenges remain to the genuine implementation of 2272, not least the fear felt by SEA survivors and the lack of straightforward, confidential mechanisms to report and receive care and support. Moreover, UN peacekeepers remain under the jurisdiction of their home countries, where appetite for pursuing SEA cases may be minimal. Furthermore, state obligations to respond to survival sex do not currently exist, which has left a 'survival sex legal loophole' (Mudgway, 2017).

Funding for the WPS Agenda

This is a challenging subject to disentangle, because many interventions are subsumed under 'gender equality' or other markers. It is difficult to ascertain what proportion/sub-set of WPS funding might be specifically for VAWG actions (see Chapter 9 for a detailed discussion).

> In 2012–13, only 2% of all aid to peace and security in fragile states and economies targeted gender equality as a principal objective. Women's organisations in fragile contexts lack access to sustainable funding despite their vital role in building peace. In 2012–13, USD 130 million went to

women's equality organisations and institutions – a tiny amount compared with the USD 31.8 billion of total aid to fragile states and economies.

(OECD DAC, 2015, p. 1; see also Denney & Domingo, 2013; ICAI, 2019; WILPF, 2019a)

All too often, women's organisations that are dedicated to WPS receive short-term project funding rather than core, longer term financing. Subsequently, much time and energy are expended on annual funding submissions. This is despite several of the WPS UNSCRs not only highlighting the pivotal role of CSOs, but also calling on UN member states to provide adequate funding (e.g. UNSCR 2242 in 2015).

The 2015 Global Study on UNSCR 1325 (UN Women, 2015) recommended the establishment of a dedicated fund to address the financing gap for women's engagement in peace and security activities. The **Global Acceleration Instrument** (GAI) on WPS and Humanitarian Action was launched in February 2016 (GAI, 2015; also Peace Women 2015). Since August 2017, the GAI operates as the **Women's Peace and Humanitarian Fund** (WPHF – a pooled funding mechanism).

The core mandate of the WPHF is to steer resources directly to CSOs working on WPS efforts. GAI allocated 50% of funds; it is unclear if that proportion continues under the WPHF. Total WPHF funds as of the end of 2018 amounted to almost USD 14 million (WPHF, 2019), patently an extreme shortfall vis-à-vis need.

The WPHF is positioned as a potential tool for donors to fund three of the Grand Bargain work streams: participant revolution, the 'humanitarian-development nexus', and localisation. Data appear to be unavailable on the extent to which any such funds have been allocated through the WPHF.

Key WPS Agenda gaps

Effective and measurable mainstreaming of the WPS Agenda into conflict prevention, peacebuilding and post-conflict development, remains patchy (GAPS, 2019a; GWI, IRC, & CARE, 2018; Kirby & Shepherd, 2016). **Key gaps** from 1325 onwards (as defined by advocates, activists, and practitioners) include:

- **Inadequate focus on the entirety of VAWG prevention and response in the WPS Agenda** The four pillars of the WPS Agenda are grounded in focus on GBV/CRSV, not VAWG. It is only relatively recently that focus has expanded, to encompass issues such as IPV in conflict settings, VAWG against women's human rights defenders, and GBV being used as a weapon against any person (see, e.g., GAPS UK, 2019a, 2019b; WILPF, 2019a). The dangers inherent in potential dilution of VAWG focus resonate in this context.
- Focus on CRSV leads to further questions: might such prioritisation result in lack of attention to the need to address all forms of VAWG? A synthesis brief

that reviewed new evidence on VAWG in conflict and humanitarian settings found that prevalence of IPV was higher than that of non-partner sexual violence. In three sites in South Sudan, IPV rates were between 54% and 73%, while rates for non-partner sexual violence (although horrific) were lower at between 28% and 33% (both for ever-partnered women) (IRC, GWI, & CARE, 2018a. See further GWI & IRC, 2016; GWI, IRC, & CARE, 2018b; What Works, 2017).[5]

- It is increasingly acknowledged that attention to **the intersectionality of gendered experiences in conflict and in WPS processes** is essential. In conflict, issues of gender, sexuality, disability, ethnicity, religion, class, education and other factors may have profound implications in terms of vulnerability to VAWG and other gendered violence.

- **Women are portrayed as victims, not as survivors with agency and potential active agents for peace**. Gender equality has been shown to be the number one predictor of resilient and peaceful communities. Women's participation increases the probability of a peace agreement lasting at least two years by 20% (see, e.g., UN Women, 2015). Continuation of patriarchal systems and pigeonholing of (all) women perpetuates inequality (WILPF, 2019b; also, Florea Hudson, 2013; NGO WG, 2017).

- **Institutional and structural changes at all levels do not match declarations, commitments, policies, guidelines**. UN Secretaries General and other pivotal WPS actors feel the need repeatedly to re-emphasise the importance of the WPS Agenda, highlight the gaps, and stress the need for proper financial and human resource commitment. There is a disconnect between rhetoric and policy and actual practice, with the commitment of WPS actors from all sectors seldom being matched by sufficient resources.

- **Structural obstacles to gender equality and VAWG prevention and response actions** in the context of WPS are too often side-lined in debates and pronouncements. Despite many examples of genuine good practice on a range of issues at policy level, there is far too much gender blindness at the core of many WPS actions. Human rights continue frequently to be 'the rights of man'.[6]

- **UNSCR 2493**: The fact that a UNSCR was required in 2019 to 'rebuild consensus' and 're-affirm' commitment to the WPS Agenda indicates that action and financial disbursements do not match stated commitments. It further suggests lack of coherent, coordinated engagement to ensure that WPS becomes truly mainstreamed in peace-making and peacebuilding.[7]

National Action Plans on 1325/WPS: gaps

While there is much evidence of clarity, prioritisation, and action coming out of NAP development, there is need for (re)focus on aspects of the Agenda if (some) NAPs are not to become primarily rhetorical statements.

CSOs and WROs must participate in NAP formulation, monitoring and reporting. Women's voices must be heard, and their testimonies acted upon. The lack of effective integration of civil society expertise, commitment, and testimony into the development and implementation of NAPs is a major stumbling block to genuine inclusion of all perspectives, as is inadequate funding (GAPS UK, 2019b). Engaging with civil society, i.e. the actions led by the UN agencies and donor partners working more effectively and collaboratively with CSOs, has resonance in terms of 'localisation' (see also Chapter 5).

More coherent work is needed to strengthen WPS through NAPs that effectively promote action throughout the continuum of conflict to peacekeeping and beyond. Achievements in WPS can be lost if a country returns to conflict or experiences a humanitarian emergency and does not continue peace-making and peacekeeping activities (see FCO, 2017 re: the Middle East and North Africa).

Closer integration with SDGs 5 and 16 is needed, e.g., through including NAPs in SDG reviews and using the development of a new NAP to mainstream such action. Only a few NAPS current in 2020 explicitly make the connection between SDGs 5 and 16 and the wider WPS Agenda (e.g. Canada, Germany, Sweden). Further gaps include:

- **Absence of proper focus on WPS in SDGs 5 and 16**: the UNSC has frequently affirmed that mainstreaming gender into all aspects of peace and security, and genuine participation of women in peace-making and peacebuilding, are essential to achieving lasting peace, yet SDG 16 does not reflect such sentiments. There is no read across between SDGs 5 and 16. None of the 12 targets of SDG 16 explicitly refers to gender, yet none can be comprehensively and equitably achieved without action on gender issues. Although a number of the 23 indicators of SDG 16 refer to disaggregation by sex and age, there is no closer consideration of gender differentials, nor of specific WPS factors (IWDA, 2016).[8]
- **Peace agreements** continue to be adopted without provisions for the stated objectives and needs of women and girls; attacks against Women's Human Rights Defenders, humanitarians, and peacebuilders are all on the rise; and survivors are left without support or justice. Women's rights and gender equality must not be treated as mere adjuncts to peacebuilding but integral components of a lasting peace.
- In the often-hyper-masculinised world of security and conflict, **WPS issues may be seen as a 'soft agenda'**. One example is that despite increasing numbers of women acting as UN peacekeepers, as police officers, and in other security roles, they are often to be found in 'traditional' female positions, e.g., as community liaison officers on women's issues (Kirby & Shepherd, 2016; Ryan & Basini, 2017; for examples of gender-blind approaches, see papers in NATO, 2019).
- **Use of gender expertise** remains limited at most levels in peace-making policy development, in UN peace operations and in Disarmament,

Demobilisation, and Re-integration (DDR) initiatives. Increasing women's participation in the security sector could assist gender mainstreaming in Security Sector Reform (SSR). Any coordinated, effective action to develop gender-responsive structures within SSR to advance the WPS Agenda necessitates moving beyond just counting numbers of women.

- **Disarmament**: Minimal attention to this in WPS has hampered concrete steps and positive change – not least because, despite demands for action, sales of arms have expanded since 2000. The proliferation of weapons exacerbates the dangers of VAWG. In 2018, the UN called (again) for action on the Arms Trade Treaty gender criterion, which requests that states refrain from authorising arms exports if there are 'overriding' risks of VAWG.

- **Preventing and countering violent extremism (P/CVE)**: The P/CVE thrust of much global security focus has led to a blurring of attention on WPS priorities. WPS can become conflated with national, regional, or global security priorities. Short-term 'hard security' measures take precedence over longer term work to bring about social change. P/CVE cannot be allowed to (or allowed to further) undermine focus on women's rights and gender equality. Effectively countering violent extremism requires participation by all; current approaches are seen as counterproductive to women's engagement (GAPS UK, 2018).

- UNSCR 1325 nowhere mentions **men and boys**, whether as perpetrators of VAWG, as products of patriarchal societies that enable, even justify, such violence, as living examples of 'hyper masculine' codes and behaviours and social norms that perpetuate male power – or indeed as supporters of women's rights.

- A more inclusive approach to WPS might allow space for engagement by male survivors of sexual violence and more targeted work on social norms that put men at risk, such as homophobic attitudes that encourage such acts. A too rigid acceptance that social norms everywhere and always perpetuate male dominance and patriarchy may limit opportunities for more innovative and inclusive actions (for varying emphases, see, e.g., GWI, IRC, & CARE, 2018a, 2018b; Kirby & Shepherd, 2016; Spangaro et al., 2013; Swaine Spearing, Murphy, & Contreras-Urbina, 2019; the WILPF website[9]).

- Only a few DDR (or indeed other peace-making/WPS) programmes have developed concrete initiatives to **transform violent masculinities**. Yet such attention is essential if peaceful societies are to be built and sustained. In conflict, the militarisation of masculinity, grounded in profound gender inequalities and societal acceptance of VAWG, perpetuates both. Too often, the gendered dimensions of power, and how violence is used to maintain them, receive little attention in WPS, peace-making and peacebuilding (Duriesmith, 2017).

- In recent years there has been growing (but so far limited) attention to the **interconnections between WPS, VAWG in conflict, socio-economic and ecological inequalities, and post-colonialism** – and indeed to 'the coloniality of power' (Davies & True, 2018; WILPF, 2019a).

Initiatives to counter CRSV: UN Action and PSVI

UN Action against Sexual Violence in Conflict[10]

Since 2007, UN Action against Sexual Violence in Conflict (UN Action) has sought to unite the UN system to achieve the goal of ending CRSV. UN Action was created in response to requests from WROs, CSOs, and VAWG survivors for the UN to act more coherently. The impetus for UN Action remains to reduce internal UN fragmentation of efforts and more effectively to synergise work on sexual violence prevention and response activities (MPTF & UNDP, 2018, 2019; UNSG, 2019).

The raison d'être of UN Action (as per its website) is to achieve results by

> amplifying advocacy, improving co-ordination and accountability, and supporting country efforts to prevent conflict-related sexual violence and respond effectively to the needs of survivors.

The Chair of UN Action is the Special Representative of the Secretary-General on Sexual Violence in Conflict (the SR-SVC); the UNSC holds at least one open debate on sexual violence in conflict every year.

The Multi Partner Trust Fund (the MPTF) was set up in 2008. As of end 2019 there were 13 UN members of UN Action, including UNDP, UN Women, UNICEF, UNHCR, WHO, and UN OCHA. The total budget for that year was close to USD 50 million (for information on UN Action projects, see UNSG, 2019; also, annual reports of MPTF, 2010–2019).[11]

The UN Action team of experts

The Team of Experts on the Rule of Law and Sexual Violence in Conflict (the ToE) was created by UNSCR 1888 (2009) and revisited in 2019 by UNSCR 2467. The ToE remit is to assist national authorities to strengthen the rule of law and to achieve criminal accountability for CRSV. UN Action created a dedicated window for the ToE within the MPTF, which allows donors to earmark funds specifically for its work. While UN Action is not a field-based mechanism, the ToE does deploy regularly to the field (ToE annual reports).

UNSCR 1888 acknowledges CRSV as a threat to peace and security, noting that many UN member states continue to require assistance to develop legal instruments and address CRSV. The ToE is the only globally mandated entity to provide such support; it reports to the SR-SVC.

ToE work covers: (i) criminal investigations and prosecutions; (ii) military justice; (iii) legislative reform; (iv) protection of victims and witnesses; (v) reparations for survivors; and (vi) security sector oversight. The ToE also works at regional and global levels, e.g., with the African Union and the International Criminal Court.

Is there coherence between the work of UN Action, the ToE, and the WPS Agenda?

Annual UN Action reports are published by the Secretary General's Special Representative. These reports, the first of which was published in January 2012, have raised awareness; they are based on country-level evidence that is deemed by the Special Representative's office to be robust. The reports have contributed significantly to the evidence base and the global debate and actions on CRSV.

A review of the first five years (2007–2012) of UN Action found laudable engagement and achievements. However, the review indicates at best limited coherence of UN Action's activities with the wider WPS Agenda, as well as concerns that the adoption of the term 'conflict-related sexual violence' may have diluted focus from wider GBV/VAWG and the overall WPS Agenda (O'Gorman, 2013). Many of those points continue to be extremely relevant.

A major study on the first 15 years of the WPS Agenda makes minimal reference to UN Action or to the ToE (UN Women, 2015): comments are on the need for increased funding, greater coherence, and coordination of UN Action's work. There is mention of work undertaken by the ToE, e.g., in the DRC and in Guinea (Conakry), in both instances to address sexual violence perpetrated by military personnel. There is no discussion of whether, and if so, how, the UN Action and the ToE have supported, facilitated, or expanded the WPS Agenda, beyond their positioning as mechanisms to address CRSV.[12]

The UN Women report highlights an important and ongoing issue: there should be far more coherence and crosscutting initiatives between WPS and VAWG prevention and response in all humanitarian emergencies (i.e. not solely conflict).

The **UN Action Theory of Change** was updated in 2018 (MPTF & UNDP, 2019). It refers minimally to linking to other initiatives, whether in conflict or during transition to peaceful development. The Theory of Change appears to position VAWG survivors as primarily passive recipients of support, rather than as potential active agents in their own lives and in peace-making and beyond. It is woefully silent on civil society participation in WPS, and the potential benefits of effective partnerships.

The Preventing Sexual Violence in Conflict Initiative[13]

PSVI was set up in 2012 by the UK. It aims to strengthen and support international efforts responding to sexual violence in conflict. As PSVI champion (with Angelina Jolie, Special Envoy to UNHCR) William Hague, then UK Foreign Secretary, stated: 'we very deliberately invoked a high ideal – the eradication of the use of rape as a weapon of war'. Thus, IPV and other forms of VAWG were not part of the initial PSVI focus and are not so today.

PSVI seeks to enhance the capacity of countries, institutions, and communities to support survivors and end impunity for perpetrators. In 2014 the first Global Summit to end sexual violence in conflict resulted in a UN Declaration, currently signed by 156 member states.

PSVI established a UK Team of Experts, members of which have been deployed to a number of conflict areas, e.g., to the Syrian borderlands and to Mali. The UK ToE was cut from its 70-plus initial members to fewer than 40 in 2015. It is unclear from documentation whether, and if so, how, the PSVI ToE might have collaborated or worked with the UN Action ToE; the range of expertise and remits for the teams appear similar.

Documentation indicates that PSVI has lost momentum, especially since Hague's tenure as Foreign Secretary ended in mid-2014. The PSVI team budget has fallen considerably since 2014, when it was approximately £15 million. By 2018–2019, the PSVI London team spending amounted to less than £2 million, much of which went to the UN; there were only a handful of projects at country level, amounting to less than £300,000 (ICAI, 2020).

The work and achievements of PSVI 2014–2019 were reviewed by the UK Independent Commission for Aid Impact (ICAI). Its report awards an overall amber/red rating, which means 'The programme performs relatively poorly overall against ICAI's criteria for effectiveness and value for money. Significant improvements should be made' (ICAI website).

Other key points of concern expressed in the ICAI report include issues that resonate across the entirety of the WPS/VAWG landscape. These include:

- Absence of an over-arching strategy and strategic plan
- Absence of a Theory of Change
- Short funding cycles, typically one-year, that cannot address the complexities of CRSV or survivors' needs, and are especially challenging for national, often small, CSOs
- Minimal inclusion of survivors in PSVI activities, at any stage
- Absence of an integrated, robust knowledge management system and a lesson learning approach – PSVI has not added significantly to the sum of knowledge (this area receives an ICAI red rating – 'poor performance; immediate and major changes need to be made')
- Lack of adequate overview of what the PSVI portfolio includes and what it supports
- Difficulties in establishing the extent of funding to specific PSVI/CRSV actions

The UK Government response rebuts certain of the points above, e.g., stating that it has always had a survivor-centred approach, that there is much informal lesson sharing across government and that PSVI remains a priority for the UK (UK Gov, 2020).

Concluding remarks[14]

Enhanced joint working across the WPS Agenda is essential: this is self-evident from our review of UN Action and PSVI. PSVI documentation and the 2020 ICAI report make no reference to UN Action. We have found little discussion in

132 VAWG, conflict and WPS

the literature on how UN Action and its ToE might effectively coordinate and co-operate with WPS actors, whether those are based in the UN agencies, donor partners, or indeed, and crucially, in civil society. This is very much the same case with PSVI and its own ToE.

One of the core catalysts for UNSCR 1325 and subsequent WPS SCRs was the recognition of the urgent need to acknowledge the individual and societal damage and hurt caused by GBV/VAWG in conflict. Another was the essential requirement for women to be equal participants in peace-making, peacebuilding, and security. It may be that such interaction and joint working exist and are considered so self-evident that reference is deemed unnecessary; if so, then there should be explicit review of the efficacy of such partnership – and greater accountability.

It cannot credibly be argued that resources are remotely adequate, and these already limited funding streams appear to run largely in parallel, when there might be scope for imaginative, innovative collaboration. Thus, it is important to question, for example, whether the Multi-Partner Trust Fund and the Women's Peace and Humanitarian Fund ever speak to each other, as well as how they do so and whether this results in greater effectiveness – not least because both are run out of UN Women.

A report prepared in advance of the UN Women 15-year review of UNSCR 1325 highlights two issues that are just as important today: the need for far less rhetoric and far more action, and for greater emphasis to be given to the prevention and participation pillars of WPS (GAAV, 2015).

There are tensions inherent in the WPS Agenda between prevention of sexual violence in conflict and the promotion of women as active and equal participants in the continuum of peace-making and peacekeeping activities. Are females to be passive recipients of protection, or active agents for peace? Or both? Which takes priority in the WPS Agenda, especially when it is apparent that countries and NAPs do not adhere to one defined set of priorities? The entire WPS Agenda has been described as constituting a 'norm bundle' (as uncomfortably disparate as that sounds) and as including 'fundamental norms', which refers primarily to prevention of sexual violence in conflict, and 'adjacent (or emerging) norms', i.e. women's engagement in WPS (True & Weiner, 2019; see also True, 2016).

We believe that the application of a more rigorous approach, through applying the various interrogatory stages of our proposed VAWG Mainstreaming Framework (as set out in Chapter 2), would provide an opportunity for more coherent planning that encompasses the many and varied roles potentially available to female WPS actors. It also highlights the pitfalls that are inherent in an either/or perspective whereby women are viewed as either to be protected passively or to participate actively.

Notes

1 Other relevant WPS UNSCRs: 1889 (2009); 2016 (2013); 2122 (2013); 2242 (2015).
2 Normative: support to develop, change, and/or integrate norms and standards in international and national laws, international conventions, regulatory frameworks, codes

of practice, etc. Normative work is often described as 'bridging the policy-practice divide'.

3 WILPF WPS webpages, downloaded June 2020; Permanent Mission of Germany to the UN 2020.

4 In 2004, the then UN Secretary General Kofi Annan commissioned what became known as the Zeid Report, the first internal review of SEA. For overviews of action (or not) since 2000, see Whalan (2017); also, GADN, GAPS, and UK SRHR Network (2015), Grady (2010), Kovatch (2016), Magone (2014), Stern (2015), Westendorf and Searle (2017), and UNHCR (2018).

5 This is an evidence brief from phase 1 of the DFID-funded *What Works to Prevent VAWG* programme. In September 2020, DFID was merged into the Foreign, Commonwealth, and Development Office. Uncertainty prevails for ICAI and the House of Commons' International Development Committee; the IDC is apparently to be abolished. Future opportunities for public scrutiny of UK Aid are unclear.

6 The 2018 UN Secretary General's report on sexual violence in conflict (UNSG, 2019) referred back to the UN Women WPS review. For a range of perspectives, see, e.g., Cockburn (2010, 2013), Domingo et al. (2013); Florea Hudson (2013, 2015), IWDA (2016), Jia, Gebhard, and Cham (2019), NGO WG (2017), Taylor (2018), True & Tanyag (2017), WILPF (2019b). Also, WILPF (2018) for the need for a feminist UN Security Council and Kirby and Shepherd (2015) on why feminist foreign policy is essential.

7 Thus, e.g., *Pathways for Peace. Inclusive Approaches to Preventing Violent Conflict* (World Bank, 2018) does not mention WPS and only superficially references gender. The UK response to the UNSCR 2493 vote stated: 'focus should now be on delivering on the ambition of the full existing framework of Women, Peace and Security Resolutions, and not producing more texts'.

8 E.g. the 2019 Global Sustainable Development Report (GSDR - UNDESA, 2019) barely addresses gender and has no substantive references to VAWG, GBV, IPV, or to WPS. A third of the way through the SDGs gender and VAWG-blind 'Business as Usual' is of concern. See also Ritchie, Roser, Mispy, and Ortiz-Ospina (2018) and Chapter 5 of this volume.

9 WILPF website: https://www.wilpf.org/

10 Data on UN Action and ToE are from MPTF and UNDP (2019), UNSG (2019), O'Gorman (2013), ToE (2018), UNDP (2020), UN OIOS (2018), and WILPF website.

11 Website for MPTF annual reports: https://mptf.com/annual-report/

12 Other major VAWG documents are similarly silent on any links between overall work on VAWG in humanitarian emergencies, UN Action, the ToE, and wider WPS action – as well as on the pivotal role of civil society. See, e.g., IASC (2018) and UN OIOS (2018).

13 Information on PSVI from FCO (2017), UK Gov (2020), ICAI (2020), and WILPF data.

14 Several points here, and elsewhere in this chapter, have been amplified by reading the 2018 WPS Handbook (Davies & True, 2018).

References

Awadh, M., & Shuja'adeen, N. (2019). *Women in Conflict Resolution and Peacebuilding in Yemen.* Nahj Consulting for UN Women. https://arabstates.unwomen.org/en/digital-library/publications/2019/01/women-in-conflict-resolution-and-peacebuilding-in-yemen

CEDAW. (2017). *General Recommendation No. 35 on Gender-Based Violence against Women, Updating General Recommendation No. 19.* Committee on the Elimination of Discrimination against Women. https://www.ohchr.org/en/hrbodies/cedaw/pages/gr35.aspx

134 VAWG, conflict and WPS

Cockburn, C. (2010). Gender Relations as Causal in Militarization and War: A Feminist Standpoint. *International Feminist Journal of Politics, 12*(2), 139–157. https://doi.org/10.1080/14616741003665169

Cockburn, C. (2013). War and Security, Women and Gender: An Overview of the Issues. *Gender & Development, 21*(3), 433–452. https://doi.org/10.1080/13552074.2013.846632

Davies, S., & True, J. (Eds.) (2018). *The Oxford Handbook on Women, Peace and Security.* Oxford University Press. https://doi.org/10.1093/oxfordhb/9780190638276.001.0001

Denney, L., & Domingo, P. (2013). *A Problem-Focused Approach to Violence against Women and Girls: The Political Economy of Justice and Security Programming.* Overseas Development Institute (ODI). https://www.odi.org/publications/7372-problem-focused-approach-violence-against-women-political-economy-justice-and-security-programming

Domingo, P., Holmes, R., Rocha Menocal, A., Jones, N., Bhuvanendra, D., & Wood, J. (2013). *Assessment of the Evidence of Links between Gender Equality, Peace-Building and State-Building: Literature Review.* Overseas Development Institute (ODI). https://www.odi.org/sites/odi.org.uk/files/odi-assets/publications-opinion-files/8767.pdf

Duriesmith, D. (2017, December 15). *Engaging Men and Boys in the Women, Peace and Security Agenda: Beyond the 'Good Men' Industry* (LSE WPS Working Paper Series 11/2017). London School of Economics; Centre for Women, Peace and Security. https://blogs.lse.ac.uk/wps/2017/12/15/engaging-men-and-boys-in-the-women-peace-and-security-agenda-beyond-the-good-men-industry-david-duriesmith-112017/

FCO. (2017). *Now Is the Time: Research on Gender Justice, Conflict and Fragility in the Middle East and North Africa.* FCO, Oxfam and International Alert. https://www.oxfam.org/en/research/now-time-research-gender-justice-conflict-and-fragility-middle-east-and-north-africa

Ferro Ribeiro, S., & van der Straten Ponthoz, D. (2017). *International Protocol on the Documentation and Investigation of Sexual Violence in Conflict: Best Practice on the Documentation of Sexual Violence as a Crime or Violation of International Law* (2nd ed.). Foreign and Commonwealth Office (FCO). https://assets.publishing.service.gov.uk/government/uploads/system/uploads/attachment_data/file/598335/International_Protocol_2017_2nd_Edition.pdf

Florea Hudson, N. (2013). *UNSCR 1325: The Challenges of Framing Women's Rights as a Security Matter* (Policy Brief). Norwegian Peacebuilding Resource Centre (NOREF). https://reliefweb.int/sites/reliefweb.int/files/resources/4814ab8970493cca48dbbafdb b4e92bc.pdf

Florea Hudson, N. (2015). The social practice of securitizing women's rights and gender equality: 1325 fifteen years on. In J. R. Pruce (Ed.). *The Social Practice of Human Rights* (pp. 167–184). Palgrave Macmillan, London.

GAAV. (2015). *Implementing the Women, Peace and Security Agenda and Reducing Armed Violence* (A Submission for the 2015 High Level Review of the Women, Peace and Security [WPS] Agenda). Global Alliance on Armed Violence, Gender and Armed Violence Working Group. https://www.peacewomen.org/node/91641

GAI. (2015). *The Global Acceleration Instrument for Women, Peace and Security and Humanitarian Action.* Global Acceleration Instrument & UN Women. http://peacewomen.org/sites/default/files/TOR%20for%20GAI%20(1).pdf

GADN. (2019). *Members' Meeting Notes. Creating a Safe Culture for Development: A Workshop to Share the Recommendations from the Oxfam Independent Commission Report.* Gender and Development Network.

GADN, GAPS, & UK SRHR Network. (2015). *Turning Promises into Progress Report.* Gender and Development Network & Gender Action for Peace and Security, UK Sexual and Reproductive Health and Rights Network. https://gadnetwork.org/turning-promises-into-progress

GAPS UK. (2018). *Prioritise Peace: Challenging Approaches to Preventing and Countering Violent Extremism from a Women, Peace and Security Perspective.* Gender Action for Peace and Security (GAPS) UK. http://gaps-uk.org/wp-content/uploads/2018/06/GAPS-report_Prioritise-Peace-Challenging-Approaches-to-P-CVE-from-a-WPS-perspective.pdf

GAPS UK. (2019a). *Assessing UK Government Action on Women, Peace and Security in 2018.* Gender Action for Peace and Security (GAPS) UK. https://gaps-uk.org/wp-content/uploads/2019/01/Assessing-UK-Government-Action-on-Women-Peace-and-Security-in-2018.pdf

GAPS UK. (2019b). *The Ten Steps: Turning Women, Peace and Security Commitments to Implementation. Global Women, Peace and Security Consultation Findings.* Gender Action for Peace and Security (GAPS) UK. https://gaps-uk.org/wps-10-steps-2020/

Grady, K. (2010). Sexual exploitation and abuse by UN peacekeepers: A threat to impartiality. *International Peacekeeping, 17*(2), 215–228. https://doi.org/10.1080/13533311003625100

GWI & IRC. (2016). *Evidence Brief: What Works to Prevent and Respond to Violence against Women and Girls in Conflict and Humanitarian Settings?* The George Washington University, Global Women's Institute, International Rescue Committee.

GWI, IRC, & CARE. (2018a). *A New Analytical Framework for Addressing the Intersections of Violence against Women and Girls with Post-Conflict State-Building and Peace-Building Processes.* Global Women's Institute, International Rescue Committee, and CARE International. https://www.whatworks.co.za/documents/publications/209-p784-irc-what-works-framework-brief-final/file

GWI, IRC, & CARE. (2018b). *Intersections of Violence against Women and Girls with State-Building and Peace-Building: Lessons from Nepal, Sierra Leone and South Sudan.* Global Women's Institute, International Rescue Committee, and CARE International. https://www.whatworks.co.za/documents/publications/210-p784-irc-what-works-report-lr/file

IASC. (2018). *Guideline: The Gender Handbook for Humanitarian Action.* Inter-Agency Standing Committee Gender Reference Group. https://interagencystandingcommittee.org/system/files/2018-iasc_gender_handbook_for_humanitarian_action_eng_0.pdf

ICAI. (2019). *Joint Review. Part 1: Sexual Violence in Conflict. Part 2: Sexual Exploitation and Abuse by International Peacekeepers* (ICAI Approach Paper). Independent Commission for Aid Impact. https://icai.independent.gov.uk/wp-content/uploads/ICAI-Sexual-Violence-Sexual-Exploitation.pdf

ICAI. (2020). *The UK's Prevention of Sexual Violence in Conflict Initiative. Joint Review.* ICAI. https://icai.independent.gov.uk/html-report/psvi/

ICSMACC. (2019). *Committing to Change, Protecting People: Toward a More Accountable Oxfam.* Independent Commission on Sexual Misconduct, Accountability and Culture Change & Oxfam. https://www.oxfam.org/en/what-we-do/about/safeguarding/independent-commission

Inclusive Security. (2017). *Creating National Action Plans: A Guide to Implementing Resolution 1325.* Inclusive Security. https://www.inclusivesecurity.org/publication/creating-national-action-plans-a-guide-to-implementing-resolution-1325/

IRC. (2019). *Protection, Participation and Potential: Women and Girls in Yemen's War.* International Rescue Committee. https://www.rescue.org/report/protection-participation-and-potential-women-and-girls-yemens-war

136 VAWG, conflict and WPS

IWDA. (2016). *The Global Goals: Women, Peace and Security* (Policy Brief). International Women's Development Agency. https://iwda.org.au/assets/files/20160119-WPS-and-Goal-16-policy-brief_EK2.pdf

Jacevic, M. (2019, March 25). What makes for an effective WPS national action plan? *The Strategist.* https://www.aspistrategist.org.au/what-makes-for-an-effective-wps-national-action-plan/

Jia, A., Gebhard, V., & Cham, Y. (2019, March 19). UNSCR 1325: Time to Move from Letter to Spirit. *LSE Blogs.* https://blogs.lse.ac.uk/internationaldevelopment/2019/03/19/unscr-1325-time-to-move-from-letter-to-spirit/

Kangas, A., & Stevens, S. (2018). *Women, Peace and Security in Yemen: VAWG Helpdesk Research Report No. 158.* UK Aid. https://assets.publishing.service.gov.uk/media/5c5964eaed915d04352fed43/VAWG_Helpdesk_158_-_WPS_and_VAWG_in_Yemen_FINAL.pdf

Kirby, P., & Shepherd, L. J. (2016). The futures past of the women, peace and security agenda. *International Affairs, 92*(2), 373–392. https://doi.org/10.1111/1468-2346.12549

Kovatch, B. (2016). Sexual exploitation and abuse in UN peacekeeping missions: A case study of MONUC and MONUSCO. *The Journal of the Middle East and Africa, 7*(2), 157–174. https://doi.org/10.1080/21520844.2016.1192978

LSE CWPS, GAPS, & WWI. (2016). *Experts' Meeting: Sexual Violence in Conflict and the UK's Women, Peace and Security Agenda Chairs' Summary.* LSE Centre for Women, Peace and Security, Gender Action for Peace and Security and Women for Women International. http://gaps-uk.org/wp-content/uploads/2017/01/LSE-WFWI-GAPS-Experts-Meeting-SVC-and-WPS-Chairs-Summary-FINAL.pdf

Magone, C. (2014). Collecting data on sexual violence: What do we need to know? The case of MSF in the Democratic Republic of Congo. *Humanitarian Exchange, 60,* 18–20. https://odihpn.org/magazine/collecting-data-on-sexual-violence-what-do-we-need-to-know-the-case-of-msf-in-the-democratic-republic-of-congo/

MPTF & UNDP. (2018). *Ninth Consolidated Annual Progress Report on Activities Implemented under the UN Action against Sexual Violence in Conflict Fund* (Report of the Administrative Agent of the UN Action against Sexual Violence in Conflict Fund for the Period 1 January to 31 December 2017). Multi-Partner Trust Fund Office and United Nations Development Programme. https://www.un.org/sexualviolenceinconflict/wp-content/uploads/report/un-action-progress-report-2017/UN-Action-Progress-Report-2017.pdf

MPTF & UNDP. (2019). *Tenth Consolidated Annual Progress Report on Activities Implemented under the UN Action against Sexual Violence in Conflict Fund* (Report of the Administrative Agent of the UN Action Against Sexual Violence in Conflict Fund for the Period 1 January to 31 December 2018). Multi-Partner Trust Fund Office and United Nations Development Programme. https://www.un.org/sexualviolenceinconflict/wp-content/uploads/2019/06/report/un-action-progress-report-2018/20190531-2018-UN-Action-Annual-Progress-Report.pdf

Mudgway, C. (2017). Sexual exploitation by UN peacekeepers: The 'survival sex' gap in international human rights law. *The International Journal of Human Rights, 21*(9), 1453–1476. https://doi.org/10.1080/13642987.2017.1348720

NATO. (2019). *Resilience and Resolution. A Compendium of Essays on Women, Peace and Security.* NATO Secretary General: Office of the NATO Special Representative for Women, Peace and Security. https://www.nato.int/nato_static_fl2014/assets/pdf/pdf_2019_03/20190307_190308-wps-essays-en.pdf

NGO WG. (2017). *Mapping Women, Peace and Security in the UN Security Council: 2016.* NGO Working Group on WPS. https://reliefweb.int/report/world/mapping-women-peace-and-security-un-security-council-2018

O'Gorman, E. (2013). *Review of UN Action against Sexual Violence in Conflict 2007–2012. Final Report.* http://stoprapenow.org/uploads/advocacyresources/1401281502.pdf

OECD DAC. (2015). *Financing UN Security Council Resolution 1325: Aid in Support of Gender Equality and Women's Rights in Fragile Contexts.* Organisation for Economic Co-Operation and Development - Development Assistance Committee Network on Gender Equality (GenderNet). https://www.oecd.org/dac/gender-development/financingunsecuritycouncilresolution1325aidinsupportofgenderequalityand-womensrightsinfragilecontexts.htm

OSCE & LSE. (2020). *Implementing the Women, Peace and Security Agenda in the OSCE Region.* Organisation for Security and Co-Operation in Europe and London School of Economics, Centre for Women, Peace and Security. https://www.osce.org/secretariat/444577

Peace Women. (2015). *The Global Acceleration Instrument for Women, Peace and Security and Humanitarian Action.* UN Women. http://peacewomen.org/node/96798

Permanent Mission of Germany to the UN. (2020). *Monitoring Progress and Looking Ahead: Interactive Stock-Taking on High Level Commitments Made on Women, Peace and Security Ahead of the 20th Anniversary of 1325.* Document Updated 29/1 2020.

Ritchie, H., Roser, M., Mispy, A., & Ortiz-Ospina, E. (2018). *Measuring Progress towards the Sustainable Development Goals.* Our World in Data: SDG-Tracker.org website. https://sdg-tracker.org/

Ryan, C., & Basini, H. (2017). UNSC Resolution 1325 national action plans in Liberia and Sierra Leone: An analysis of gendered power relations in hybrid peacebuilding. *Journal of Intervention and Statebuilding, 11*(2), 186–206. https://doi.org/10.1080/17502977.2017.1337337

Spangaro, J., Adogu, C., Ranmuthugala, G., Davies, G. P., Steinacker, L., & Zwi, A. (2013). *What Is the Evidence of the Impact of Initiatives to Reduce Risk and Incidence of Sexual Violence in Conflict and Post-Conflict Zones and Other Humanitarian Crises in Lower and Middle Income Countries? A Systematic Review.* University of London; Institute of Education, Social Science Research Unit EPPI-Centre. http://eppi.ioe.ac.uk/cms/Portals/0/PDF%20reviews%20and%20summaries/Conflict%20zones%202013Spangaro%20report.pdf

Stern, J. (2015). *Reducing Sexual Exploitation and Abuse in UN Peacekeeping. Ten Years after the Zeid Report* (Civilians in Conflict: Policy Brief 1). The Stimson Center. https://www.stimson.org/wp-content/files/file-attachments/Policy-Brief-Sexual-Abuse-Feb-2015-WEB_0.pdf

Swaine, A., Spearing, M., Murphy, M., & Contreras-Urbina, M. (2019). Exploring the intersection of violence against women and girls with post-conflict statebuilding and peacebuilding processes: A new analytical framework. *Journal of Peacebuilding & Development, 14*(1), 3–21. https://doi.org/10.1177/1542316619833877

Taylor, S. (2018, October 31). Why women, peace and security? Why now? *International Peace Institute; Global Observatory Blog.* https://theglobalobservatory.org/2018/10/why-women-peace-and-security-why-now/

ToE. (2018). *Annual Report 2017: Team of Experts Rule of Law/Sexual Violence in Conflict.* UN Office of the High Commissioner for Human Rights and the Office of the Special Representative of the UN Secretary General on Sexual Violence in Conflict. https://www.un.org/sexualviolenceinconflict/wp-content/uploads/Team-of-Experts-on-Rule-of-Law-Sexual-Violence-in-Conflict-Annual-Report-2017.pdf

True, J. (2016). Explaining the global diffusion of the women, peace and security agenda. *International Political Science Review, 37*(3), 307–323. https://doi.org/10.1177/0192512116632372

True, J., & Tanyag, M. (2017). Global violence and security from a gendered perspective. In A. Burke, & R. Parker (Eds.). *Global Insecurity: Futures of Global Chaos and Governance* (pp. 43–63). Palgrave Macmillan. https://doi.org/10.1057/978-1-349-95145-1_3

True, J., & Wiener, A. (2019). Everyone wants (a) peace: The dynamics of rhetoric and practice on 'Women, Peace and Security'. *International Affairs, 95*(3), 553–574.https://doi-org.eres.qnl.qa/10.1093/ia/iiz027

UK Gov. (2018). *UK national action plan on women, peace and security 2018 to 2022.* Foreign and Commonwealth Office, Department for International Development and the Ministry of Defence. https://www.gov.uk/government/publications/uk-national-action-plan-on-women-peace-and-security-2018-to-2022

UK Gov. (2020). *HMG Response to the Independent Commission on Aid Impact Recommendations on the UK's Prevention of Sexual Violence in Conflict Initiative, January 2020.* UK Government/UK Aid. https://icai.independent.gov.uk/wp-content/uploads/Independent_Commission_for_Aid_Impact_review_on_PSVI.pdf

UN OIOS. (2018). *Evaluation of the Offices of the Special Representatives of the Secretary General for Children and Armed Conflict, for Sexual Violence in Conflict and on Violence Against Children.* UN Office of Internal Oversight Services Inspection and Evaluation Division.

UN Women. (2015). *Preventing Conflict, Transforming Justice, Securing the Peace. A Global Study on the Implementation of UNSCR 1325.* UN Women Peace and Security Section. https://reliefweb.int/report/world/preventing-conflict-transforming-justice-securing-peace-global-study-implementation

UNDESA. (2019). *The Future Is Now. Science for Achieving Sustainable Development. Global Sustainable Development Report 2019.* Report Written by the Independent Group of Scientists 2019 and Co-Ordinated by the UN Department of Economic and Social Affairs, ISC, IAP, and WFEO. https://sustainabledevelopment.un.org/content/documents/24797GSDR_report_2019.pdf

UNDP. (2020). *UN Action against Sexual Violence. Financial Reporting on Sources and Use of Funds for the Period Ending 31 December 2019.* New York: UNDP.

UNHCR. (2018). *Our Fight against Sexual Misconduct: 2018 in Review.* United Nations High Commissioner for Refugees. https://www.unhcr.org/5c51a5d34.pdf

UNSG. (2019). *Conflict-Related Sexual Violence: 2018 Report of the UN Secretary General.* Office of the Special Representative of the UN Secretary General on Sexual Violence in Conflict. http://undocs.org/en/S/2019/280

Westendorf, J. K., & Searle, L. (2017). Sexual exploitation and abuse in peace operations: Trends, policy responses and future directions. *International Affairs, 93*(2), 365–387. https://doi-org.eres.qnl.qa/10.1093/ia/iix001

Whalan, J. (2017). *Dealing with Disgrace: Addressing Sexual Exploitation and Abuse in UN Peacekeeping* (Providing for Peacekeeping 15). The International Peace Institute. https://www.ipinst.org/wp-content/uploads/2017/08/IPI-Rpt-Dealing-with-Disgrace2.pdf

What Works. (2017). *No Safe Place: A Lifetime of Violence for Conflict-Affected Women and Girls in South Sudan. Main Results Report.* What Works to Prevent VAWG Programme. https://www.rescue-uk.org/sites/default/files/document/1580/southsudanlgsummaryreportonline.pdf

WILPF. (2018). *Towards a Feminist Security Council. A Guidance Note for Security Council Members.* Women's International League for Peace and Freedom (Peace Women). https://www.peacewomen.org/sites/default/files/WILPF_Feminist%20Security%20Council%20Guide_Print.pdf

WILPF. (2019a). *Open Letter to the Friends of 1325: Recommendations for the September 2019 UN General Assembly High Level Political Forum (HLPF) Sustainable Development Summit.* Women's International League for Peace and Freedom (Peace Women). https://www.peacewomen.org/node/103661

WILPF. (2019b). *Five Key Issues*. Women's International League for Peace and Freedom (Peace Women).

World Bank. (2018). *Pathways for Peace. Inclusive Approaches to Preventing Violent Conflict*. The World Bank Group. https://openknowledge.worldbank.org/handle/10986/28337

WPHF. (2019). *Annual Report. January - December 2018*. Women's Peace and Humanitarian Fund. https://reliefweb.int/report/world/women-s-peace-and-humanitarian-fund-annual-report-january-december-2018

7

THE RULE OF LAW, WOMEN'S RIGHTS, AND VAWG PREVENTION AND RESPONSE

Introduction

This chapter addresses a number of areas relating to VAWG and the rule of law. To begin, we summarise the legal context of VAWG, including international mechanisms, principles, and national laws. We consider how individual countries address such matters, and whether provisions have resulted in reduction of VAWG and wider gender inequality. Next, we consider the work done over the past three decades by a wide range of advocates and activists to advance, introduce, and then consolidate international mechanisms in order to prevent and respond to VAWG at all levels. As illustrative examples, we first shine a spotlight on femicide, secondly consider the 2015 Report on the UK by the UN Special Rapporteur on VAWG, and thirdly provide an extended Case Study of Rwanda. For Rwanda, we focus on the situation as regards legal provisions and VAWG prevalence at the national level. In the conclusion, we set out a number of key questions and comments on the current status of VAWG prevention and response as supported – or not – by the rule of law.

International mechanisms addressing VAWG

We look here at the extent to which such processes and the growing corpus of international law have led to improvements in VAWG prevention. Much has been achieved in the past few decades to bring VAWG out from the shadows of 'domestic' violence and to place it in the public sphere, regarding accountability of individual perpetrators and of states (Aziz & Moussa, 2014).

DOI: 10.4324/9780429280603-7

CEDAW

The 1979 Convention on the Elimination of All Forms of Discrimination Against Women (CEDAW) was the first legally binding international instrument for the protection of women's rights.

An independent global CEDAW Committee monitors implementation of the Convention. States Parties (country signatories) are asked to submit reports at least once every four years, providing updates on compliance with Convention obligations. Non-government actors are also encouraged to submit 'Shadow Reports', independent documents addressing discrimination and violations of Convention commitments.

CEDAW did not initially address violence against women, but it is an evolving Convention; CEDAW Committees have supported INGOs and national CSOs working on gender equality and VAWG prevention, making the Convention a mechanism for linking the local to the global to back changes to national laws on women's rights.

CEDAW has promoted more informed attention by states and civil society to national legal standards and (to a lesser extent) social norms about VAWG and gender equality, and the linkages between those and international laws, norms, and principles.

CEDAW General Recommendations (GRs) have sharpened focus on GBV (the definition used by CEDAW). It is of note, however, that GRs are not legally binding.[1]

While the global CEDAW Committee has not explicitly considered intersectionality, it has, in the past few years, begun to address how a woman's (self) identification with regard to race or ethnicity, her minority status, age, sexuality, status as a refugee or IDP, being (or having been) enslaved or otherwise deprived of liberty, might resonate in terms of discrimination and VAWG (Allen Dale, 2018; Campbell, 2016).

How effective is CEDAW?[2]

CEDAW places States Parties under 'positive obligation', i.e. to take action to enable women to enjoy their full human rights under international law. One such obligation could be ensuring not only enrolment of girls in school, but their retention in education.

187 States Parties are CEDAW members; more than 50 have lodged certain reservations and/or objections. Therefore, while a State Party is legally obliged to take all appropriate measures to eliminate discrimination against women, there is room for manoeuvre. Ratifying countries have interpreted CEDAW obligations in a wide variety of ways, ranging from reluctant engagement to active incorporation.

There are indications that CEDAW can positively affect national legal protections against VAWG. As the time since a country ratified CEDAW increases, there is more likelihood (ca. 23%) that it will adopt full legal protections; conversely, countries that have placed a 'full reservation' on CEDAW Article 2[3] have weaker national VAWG and marital rape laws (Richards & Haglund, 2015). The reasons are not clear: might CEDAW promote actions that might not otherwise be taken? And are Shadow Reports effective for holding governments to account?

142 The rule of law

Vienna 1993 and Beijing 1995

1993 and 1995 were watersheds for women's rights and the acknowledgement that violence against women is not solely a domestic act. After 1995, IPV could no longer easily be dismissed as a private issue, beyond recourse to justice. The Global Campaign for Women's Human Rights was one grouping that provided a rallying point for civil society leading up to the Vienna World Conference on Human Rights (Fraser & Wood, 2018; Htun & Weldon, 2012; Klugman et al., 2014; World Bank, 2017). After Vienna, the UN established the offices of the Special Rapporteur on Violence against Women and the UN High Commissioner for Human Rights.

The 1995 Beijing Declaration and the Platform for Action (PoA) were the chief outcomes of the 4th World Conference on Women. The PoA is 'an agenda for women's empowerment'; its contents continue to be fundamental pre-requisites for equality. The PoA Strategic Objective D (Violence Against Women) and Actions D1–D3 address key issues. The 'girl child' is singled out for specific attention in the PoA. The PoA sets out standards for actions to be implemented by national governments, the UN system and civil society, and provides the first global commitment to gender mainstreaming. And as was reiterated at Beijing by the then US First Lady Hillary Clinton: '*Human rights are women's rights and women's rights are human rights*'.

In 2020, the year of Beijing +25, there was in-depth evaluation of what has been achieved in terms of women's and girls' equality and what are the opportunities for them to live lives free from violence – and how to prevent 'one size fits all (women and girls)' approaches. One example is that adolescent girls' voice, agency and experiences are still under-represented in international commitments (including the SDGs). At the national level, they are often legally defined as minors without agency (yet can, in many countries, be married at a young age). Unmarried female adolescents in particular have little space for engagement.

The Rome Statute and the International Criminal Court

The 1998 Rome Statute that established the International Criminal Court (effective 2002) sets out violence against women and children as an offence under war crimes, for which ratifying States Parties (123 as of 2020) have obligations (see Clark, 2019, for a critique of the ICC; OSF, 2018, provides a more positive review).

As of 2020, there had been no successfully upheld conviction at the ICC for sexual violence in conflict. The current ICC Prosecutor has emphasised that on her watch sexual violence as a weapon of war will be actively pursued (ICC, 2014). The Dennis Mukwege Foundation claims, as do other actors in the field of VAWG prevention in conflict, that while the structures exist, VAWG as a war crime has been consistently downplayed at the ICC (Dr Mukwege shared the 2018 Nobel Peace Prize with the Yazidi advocate and VAWG survivor Nadia Murad).

Regional commitments

Numerous regional commitments underscore the importance of achieving gender equality (though not always prioritising VAWG issues). These include the 2003 African Union Maputo Protocol on the Rights of Women in Africa; the 1994 Inter-American Convention of Belem Do Para on the Prevention, Punishment, and Eradication of Violence against Women; the 2011 European Convention on Preventing Violence against Women and Domestic Violence; and the Pacific Islands' Forum Gender Equality Declaration of 2012.

As is the case for all international statutes, conventions, and commitments, implementation and accountable tracking of actual impacts remain challenging, patchy, and all too often limited by lack of dedicated financial and human resources.

The UN Team of Experts

The UN Action Team of Experts (the ToE) on the Rule of Law and Sexual Violence in Conflict (based on the Women, Peace, and Security Agenda) is a global initiative to tackle conflict-related sexual violence (CRSV) through supporting implementation of legislation. The ToE came about through UNSCR 1888 (2009), and its remit is to assist national authorities to ensure criminal accountability for perpetrators of CRSV (see Chapter 6 for a detailed discussion of WPS, the ToE, and other CRSV initiatives).

The SDGs[4]

All 193 UN members signed up to the 2030 Agenda for Sustainable Development and the 17 SDGs, which came into force in September 2015 after much fierce debate, not least on gender equality and VAWG. The express ambition of the SDGs is *to leave no-one behind*.

Gender equality is a goal in its own right (SDG 5), and it is mainstreamed across all 17 SDGs, reflected in 45 targets (of the total 169) and 54 gender-specific indicators. SDG 5 represents a hard-won victory for activists and advocates. Alongside the gender-focused goal, SDG 16 addresses forms of violence and, as such, the SDGs represent a marked advancement on the Millennium Development Goals, which did not include specific VAWG focus. The SDG foregrounding of gender and violence provides opportunities for earmarked human and financial investments in actions to prevent VAWG. There is hope that achievement of relevant targets and indicators may provide impetus for truly gender equal progress on all 17 SDGs.[5]

How well are the SDGs doing?

2020 marked one-third of the way through implementation of the SDGs, and concerns were raised on a wide range of issues. Data demands are onerous for many countries, and this is further hampered by the vagueness of indicators: Equal

Measures 2030 (2018) states that only 15 of the 53 gender indicators are well defined enough to measure. Thus, many data gaps remain. Moreover, few gender indicators include men; one is 16.2.3 (proportion of young women and men aged 18–29 years who experienced sexual violence by age 18). Because there are 53 gender indicators, governments might, perhaps, cherry pick those that are easier to measure and, potentially, to achieve. Many low- and middle-income countries are unlikely to achieve many of the SDG targets, and the World Economic Forum has suggested that true economic parity between men and women might not be achieved until 2277 (see O'Donnell & Kenny, 2020). This raises the question, will the 'unfinished business' left by the MDGs still remain after the SDGs deadlines have passed? For example, projections in 2015 on the opportunities for achievement of SDG 5, indicator 5.3.1 (child marriage) are bleak: it is estimated that progress globally needs to be eight times faster to meet the deadline of 2030 (Nicolai, Hoy, Berliner, & Aedy, 2015; also, UN Women, 2018).

The SDGs are viewed by many practitioners as having become a lucrative business, with negative implications for progress and quality of work on VAWG. New players, often with minimal expertise, have entered the 'market', often helping to make small, local women's organisations and VAWG prevention CSOs even more invisible. The danger of work on VAWG prevention and response becoming less focused on transformative action, and taking a less feminist approach, is seen as real – how can VAWG be genuinely addressed without significant transformation? (see, e.g., COFEM, 2017, 2019; Fulu, 2017).

Legal instruments addressing VAWG

The due diligence principle[6]

This holds states accountable for human rights abuses, including violence against women, committed by state and non-state actors. The Principle has set a benchmark for activists seeking to support and monitor implementation of national level legislation and to hold governments and other state agents accountable. CEDAW Article 2 (3) applies an obligation of due diligence.

The Principle states that a government has a duty to protect women from violence and to enforce relevant laws. There is a requirement to establish a legal framework that enables criminal prosecutions for VAWG. A government failing to take such measures can be deemed complicit in human rights abuses. States ideally have obligations for the 'five Ps': **protection** of survivors; **prosecution of** perpetrators; appropriate **punishment**; **provision** of adequate reparations to survivors; effective **prevention** campaigns (World Bank, 2015; also, Aziz & Moussa, 2014).

Laws that address VAWG: how widespread and genuinely gender equal are these at national level?

'Domestic violence' is the term most commonly used in discussions of legislative action against VAWG. But definitions of what constitutes 'domestic violence'

The rule of law **145**

differ markedly between countries and legal systems. There is a confusing array of terms and definitions, and of the scope of such legislation, with certain types of violence, such as economic violence, seldom being addressed (Iqbal, 2015). There is modest yet increasing evidence that legislation addressing violence, however defined and however incomplete, can offer a degree of protection and some redress (Klugman, 2017; Richards & Haglund, 2015 provide additional analysis).

Set against the positive aspects of legislation and expanding national attention to combatting all forms of VAWG, are the legal and policy frameworks that continue to discriminate *against* equality of women and girls in terms of their rights, and by extension underpin the continuation of VAWG. There is frequent disconnection between legal instruments and actual achievement of greater gender equality and freedom from all forms of VAWG. This is not a fringe issue in a few outlier states; as noted in a 2017 assessment of 173 countries, the problem is so widespread that it is, in fact, a global norm:

- 155 countries (90% of those whose legal provisions were surveyed) have legal provisions that discriminate against women;
- Laws or customary practices in 102 countries deny [all or some] women the same rights, including inheritance, to land as men;
- 100 countries place legal restrictions on the types of jobs women can have; and
- 19 countries legally oblige a wife to obey her husband.

(IDLO, 2017)

> Over the past 25 years, progress has been made in gender equality through the creation of new legislation and the reform of existing laws. Still, troublesome gaps remain. This was the conclusion of a study of data collected in 2018 and covering four areas of law in 53 countries... In the area of violence against women, legal gaps were found in over one quarter of the countries... Of those countries, 68% lacked rape laws based on the principle of consent.
>
> *(UN, 2019, p. 33)*

Research into child marriage (specified in that study as under 18) found that 117 countries allow such marriage and many countries setting the minimum age at 18 allow exemptions. There are often different marriageable ages for girls and boys. In Sudan, a girl may be married at ten, while for a boy the age is 15 or 'at puberty'; in the Philippines, a Muslim girl may be married 'at puberty'. There is no minimum age below which a girl cannot be married in Saudi Arabia, Somalia, or South Sudan (Pew Research Center, 2016).

Shining a spotlight on femicide

Femicide describes the gender-related killing of women and girls. Such killings are rooted in the unequal power structures that shape existence for women and girls, their subordination, rigidly imposed gender roles, and requirements to behave 'correctly'. Femicide is a broad category that encompasses murder by an intimate partner, dowry deaths, so-called 'honour' killings, targeted murder of women and girls in conflict settings. The former UN Special Rapporteur on VAWG, Rashida Manjoo, has stated that femicide is 'the most violent manifestation of discrimination against women' (AHR, 2018; UNGA, 2012, p. 1; UNODC, 2018; WHO, 2012). But there are differing definitions of what constitutes femicide and, indeed, this may be the challenge that needs to be overcome if a precise legal and judicial focus is to emerge and robust evidence is to be collected. Disaggregated data that separate out instances of femicide from other deaths of women and girls are seldom available, even in countries with strong legal data management (Lappi-Seppälä & Lehti, 2016; Small Arms Survey, 2016).

The data that are available tell us that Latin America and the Caribbean have the highest global rates of femicide (Small Arms Survey, 2016). All countries in the region have ratified the 1994 Belem do Para Convention, but during 2016 an estimated seven women per day were killed in Mexico alone because of their gender (UN Women, 2017). According to the Economic Commission for Latin America and the Caribbean, an average of 12 women are murdered each day across the region. Even these figures, as high as they are, exclude Brazil due to data limitations, despite it having one of the worst VAWG records globally. In South Africa, 57% of all women who were killed in 2013 were murdered by their intimate partner (Abrahams, Mathews, Martin, Lombard, & Jewkes, 2013). In Jordan there are between 15 and 20 so-called 'honour' killings each year, and there were 24,771 (known) dowry deaths in India between 2012 and 2015 (Global Americans, 2020). There are certainly also many incidences of femicide that are invisible in the data. For example, identifying acts of femicide in conflict (e.g. in Syria or South Sudan) may be an insurmountable task. Also, the risks associated with being a woman intersect with additional vulnerabilities, which is also often invisible in the research. For example, data on the instances and rates of femicide where a woman is known to be, or labelled, as lesbian (or somehow 'other' in terms of her sexuality) are difficult to find. In South Africa this type of femicide can be linked to other forms of violence described as a 'corrective attack', which can include gang rape, and often results in death.

In the past decade, much has been done to address femicide and to put in place legal mechanisms at global, regional, and national levels. In 2014, UN Women and the Central America Regional Office of the UN High Commissioner for Human Rights published the detailed and comprehensive *Latin American Model Protocol for the investigation of gender-related killing* (OHCHR, 2014). Also, in 2014, the UN General Assembly adopted Resolution 68/1919 on *Taking action against gender-related killing of women and girls*.

The current UN VAWG Special Rapporteur called in 2016 for countries to collect data and determine gaps in legislation and failures in implementation of existing laws, as well as preventive measures (UNGA, 2016). Argentina is one country to have established a Femicide Observatory, and 16 Latin American countries now have femicide laws, with Costa Rica leading the way in 2007.

Some key gaps between VAWG policy, practice, and social norms

One critique of the global gender equality and VAWG system and international and national laws is that these are usually based on Western narratives, too frequently defined solely or mainly by male jurists and policymakers and applying gender (male) bias. A related argument is that legislators do not fully understand the deep roots and meanings of social norms – indeed, that they themselves are shaped by such unequal attitudes and behaviours. The 'sanctity' of customary law can become a useful instrument to blunt specific actions on VAWG (IDLO, 2017).

Such biases are brought into sharp focus when sexual rights are considered (Lalor, Mills, Sánchez-García, & Haste, 2016). Within access to justice work there is a necessary balancing act that must be performed between challenging customary law (which may not always be as venerable or as immutable as appears at first sight) and what might be deemed the imposition of a 'modern' and/or 'Western' legal system (Deng, 2013; Heise & Kotsadam, 2015; IDLO, 2013; UN DESA, 2010).

Box 7.1 Legislation on VAWG: key findings from a systematic review of 80 countries and territories

- Most laws do not incorporate key components as recommended by the UN and PAHO after the 2005 WHO multi-country study on women's health and 'domestic violence'. Such components include: identification of women [and girls] as primary legislative beneficiaries; clear definition of what constitutes VAWG; clear definition of different types of VAWG; multi-sectoral approaches.
- Few countries specifically identify women [and very seldom girls] as the primary beneficiaries of their VAWG/GBV legislation, including those that label their legislation 'domestic violence' law (n = 51). Only two countries explicitly mention women as complainants/survivors.
- 49% of countries/territories include definitions of the main forms of VAW in their legislations (economic, physical, psychological, and sexual).
- 97% of national laws highlight the role of the judicial system, followed by that of social services (60%) and the police (44%). Only 35% mention the health sector. In Africa, most VAW/G legislation refers only to the police and judicial systems. In Asia, VAW/G legislation mainly emphasises the role of the police and the judicial system, with the occasional reference to social services, health services, and the education system.

(Largely derived from Fraser & Wood, 2018, p. 7; also informed by Garcia-Moreno et al., 2005)

148 The rule of law

Legal practitioners and others dealing with the aftermath of VAWG may (and do) exhibit bias by interpreting and even bending the law to be coherent with their own social norms and gender perceptions. Where IPV is considered 'normal' if a wife 'fails' to provide certain domestic and/or sexual services, a police officer or legal representative may demonstrate such bias.[7]

In many contexts (including 'restorative justice' approaches, where survivors of VAWG may be supported to seek community-based redress), there may be countless unreported instances of women and girls keeping their heads down and not reporting violence for fear of wider societal consequences. Such survivors may come to the conclusion that it is 'better' to remain within one's community and not be ostracised, rather than make a complaint, receive redress (possibly), and then have to return to the self-same situation, facing further potential violence and stigma (for a discussion of aspects of social norms, see Alexander-Scott, Bell, & Holden, 2016; Asubiario-Dada & Gaynor, 2017; Jewkes, Stern, & Ramsoomar, 2019; Stern, Heise, & McLean, 2018a, 2018b; Stubbs, 2014; UN Women, IDLO, World Bank, Task Force on Justice, 2019).

The depth and extent of patriarchy, how that informs customary systems and social norms, and how all of these might be highly resistant to change cannot be underestimated. It is also important to consider, however counter-intuitive and uncomfortable this might feel, situations where patriarchy might enable women and girls to live better lives than otherwise possible (Hughes, Marrs, & Sweetman, 2016). Nobody can argue that one size fits all in terms of legal provisions and access to justice for VAWG survivors.

VAWG and justice in the UK

To provide perspective on the challenges and complexities of obtaining justice for survivors of VAWG, the all too frequent gap between policy, legislation, and actual implementation, as well as an indication of how deep rooted and intransigent inequitable social norms and gender biases can be, let us consider the UK. In early 2014, the UN VAWG Special Rapporteur visited the UK, consulting with civil society actors, activists, and survivors. She met many UK Government justice and other representatives, as well as officers of the four legal jurisdictions within the UK[8] (see also EHRC, 2019). Key points made in the Special Rapporteur's report include the following:

- 87% of those who had experienced the most 'serious sexual offences' in England and Wales in 2011–2012 did not tell the police;
- deep concerns were raised by those working with Black, Asian, and Minority Ethnic girls and women about the specific challenges they faced in reporting sexual violence and receiving support;
- the inadequacy of Home Office assessments to identify female asylum seekers' past experience of violence was highlighted; and
- The steps taken by local authorities and the government in moving from gender-specific to gender-neutral approaches were perceived by the Special

Rapporteur as retrograde, as they can disregard the need for special services and expertise to address the reality that women and girls suffer most violence

(see e.g., UN OHCHR, 2019)

And the following statement summarises how, regardless of whether in a developing context or not, barriers to justice for women and girls who are survivors of VAWG not only exist, but are widespread:

> *Many individuals stated... that the justice system is not effectively equipped, or responsive, to address the specific needs of women and girl survivors of violence. The justice system* [is not considered] *a viable option to obtain remedies for several reasons, ranging from the inadequate police responses,... the lack of co-ordination among the various State agencies [contributes] to the low levels of prosecution and the negligible conviction rates.*
>
> *(UNGA, 2015, p. 23)*

The number of rape cases referred to the Crown Prosecution Service (the CPS, covering England and Wales) by the police for charging decisions fell by 32% in the year to September 2019, while prosecutions by the CPS fell by 26% and convictions by 21% (CPS, 2020). The 2018 (UK) Femicide Census found that 91 of the 149 women murdered in the UK in 2018 (61%) were killed by their current or former intimate partner (Long & Harvey, 2020).

Rwanda case study[9]

Here, we take a closer look at the work addressing gender inequality and VAWG undertaken in Rwanda since the 1994 genocide. In the late 1980s and early 1990s, women in the country were perceived as either *'virtuous wives, timid virgins or loose women'* (Jefremovas, 1991). Married women required their husbands' consent to buy land, and husbands could withdraw money from their wives' bank accounts without permission. While unmarried women legally had equal rights, they were *de facto* the wards of their fathers and brothers. But in the aftermath of the 1994 genocide, many women and girls had to take on new roles in both domestic and public spheres and assume economic responsibility for their households. This continues: in 2004 UNICEF calculated that there were 42,000 child-headed households in Rwanda, and the 2014–2015 Demographic and Health Survey (the DHS) indicated that 30% of households in the country are female headed.

It has been estimated that perhaps 200,000 women and girls experienced sexual violence during the genocide, and an unknown number became HIV positive (Mukamana & Brysiewitz, 2008, discuss VAWG during the genocide; for gender aspects of the HIV epidemic, see Bloom, Cannon, & Negroustoueva, 2014; Rwanda Biomedical Centre, 2014).

150 The rule of law

Government of Rwanda initiatives addressing gender equality and VAWG[10]

Rwanda has legislated for gender equality and freedom from VAWG to such an extent that it is unparalleled in Africa and, indeed, almost everywhere else. Such actions began as the country rebuilt itself after manmade catastrophe. The 2015 *Gender Development Index* ranked Rwanda second globally, with the lowest level of gender inequality in sub-Saharan Africa (UNDP, 2015). The *Mo Ibrahim Index* 2016 ranks Rwanda first in Africa for absence of gender discrimination, and the 2016 *Global Gender Gap Report* also recognised Rwanda as the leading country for women's labour force participation, wage equality, primary and secondary school enrolment of girls, and women's representation in parliament (WEF, 2016). That said, while Rwanda was placed first in Africa and fourth globally for wage equality in the 2017 *Global Gender Gap Report*, it is sixth with respect to estimated earned income and seventh for economic participation and opportunity (WEF, 2017). Moreover, male/female wage differentials remain significant, and unpaid care work and agricultural tasks are undertaken primarily by women and girls.

Rwanda is a signatory to CEDAW, the UN Declaration on the Rights of the Child and regional commitments, such as the African Charter on Human and People's Rights (1986), the Maputo Protocol (2003), the International Conference on the Great Lakes Region (ICGRL) Protocol on the Prevention of Sexual Violence against Women and Children (2006), and the Kampala Declaration on SGBV (2011). To date, Rwanda has implemented two UNSCR 1325 NAPs (see MIGEPROF, 2018a). Under the 2010 Kigali Declaration, the Rwanda National Police, military, and correctional services began working together to end VAWG.

Female representation

After the 2018 election, Rwanda leads the world in terms of female representation in government: 61.3% of MPs are female, as are 38% of Senators and 50% of Ministers. However, female representation is less advanced at lower levels; at the district level women tend to occupy 'softer' positions. For example, women represent 20% of district Vice-Mayors in charge of economic affairs, but 76.7% of those in charge of social affairs (Barnes & Burchard, 2012; Burnet, 2008, 2011; Coffé, 2012; Hansén, 2017).

Rwanda has a **national gender machinery**, which was fully instituted in 2003: the Ministry of Gender and Family Promotion (MIGEPROF), the Gender Monitoring Office (the GMO), the National Women's Council (the NWC – with branches down to village level) and the Rwanda Women's Parliamentary Forum (FFRP). These institutions seek to work together to coordinate policy development and implementation, VAWG prevention and redress, applying, monitoring and evaluating gender mainstreaming, and overall protection of women's and children's rights.

Gender equality in the law and Constitution of Rwanda[11]

- The **Constitution** was updated in 2003, in the build-up to which women's CSOs advocated successfully for attention to gender equality. The current Constitution (2016) enshrines equal rights by guaranteeing women at least 30% of posts in decision-making bodies at all levels. It also contains provisions to prohibit all forms of discrimination against women.
- **Gender budgeting** was introduced in 2003, with the explicit aim of mainstreaming gender at all levels of government. The 2013 Law on State Finances and Property institutionalised gender budgeting. However, there are ongoing challenges to overcome if truly effective national implementation is to be achieved. These include lack of human resources, (over) reliance on aggregate data and insufficient gender analysis, and lack of engagement with CSOs.
- The **Labour Law 13/2009** enacted the principle of equal pay for equal work. Gender discrimination and GBV in the workplace are illegal, and there are legal provisions to ensure that support is provided for pregnant women and mothers. However, there are still many areas that have not been addressed or, in some cases, have since been rolled back. In 2009, the majority female Parliament approved reductions in paid maternity leave (down from 12 weeks to six weeks) for women in the formal private sector. No explanation for the change appears to have been provided. CSOs advocated in vain against such changes. Women in the informal sector (the majority) have no such provisions and few labour protections. While the Labour Law was updated in 2018 (66/2018), it does not appear that gender issues were revisited. Women's unpaid labour is unacknowledged.
- The **Land Law 43/2013** addresses equal rights for legally married (or widowed) spouses regarding land access, ownership, and use. Girls and boys have equal rights of inheritance, but the Law prohibits splitting land into parcels of less than one hectare, which affects a large majority of Rwandan households. In such situations, the family council decides under whose name the land will be registered.[12] Significant issues remain, most notably the rights of women in informal and polygamous union, and their children,[13] and women's rights to land may often be more symbolic than actual.

Laws addressing VAWG prevention and response

- **Law No. 59/2008** on Prevention and Punishment of Gender-based Violence enacts a minimum penalty of six months' imprisonment, while sexual abuse or rape may result in a life sentence. The Law prescribes heavy punishment for child defilement, marital rape, sexual violence, and spousal harassment, and provides for the prevention of GBV, and protection and relief of survivors.
- Concerns have been raised about the provisions of **Article 39** (administration of property confiscated from a perpetrator). There have been calls for

152   The rule of law

it to be reviewed, specifically to protect women living in informal and polygamous unions (Mwendwa Mechta, Buscagli, Bikesha, & Routte, 2016).

- The Law is supported by the provisions of the 2011 National Policy against GBV; its over-arching objective is to eliminate gender-based violence 'through the development of a preventive, protective, supportive and transformative environment' (GMO, 2019, p. 10).

- Legal provisions have been expanded: **Law 68/2018**, for example, defines four types of GBV – bodily, economic, sexual, and psychological. The same law also removed several barriers to legal and safe abortion. The Rwandan Youth Action Movement led partially successful advocacy to bring about this legislative change.

- A 2005 study estimated that 50% of obstetric complications were due to spontaneous or induced abortions. The **2012 Penal Code** revision had allowed abortion to save life, or to protect physical or mental health where the pregnancy is the result of rape, incest, or forced marriage (Republic of Rwanda, 2012). An interpretation could be that only women and girls who experience rape can hope to exercise their reproductive right to safe abortion. The onus is upon the woman or girl to prove rape.

- Obtaining a legal abortion may be especially challenging for the poor, the rural, and the less well educated (Basinga et al., 2012; Umuhoza, Oosters, van Reeuwijk, & Vanwesenbeeck, 2013). But terminations must be performed by a doctor, and as of 2016 Rwanda had only one doctor per 10,055 people (according to Rwanda Medical & Dental Council figures). It has also been suggested that health workers' attitudes may limit access (Påfs et al., 2020).

- **Law 27/2016** (which refers to Matrimonial Regimes, Donations, and Successions) strengthens widows' and ('legitimate') children's rights to inheritance. Nonetheless, provisions remain that limit women's equal rights. The Law permits bride price. It offers little protection of inheritance and property rights in the case of separation or death of the partner for women in informal unions. A childless widow in informal union may be especially vulnerable to asset loss. Research suggests that some community GBV Committees may encourage women in informal unions who experience IPV to enter into civil marriage with the perpetrator in order to secure greater societal protections (Stern & Mirembe, 2017). Despite its ubiquity, an informal union can brand a woman as socially unacceptable while men escape such condemnation.

Rates of VAWG in Rwanda[14]

Despite legal provisions and actions, VAWG continues to be a significant problem in Rwanda, with high rates compared to many African countries. The 2014–2015 DHS provides the most recent overview of the extent of the issue: 22% of women and 5% of men aged 15–49 have ever experienced sexual violence; 20.7% of women had experienced IPV from a current or former intimate partner during the 12 months that preceded the DHS, and 34% have ever experienced such violence. The DHS also discusses other apparently widespread forms of violence, such as economic violence where women do not have control over their earnings, where allocation of assets when separating, divorced or widowed may be unequal, and where women's participation in decision-making is limited (Mannell & Jackson, 2014; NISR, MOH, & ICF International, 2015).

Societal barriers to addressing VAWG and achieving gender equality

Evidently, legal provisions alone are not sufficient to end VAWG; this is partly because societal barriers that resulted in the laws being made remain prevalent. One graphic example of such challenges is that adolescent girls and young women, who have benefitted from 25 years of attention to gender equality and VAWG prevention, suffer from, but also sometimes hold, harmful attitudes and beliefs around behaviours. For example, the 2014–2015 DHS (NISR, MOH, & ICF International, 2014) states that 33% of girls aged 15–19 have experienced physical or sexual violence, and 45% in the same age group believe 'wife beating' is justified under certain circumstances.

These lingering beliefs, sometimes called 'sticky social norms', and the continued strength of patriarchy mean that VAWG remains acceptable to many. As such, legal measures are often ignored, and community members may shun women who report violence by their husband (Berry, 2015; Isimbi, Manzi Simpunga, & Domingo, 2018). Perhaps the government has trusted too much to laws and programmes effecting social norm change on VAWG and gender equality, rather than seeking to address deeply rooted patriarchy and power hierarchies? There is a clear disjuncture between law, policy, and the constitution, and the lived experience of women in Rwanda, and this demonstrates the importance of embedding a VAWG Mainstreaming Framework in development practice, as well as potentially in the implementation of laws and policy. For example, if the rolling back of maternity entitlements were viewed through a VAWG lens, a different decision may have been reached because lack of such leaves some women particularly at risk of specific forms of violence or abuse.

The 'certain circumstances' that large numbers of women appear still to believe make wife beating acceptable are wide ranging; they include burning food, leaving the home without informing one's husband, and refusing to have sex (see Mannell, Jackson, & Umutoni, 2015; NISR, MOH, & ICF International, 2015). Significant numbers of women may choose silence and compliance in order to live their lives relatively free of violence, even as a form of agency – preferring to be a 'good wife', with all the social acceptance that position brings. Such choices raise many problematic questions about the degree of true autonomy and choice inherent in a decision to remain. A woman may employ a type of self-preservation (and preservation also of her children), by remaining in a violent relationship, perhaps balanced against what might be a very real fear of the unknown.

There has been little research on male views. One study indicates that many men believe the new laws on land rights and matrimony, by favouring women, have weakened their position and their roles in the private and public spheres. The social construction of masculinity, which is linked inextricably in many Rwandans' minds to male dominance in the domestic sphere and control in the public arena, no longer seems quite so stable (Kagaba, 2015). Research from 2010 suggests that over 90% of men and women at the time felt the 2008 GBV Law to be too harsh. Fears were expressed that women would lose respect for their husbands, fathers, and brothers, to the point where they would leave the house without permission and use 'provoking language' (Aggee, 2013; RWAMREC, 2010, p. 44). Women's behaviour was seen as the catalyst for male violence, and these views resonate with studies examining the impacts of the *Indashyikirwa* programme, which sought to reduce experience of IPV among women and perpetration among men in Rwanda (Dunkle, Stern, Heise, & Chatterji, 2019; Stern, Heise, & McLean, 2018a, 2018b, 2018c).

Discussion of such backlash is limited in the Rwandan literature. There are indications that some male adolescents and young men resent what they consider to be disproportionate 'favouring' of girls (Stavropoulou & Gupta-Archer, 2017). Gender relations, gender negotiation, and social norms apply to men too. Men wishing to marry must pay bride price and are expected in rural areas to build a house for their bride. This is considered a major reason why many enter into informal unions. One study suggests that being unable to fulfil the traditional criteria that facilitate legal marriage implies for men 'a failed transition to manhood' (Debusscher & Ansoms, 2013, p. 1121).

Concluding remarks

The balancing of VAWG legislative processes and implementation with proper, effective attention to social norm change is extraordinarily challenging, as this chapter demonstrates. To conclude, we offer the following questions and comments that have emerged out of the observations in this chapter, all of which could be better addressed were VAWG to be effectively mainstreamed into development research, programming, implementation, and various levels of decision-making:

1. Can legislation against VAWG ever be effectively implemented when the provisions are seen as overturning or diluting what may be cherished traditions and customary laws and practices – some of which will perpetuate VAWG and toleration of such violence?
2. To what extent should there be consideration of incorporating customary practices into VAWG legislation (e.g. allowing a parallel system, often with widely different strictures and sanctions, to survive), and how might this work in practice?
3. How transformational should VAWG legislation be? Is there ever an argument to retain or somehow incorporate social norms and practices that are inimical to genuine sanctions against VAWG?

4. How, and to what extent, should VAWG legislation seek to include individuals identifying as lesbian, gay, bisexual, transsexual, queer, or intersex (LGBTQI)?
5. What needs to be done to ensure people are educated about their rights, responsibilities, and the sanctions relevant to VAWG prevention, mitigation, and redress?
6. In situations where many people (including women and girls), and perhaps even the majority of the population, tolerate, accept, even support, VAWG, what are the most effective and inclusive approaches to working towards social norm and institutional change, so that there is both space for reporting VAWG and a non-prejudicial response from police, health workers, those involved in the judicial process?
7. How can interventions guard against backlash, either in terms of increased VAWG or elements of society seeking to nullify or dilute VAWG legislation and other provisions, such as a responsive police force and health system? How can any such backlash, which has dangerous consequences for women and girls and for VAWG prevention and redress advocates, be prevented or mitigated against?
8. Why do so few laws globally acknowledge the intersectionality of women and girls' lived experiences and the range of vulnerabilities they experience?
9. Why is consideration of intersectionality necessary when seeking to prevent VAWG and promote gender equality?

Though it is not the intention of this chapter to answer all these questions definitively, there are several points that highlight the need for considering these questions through a VAWG Mainstreaming Framework and doing so through an intersectional lens. First it is crucial to acknowledge that a blanket definition of what it is to be a 'woman' ignores intersecting factors, including class, location, age, education, and life cycle experiences. That is to say, any one female will exist at the intersection of several (and differing) identities and oppressions. To take one example, elite women may well have far greater access to and control over rights than rural peasant farmers. Studies from many countries describe how non-elite women express hopelessness, fears of poverty, drudgery, and gaps between expectations and reality regarding their hopes and aspirations for themselves and their children. Access to land, labour tasks or involvement in decision-making processes are structured along various axes, including gender, class, age, marital status, education, ethnicity, household composition, and social status. Little attention is given to survivors of violence or at-risk groups. Older women, often widowed, are a seldom considered grouping, as are LGBTQI women and girls, migrant women and women, and girls with disabilities. All may potentially be at risk from IPV, coercive control, and non-partner violence.

All of the above means that there exists a disjuncture between VAWG legislation and the lived experience of women, and this can at times be so great that the reality of women's lives barely reflects the legal framework in which they

156 The rule of law

exist. As pointed out in the case study, such interventions are promoted, have been legislated for, and are actively supported by the Rwandan government, by the national gender machinery, and by local structures, yet resistance to change is widespread and deeply embedded. A critical entry point to addressing this is social norm change but as noted above, the 'sticky social norms' that are upheld by both women and men in society can also represent the most difficult barriers to overcome. Moreover, if adequately considered in the design and implementation phases of development intervention, they may lead to failure or, worse, increased levels of VAWG.

Notes

1 GRs 19 (1992): 'due diligence'. GR 30 (2013): conflict and UN SCR 1325. GR 35 (2017): updates. GR 19: asserts that the prohibition of GBV has evolved into customary international law principle (CEDAW, 2013, 2017; IDLO, 2013, 2017; Richards & Haglund, 2015; UN Women, 2015).
2 For the positives and negatives of CEDAW, see, e.g., Mullins (2018), El-Masri (2012), Englehart and Miller (2014), Hodson (2014), Klugman (2017), Raday (2012), and Zwingel (2005).
3 CEDAW Art. 2 states: 'States Parties condemn discrimination against women in all its forms, agree to pursue by all appropriate means and without delay a policy of eliminating discrimination against women'.
4 For reflections on SDG progress, see DFID (2017), Donoghue and Khan (2019), Equal Measures 2030 (2018), Fulu (2017), Kusuma and Babu (2017), Manuel and Manuel (2018), Nicolai, Hoy, Berliner, and Aedy (2015), Samman, et al. (2018), SDGs Reports UN (2016, 2017, 2018, 2019), and Zamora et al. (2018).
5 However, the 2018 and 2019 UN Sustainable Development Reports, which collate global evidence on progress, or its lack, across all 17 SDGs, make few references to gender. These brief reports provide little evidence of a genuinely crosscutting approach to gender equality or to VAWG.
6 There is a wide literature on the principle of due diligence and its centrality in legal provisions to address VAWG. See, e.g., Aziz and Moussa (2014), IDLO (2013, 2017), Klugman et al. (2014), Klugman (2017), World Bank (2015, 2017).
7 For publications addressing these topics globally/for countries and regions, see, e.g., Arango, Morton, Gennari, Kiplesund, and Ellsberg (2014), Commonwealth Secretariat (2019), Criado-Perez (2019), ELF (2018), Htun and Weldon (2012), IDLO (2013, 2017), KAFA and Oxfam (2017), Mandal (2014), and RoU (2016).
8 The Special Representative's report was strongly contested by the UK Government.
9 For reasons of space and because this chapter primarily addresses legal mechanisms and instruments, the Rwanda case study does not include discussion of the *Isange* initiative, a one-stop centre (OSC) approach to provision of health and psychosocial services for survivors of VAWG. *Isange* OSCs also provide access to police officers trained in VAWG response and to legal services. The intention is to publish an extensive study of *Isange* in a paper on advocacy actions (including health advocacy) in support of VAWG prevention and response.
10 There is no space here for the views of those who disagree with the majority positive perceptions of the Rwandan environment when it comes to governance, rule of law, civil liberties, and degree of freedom vs. authoritarianism. See Bauer and Burnet (2013), Burnet (2008, 2011), Debusscher and Ansoms (2013), HRW (2020). Of relevance is that some observers critical of the Rwandan government acknowledge efforts made to achieve greater gender equality – although there are different views as to efficacy.

11 We draw on a wide range of documents, including Abbott and Malunda (2015), Abbott, Mutesi, and Norris (2015), Ansoms (2009), Booth and Golooba-Mutebi (2012), CARE (2019), Coffé (2012), Debusscher and Ansoms (2013), Hansén (2017), Hughes and Tripp (2015), Orrnert (2018), Republic of Rwanda (2008, 2017, 2018), GMO (2016, 2017, 2018, 2019), MIGEPROF (2018a, 2018b), Republic of Rwanda NPPA (2016, 2017), US Department of State (2016).
12 'Family councils/courts' are groupings of family members, predominantly (but seemingly not exclusively) male. Evidence is limited as to these groups' power and authority and whether judgements are gender equal, fair, accepted by not only those on whom judgement is being made but the wider community. See Dunkle, Stern, Heise, & Chatterji (2019), Stern and Mirembe (2017), Stern et al. (2018a, 2018b, 2018c).
13 Definitions and data are imprecise; the 2014–2015 DHS states that 17% of women aged 15–49 are in informal unions (and 7% in polygamous union); Berry (2015) has upwards of 60%.
14 The most common term used in reports and papers is gender-based violence; the DHS uses 'domestic violence'.

References

Abbott, P., & Malundam, D. (2015). *The Promise and the Reality: Women's Rights in Rwanda* (Oxford Human Rights Hub. Working Paper No. 5). https://doi.org/10.2139/ssrn.2710729

Abbott, P., Mutesi, L., & Norris, E. (2015). *Gender Analysis for Sustainable Livelihoods and Participatory Governance.* Oxfam International. https://www.africaportal.org/publications/gender-analysis-for-sustainable-livelihoods-and-participatory-governance-in-rwanda/

Abrahams, N., Mathews, S., Martin, L. J., Lombard, C., & Jewkes, R. (2013). Intimate partner femicide in South Africa in 1999 and 2009. *PLoS Medicine, 10*(4), e1001412. https://doi.org/10.1371/journal.pmed.1001412

Aggee, S. (2013). *Sexual and Gender-Based Violence Baseline Study in 13 Districts.* RWAMREC, Funded by Norwegian People's Aid. http://www.rwamrec.org/IMG/pdf/baseline_study_on_gbv_may_2013-_rwamrec.pdf

AHR. (2018). *Femicide.* The Advocates for Human Rights. https://www.stopvaw.org/femicide

Alexander-Scott, M., Bell, E., & Holden, J. (2016). *DFID Guidance Note: Shifting Social Norms to Tackle Violence against Women and Girls (VAWG).* Department for International Development (DFID). https://www.gov.uk/government/publications/shifting-social-norms-to-tackle-violence-against-women-and-girls

Allen Dale, A. (2018). *Intersectional Human Rights at CEDAW: Promises, Transmissions and Impacts.* Doctoral dissertation, University of York, Osgoode Hall Law School. https://digitalcommons.osgoode.yorku.ca/phd/43

Ansoms, A. (2009). Re-engineering rural society: The visions and ambitions of the Rwandan elite. *African Affairs, 108*(431), 289–309. https://doi.org/10.1093/afraf/adp001

Arango, D. J., Morton, M., Gennari, F., Kiplesund, S., & Ellsberg, M. (2014). *Interventions to Prevent or Reduce Violence against Women and Girls: A Systematic Review of Reviews World Bank Women's Voice, Agency and Participation Research Series.* World Bank. https://gsdrc.org/document-library/interventions-to-prevent-or-reduce-violence-against-women-and-girls-a-systematic-review-of-reviews/

Asubiario-Dada, W., & Gaynor, C. (2017). *Thinking and Working Politically for Legal Reform on Gender Equality.* Voices for Change Legacy Paper. UK Aid. https://www.sddirect.org.uk/media/1919/1624-v4c-lp-gender-equality-web-1.pdf

158 The rule of law

Aziz, Z. A., & Moussa, J. (2014). *Due Diligence Framework: State Accountability for Eliminating Violence against Women*. Due Diligence Project. http://www.peacewomen.org/node/98159

Barnes, T. D., & Burchard, S. M. (2013). "Engendering" politics: The impact of descriptive representation on women's political engagement in Sub-Saharan Africa. *Comparative Political Studies, 46*(7), 767–790. https://doi.org/10.1177%2F0010414012463884

Basinga, P., Moore, A. M., Singh, S. D., Carlin, E. E., Birungi, F., & Ngabo, F. (2012). Abortion incidence and postabortion care in Rwanda. *Studies in Family Planning, 43*(1), 11–20. https://doi.org/10.1111/j.1728-4465.2012.00298.x

Bauer, G., & Burnet, J. E. (2013). Gender quotas, democracy, and women's representation in Africa: Some insights from democratic Botswana and autocratic Rwanda. *Women's Studies International Forum, 41*(2), 103–112. https://doi.org/10.1016/j.wsif.2013.05.012

Berry, M. E. (2015). When "bright futures" fade: Paradoxes of women's empowerment in Rwanda. *Signs: Journal of Women in Culture and Society, 41*(1), 1–27. https://doi.org/10.1086/681899

Bloom, S., Cannon, A., & Negroustoueva, S. (2014). *Know Your HIV/AIDS Epidemic from a Gender Perspective: Rwanda Report*. MEASURE Evaluation. https://www.measureevaluation.org/resources/publications/tr-14-98

Booth, D., & Golooba-Mutebi, F. (2012). Developmental patrimonialism? The case of Rwanda. *African Affairs, 111*(444), 379–403. https://doi.org/10.1093/afraf/ads026

Burnet, J. E. (2008). Gender balance and the meanings of women in governance in post-genocide Rwanda. *African Affairs, 107*(428), 361–386. https://doi.org/10.1093/afraf/adn024

Burnet, J. E. (2011). Women have found respect: Gender quotas, symbolic representation, and female empowerment in Rwanda. *Politics & Gender, 7*(3), 303–334. https://doi.org/10.1017/S1743923X11000250

Campbell, M. (2016). *CEDAW and Women's Intersecting Identities: A Pioneering Approach to Intersectional Discrimination* (Oxford Human Rights Hub. Working Paper Vol. 2, Number 3). University of Oxford. https://ohrh.law.ox.ac.uk/wordpress/wp-content/uploads/2015/07/Working-Paper-Series-Vol-2-No-3.pdf

CARE. (2019). *Policy Brief: Update of Rwanda's Gender-Based Violence Policy*. CARE. https://www.carenederland.org/wp-content/uploads/2019/12/GBV-Policy-Revision-Briefing_-Rwanda_clean.pdf

CEDAW. (2013). *CEDAW: General Recommendation No. 30 on Women in Conflict Prevention, Conflict and Post-Conflict Situations*. United Nations: Committee on the Elimination of Discrimination against Women. https://www.ohchr.org/documents/hrbodies/cedaw/gcomments/cedaw.c.cg.30.pdf

CEDAW. (2017). *General Recommendation No. 35 on Gender-Based Violence against Women, Updating General Recommendation No. 19*. Committee on the Elimination of Discrimination against Women. https://www.ohchr.org/en/hrbodies/cedaw/pages/gr35.aspx

Clark, P. (2019, March 19). *Why International Justice Must Go Local: The ICC in Africa*. Africa Research Institute: Counterpoints. https://www.africaresearchinstitute.org/newsite/publications/why-international-justice-must-go-local-the-icc-in-africa/

COFEM. (2017). *Funding: Whose Priorities? Feminist Perspectives on Addressing Violence against Women and Girls Series*, Paper No. 4. Coalition of Feminists for Social Change. https://raisingvoices.org/wp-content/uploads/2013/03/Paper-4-COFEM.final_.sept2017.pdf

COFEM. (2019). *Feminist Movement Building: Taking a Long-Term View. Feminist Pocketbook* (Tip Sheet 10). Coalition of Feminists for Social Change. https://cofemsocialchange.org/wp-content/uploads/2018/11/TS10-Feminist-movement-building-Taking-a-long-term-view.pdf

Coffé, H. (2012). Conceptions of female political representation: Perspectives of Rwandan female representatives. *Women's Studies International Forum, 35*(4), 286–297. https://doi.org/10.1016/j.wsif.2012.05.004

Commonwealth Secretariat. (2019). *Gender Equality in the Commonwealth 2018/19* (Paper Prepared for the 12th Commonwealth Women's Affairs' Meeting Nairobi 19–20 September, 2019). Commonwealth Secretariat. https://thecommonwealth.org/sites/default/files/inline/WAMM%2819%294a%20-%20Gender%20Equality%20in%20the%20Commonwealth%202018%2019.pdf

CPS. (2020). *Data Summary Quarter 2 2019–2020.* Crown Prosecution Service. https://www.cps.gov.uk/publication/cps-data-summary-quarter-2-2019-2020

Criado-Perez, C. (2019). *Invisible Women: Exposing Data Bias in a World Designed for Men.* London: Chatto and Windus.

Debusscher, P., & Ansoms, A. (2013). Gender equality policies in Rwanda: Public relations or real transformations? *Development and Change, 44*(5), 1111–1134. https://doi.org/10.1111/dech.12052

Deng, D. (2013). *Challenges of Accountability: An Assessment of Dispute Resolution Process in Rural South Sudan.* South Sudan Law Society. https://www.icnl.org/research/library/south-sudan_sslsdeng/

DFID. (2017). *Agenda 2030: The UK Government's Approach to Delivering the Global Goals for Sustainable Development - At Home and Around the World.* Department for International Development (UK Aid). https://www.gov.uk/government/publications/agenda-2030-delivering-the-global-goals

Donoghue, D., & Khan, A. (2019). *Achieving the SDGs and 'Leaving No-One Behind': Maximising Synergies and Mitigating Trade-Offs* (ODI Working Paper 560). London: Overseas Development Institute. https://www.odi.org/sites/odi.org.uk/files/resource-documents/12771.pdf

Dunkle, K., Stern, E., Heise, L., & Chatterji, S. (2019). *The Impact of Indashyikirwa: An Innovative Programme to Reduce Partner Violence in Rural Rwanda* (What Works Evidence Brief). The What Works to Prevent VAWG Programme (WW-VAWG). https://www.whatworks.co.za/resources/policy-briefs/item/651-impact-of-indashyikirwa

EHRC. (2019). *Women's Rights and Gender Equality in 2018: Update Report. Formal Submission to the Committee on the Elimination of All Forms of Discrimination against Women, in Response to the UK List of Issues.* Equality and Human Rights Commission. https://www.equalityhumanrights.com/sites/default/files/womens-rights-and-gender-equality-in-2018-summary-update_report-long-version.pdf

El-Masri, S. (2012). Challenges facing CEDAW in the Middle East and North Africa. *The International Journal of Human Rights, 16*(7), 931–946. https://doi.org/10.1080/13642987.2011.629096

ELF. (2018). *Manual on the Law Relating to Violence against Women: England and Wales; Greece; Ireland; Italy; Northern Ireland; Poland; Spain.* European Lawyers' Foundation (Funded by the EU). https://www.consiglionazionaleforense.it/documents/20182/0/Manual+on+the+law+relating+to+violence+against+women.pdf/373786e2-4af0-4579-8f14-629c28834679

Englehart, N. A., & Miller, M. K. (2014). The CEDAW effect: International law's impact on women's rights. *Journal of Human Rights, 13*(1), 22–47. https://doi.org/10.1080/14754835.2013.824274

Equal Measures 2030. (2018). *Data Driving Change: Introducing the EM2030 SDG Gender Index.* Equal Measures 2030 and Partners. https://data.em2030.org/wp-content/uploads/2018/09/EM2030-2018-Global-Report.pdf

160 The rule of law

Fraser, E., & Wood, S. (2018). *VAWG Legislation* (VAWG Helpdesk Research Report 156). Department for International Development (DFID) (UK Aid). https://www. sddirect.org.uk/media/1520/vawg-helpdesk-156-legislation.pdf

Fulu, E. (2017). *Reflections on the VAWG Research Field* (Opening Plenary Rio de Janeiro: Sexual Violence Research Initiative Forum, 2017). https://www.svri.org/blog/ reflections-violence-against-women-and-girls-research-field

García-Moreno, C., Jansen, H., Ellsberg, M., Heise, L., & Watts, C. (2005). *WHO Multi-Country Study on Women's Health and Domestic Violence against Women.* World Health Organization. https://www.who.int/reproductivehealth/publications/violence/ 24159358X/en/

Global Americans. (2020). *Solidarity with the People? Femicide and International Women's Rights. An Epidemic of Violence in Latin America.* Global Americans. https://theglobal americans.org/reports/femicide-international-womens-rights/

GMO. (2016). *Annual Report 2014–2015.* Republic of Rwanda; Gender Monitoring Office. http://gmo.gov.rw/fileadmin/user_upload/reports/GMO_Annual_Report_ 2014_-_2015.pdf

GMO. (2017). *Annual Report 2015–2016.* Republic of Rwanda; Gender Monitoring Office. http://gmo.gov.rw/fileadmin/user_upload/reports/GMO_Annual_Report_ 2015-2016.pdf

GMO. (2018). *Annual Report 2017–2018.* Republic of Rwanda; Gender Monitoring Office. http://gmo.gov.rw/fileadmin/user_upload/reports/GMO_ANNUAL_REPORT_ 2016-2017.pdf

GMO. (2019). *The State of Gender Equality in Rwanda: From Transition to Transformation.* Republic of Rwanda; Gender Monitoring Office. http://gmo.gov.rw/fileadmin/user_ upload/Researches%20and%20Assessments/State%20of%20Gender%20Equality%20 in%20Rwanda.pdf

Hansén, J. (2017). *Political Gender Quota in Rwanda: Has Increased Female Inclusion in Politics Led to a Decrease in Domestic Gender-Based Violence?* [Senior thesis, University of Lund]. Department of Political Science. https://lup.lub.lu.se/luur/ download?func=downloadFile&recordOId=8918957&fileOId=8918958

Heise, L., & Kotsadam, A. (2015). Cross-national and multilevel correlates of partner violence: An analysis of data from population-based surveys. *The Lancet Global Health, 3*(6), e332–e340. https://doi.org/10.1016/S2214-109X(15)00013-3

Hodson, L. (2014). Women's rights and the periphery: CEDAW's optional protocol. *European Journal of International Law, 25*(2), 561–578. https://doi.org/10.1093/ejil/ chu027

HRW. (2020). *World Report 2020: Events of 2019.* Human Rights Watch. https://www. hrw.org/sites/default/files/world_report_download/hrw_world_report_2020_0.pdf

Htun, M., & Weldon, S. L. (2012). The civic origins of progressive policy change: Combating violence against women in global perspective, 1975–2005. *American Political Science Review, 106*(3), 548–569. https://www.jstor.org/stable/23275433

Hughes, C., Marrs, C., & Sweetman, C. (2016). Introduction to gender, development and VAWG. *Gender and Development, 24*(2) 157–169. https://doi.org/10.1080/135520 74.2016.1208471

Hughes, M. M., & Tripp, A. M. (2015). Civil war and trajectories of change in women's political representation in Africa, 1985–2010. *Social Forces, 93*(4), 1513–1540. https:// doi.org/10.1093/sf/sov003

ICC. (2014). *Policy Paper on Sexual and Gender-Based Crimes.* International Criminal Court; the Office of the Prosecutor. https://www.icc-cpi.int/iccdocs/otp/otp-policy- paper-on-sexual-and-gender-based-crimes--june-2014.pdf

IDLO. (2013). *Accessing Justice: Models, Strategies and Best Practices on Women's Empowerment.* International Development Law Organisation. https://www.idlo.int/publications/accessing-justice-models-strategies-and-best-practices-womens-empowerment

IDLO. (2017). *Strengthening Women's Access to Justice: Making Rights a Reality for Women and Girls. Concept Note.* International Development Law Organisation.

Iqbal, S. (2015). *Women, Business, and the Law 2016: Getting to Equal.* World Bank Group. https://openknowledge.worldbank.org/handle/10986/22546

Isimbi, R., Manzi Simpunga, D., & Domingo, P. (2018). *Policy and Legal Analysis Notes. A Review of the National Policy against Gender-Based Violence in Rwanda* (ODI Briefing Papers). London: Overseas Development Institute (ODI). https://www.odi.org/publications/11325-policy-and-legal-analysis-notes-review-national-policy-against-gender-based-violence-rwanda

Jefremovas, V. (1991). Loose women, virtuous wives, and timid virgins: Gender and the control of resources in Rwanda. *Canadian Journal of African Studies/La Revue Canadienne des études Africaines, 25*(3), 378–395. https://doi.org/10.1080/00083968.1991.10803899

Jewkes, R., Stern, E., & Ramsoomar, L. (2019). *Community Activism Approaches to Shift Harmful Gender Attitudes, Roles and Social Norms.* What Works Programme. https://prevention-collaborative.org/wp-content/uploads/2019/11/social-norms-briefWEB-28092019.pdf

KAFA & Oxfam. (2017). *A Regional Model Law on Violence against Women and Girls in the Arab Countries.* KAFA (Enough Violence and Exploitation) and Oxfam. https://views-voices.oxfam.org.uk/2018/01/model-law-tackle-violence-women/

Kagaba, M. (2015). Threatened masculinities: Men's experiences of gender equality in rural Rwanda. *Masculinities—A Journal of Identity and Culture, 3*, 55–85. http://masculinitiesjournal.org/pdf/9588-Threatened%20Masculinities.pdf

Klugman, J. (2017). *Gender-Based Violence and the Law* (World Development Report Background Paper). World Bank. https://openknowledge.worldbank.org/handle/10986/26198

Klugman, J., Hanmer, L., Twigg, S., Hasan, T., McCleary-Sills, J., & Santamaria, J. (2014). *Voice and Agency: Empowering Women and Girls for Shared Prosperity.* World Bank. https://openknowledge.worldbank.org/handle/10986/19036

Kusuma, Y. S., & Babu, B. V. (2017). Elimination of violence against women and girls as a global action agenda. *Journal of Injury and Violence Research, 9*(2), 117. https://doi.org/10.5249%2Fjivr.v9i2.908

Lalor, K., Mills, E., Sánchez-García, A., & Haste, P. (2016). *Gender, Sexuality and Social Justice: What's Law Got to Do with It?* Institute of Development Studies. https://opendocs.ids.ac.uk/opendocs/handle/20.500.12413/8878

Lappi-Seppälä, T., & Lehti, M. (2016). Global homicide mortality trends by gender, 1950–2010. In H. Kury, S. Redo, & E. Shea (Eds.). *Women and Children as Victims and Offenders: Background, Prevention, Reintegration* (Vol. 1), pp. 427–478. Cham, Switzerland: Springer International Publishing.

Long, J., & Harvey, H. (2020). *Femicide Census: Women Killed by Men in the UK. Annual Report on UK Femicides 2018.* Nia and Partners. https://niaendingviolence.org.uk/wp-content/uploads/2020/02/Femicide-Census-Report-on-2018-Femicides-1.pdf

Mandal, S. (2014). The impossibility of marital rape: Contestations around marriage, sex, violence and the law in contemporary India. *Australian Feminist Studies, 29*(81), 255–272. https://doi.org/10.1080/08164649.2014.958124

Mannell, J., & Jackson, S. (2014). *Intimate Partner Violence in Rwanda: Women's Voices.* London School of Economics; Health, Community and Development Group. http://eprints.lse.ac.uk/60014/

Mannell, J., Jackson, S., & Umutoni, A. (2016). Women's responses to intimate partner violence in Rwanda: Rethinking agency in constrained social contexts. *Global Public Health, 11*(1–2), 65–81. https://doi.org/10.1080/17441692.2015.1013050

Manuel, M., & Manuel, C. (2018). *Achieving Equal Access to Justice for All by 2030. Lessons from Global Funds* (ODI Working Paper 537). Overseas Development Institute. https://www.odi.org/publications/11161-achieving-equal-access-justice-all-2030-lessons-global-funds

MIGEPROF. (2018a). *Rwanda National Action Plan (2018–2022) for the Implementation of the United Nations Security Council Resolutions 1325 (2000) and Subsequent Resolutions.* Rwanda Ministry of Gender and Family Promotion. https://www.wpsnaps.org/app/uploads/2019/09/Rwanda-NAP-2-2018-2022.pdf

MIGEPROF. (2018b). *Gender Fact Sheet 2018.* Rwanda Ministry of Gender and Family Promotion. http://197.243.22.137/migeprof/fileadmin/user_upload/Gender_Equality_and_Women_Empowerment-Rwanda__Fact_Sheet__2018.pdf

Mukamana, D., & Brysiewicz, P. (2008). The lived experience of genocide rape survivors in Rwanda. *Journal of Nursing Scholarship, 40*(4), 379–384. https://doi.org/10.1111/j.1547-5069.2008.00253.x

Mullins, L. B. (2018). CEDAW: The challenges of enshrining women's equality in international law. *Public Integrity, 20*(3), 257–272. https://doi.org/10.1080/10999922.2017.1381542

Mwendwa Mechta, S., Buscagli, I., Bikesha, D., & Routte, J. (2016). *Decision-Making and Joint Control Rights Over Land in Rwanda.* Three Stones Consulting Ltd for International Alert. https://www.international-alert.org/publications/decision-making-and-joint-control-rights-over-land-rwanda

Nicolai, S., Hoy, C., Berliner, T., & Aedy, T. (2015). *Projecting Progress: Reaching the SDGs by 2030* (ODI Flagship Report). Overseas Development Institute. https://www.odi.org/sites/odi.org.uk/files/odi-assets/publications-opinion-files/9938.pdf

NISR, MOH, & ICF International. (2015). *Rwanda Demographic and Health Survey 2014–15.* National Institute of Statistics of Rwanda, Ministry of Health Rwanda & ICF International. https://dhsprogram.com/pubs/pdf/FR316/FR316.pdf

NPPA. (2016). *Status of GBV Cases Prosecuted: Challenges and Strategies.* Republic of Rwanda; National Public Prosecution Authority (NPPA). Government of Rwanda.

NPPA. (2017). *NPPA: Quarterly Progressive Report - July-September 2017.* Republic of Rwanda; National Public Prosecution Authority (NPPA). Government of Rwanda.

O'Donnell, M., & Kenny, C. (2020, January 13). With Ten Years to the SDG Finish Line, Laws Need to Change for Gender Equality. *Center for Global Development Blog.* https://www.cgdev.org/blog/ten-years-sdg-finish-line-laws-need-change-gender-equality

OHCHR. (2014). *The Latin American Model Protocol for the Investigation of Gender-Related Killing of Women (Femicide/Feminicide).* New York and Panama City: UN Women and the Regional Office for Central America of the UN Office of the High Commissioner for Human Rights. https://lac.unwomen.org/en/digiteca/publicaciones/2014/10/modelo-de-protocolo

OHCHR. (2019). *Protection of Victims of Sexual Violence: Lessons Learned. Workshop Report.* United Nations Office of the High Commissioner for Human Rights; Women's Human Rights and Gender Section. https://www.ohchr.org/Documents/Issues/Women/WRGS/ReportLessonsLearned.pdf

Orrnert, A. (2018). *Legislation and Policy Addressing Inequality and Redistribution in Rwanda* (Knowledge, Evidence and Learning for Development [K4D]. Help Desk Report). Department for International Development (UK Aid). https://www.gov.uk/research-for-development-outputs/legislation-and-policy-addressing-inequality-and-redistribution-in-rwanda

OSF. (2018). *Options for Justice: A Handbook for Designing Accountability Mechanisms for Grave Crimes*. Open Society Justice Initiative. https://www.justiceinitiative.org/publications/options-justice-handbook-designing-accountability-mechanisms-grave-crimes

Påfs, J., Rulisa, S., Klingberg-Allvin, M., Binder-Finnema, P., Musafili, A., & Essén, B. (2020). Implementing the liberalized abortion law in Kigali, Rwanda: Ambiguities of rights and responsibilities among health care providers. *Midwifery, 80*, 102568. https://doi.org/10.1016/j.midw.2019.102568

Pew Research Center. (2016). *Marriage Laws around the World*. Pew Research Center. https://assets.pewresearch.org/wp-content/uploads/sites/12/2016/09/FT_Marriage_Age_Appendix_2016_09_08.pdf

Raday, F. (2012). Gender and democratic citizenship: The impact of CEDAW. *International Journal of Constitutional Law, 10*(2), 512–530. https://doi.org/10.1093/icon/mor068

Republic of Rwanda. (2008). *Law No. 59/2008: Prevention and Punishment of Gender-Based Violence*. Government of Rwanda. https://www.refworld.org/docid/4a3f88812.html

Republic of Rwanda. (2012). *Organic Law 01/2012/OL of 02/05/2012*. Government of Rwanda. https://sherloc.unodc.org/cld/document/rwa/2012/penal_code_of_rwanda.html

Republic of Rwanda. (2017). *7 Years' Government Programme: National Strategy for Transformation (NST 1) 2017–2024*. Government of Rwanda. http://www.minecofin.gov.rw/fileadmin/user_upload/NST1_7YGP_Final.pdf

Republic of Rwanda. (2018). *Law No. 68/2018 Determining Offences and Penalties in General Concerning Gender-Based Violence (GBV) in All Its Forms*. Government of Rwanda. https://rwandalii.africanlii.org/content/official-gazette-n%C2%BA-special-2792018

Richards, D., & Haglund, J. (2015). *Violence against Women and the Law*. London: Routledge. https://doi.org/10.4324/9781315631295

RoU. (2016). *Summary of the Gender Book: Women's Access to Justice in Uganda*. Republic of Uganda Judiciary, Embassy of Sweden and UN Women. https://uls.or.ug/site/assets/files/1206/un_women_-_summary_of_the_gender_bench_book_2016.pdf

RWAMREC. (2010). *Masculinity and Gender-Based Violence in Rwanda: Experiences and Perceptions of Men and Women*. Rwanda Men's Resource Centre. Rwanda MenEngage Network. http://menengage.org/wp-content/uploads/2014/06/Masculinity-GBV-Rwanda.pdf

Rwanda Biomedical Centre. (2014). *Rwanda: Global AIDS Response Progress Report*. Ministry of Health; Rwanda Biomedical Centre. https://www.unaids.org/sites/default/files/country/documents//file, 94722,ru..pdf

Samman, E., Lucci, P., Hagen-Zanker, J., Bhatkal, T., Simunovic, A. T., Nicolai, S., Stuart, E., & Caron, C., (2018). *SDG Progress - Fragility, Crisis and Leaving No-One Behind*. Overseas Development Institute. https://www.econstor.eu/handle/10419/190853

Small Arms Survey. (2016). *A Gendered Analysis of Violent Deaths* (SAS Research Notes, 63). SAS. http://www.smallarmssurvey.org/fileadmin/docs/H-Research_Notes/SAS-Research-Note-63.pdf

Stavropoulou, M., & Gupta-Archer, N. (2017). *Adolescent Girls' Capabilities in Rwanda: The State of the Evidence*. Gender and Adolescence Global Evidence programme. https://www.gage.odi.org/publication/adolescent-girls-capabilities-rwanda-state-evidence/

Stern, E., Heise, L., & McLean, L. (2018a). The doing and undoing of male household decision-making and economic authority in Rwanda and its implications for gender transformative programming. *Culture, Health & Sexuality, 20*(9), 976–991. https://doi.org/10.1080/13691058.2017.1404642

Stern, E., Heise, L., & McLean, L. (2018b). *Engaging Opinion Leaders in an IPV Prevention Programme: Lessons from Indashyikirwa in Rwanda*. The What Works to Prevent VAWG programme, CARE, RWAMREC and the Rwanda Women's Network. https://insights.careinternational.org.uk/media/k2/attachments/Practice_brief_Indashyikirwa_opinion_leaders_2018.pdf

Stern, E., Heise, L., & McLean, L. (2018c). *Working with Couples to Prevent IPV: Indashyikirwa in Rwanda*. The What Works to Prevent VAWG Programme, CARE, RWAMREC and the Rwanda Women's Network. https://insights.careinternational.org.uk/media/k2/attachments/Practice_brief_Indashyikirwa_working_with_couples_2018.pdf

Stern, E., & Mirembe, J. (2017). Intersectionalities of formality of marital status and women's risk and protective factors for intimate partner violence in Rwanda. *Agenda, 31*(1), 116–127. https://doi.org/10.1080/10130950.2017.1349345

Stubbs, J. (2014). Gendered violence and restorative justice. In A. Hayden, L. Gelsthorpe, V. Kingi, & A. Morris (Eds.). *A Restorative Approach to Family Violence: Changing Tack* (pp. 199–210). Ashgate. https://doi.org/10.4324/9781315565156

Umuhoza, C., Oosters, B., van Reeuwijk, M., & Vanwesenbeeck, I. (2013). Advocating for safe abortion in Rwanda: How young people and the personal stories of young women in prison brought about change. *Reproductive Health Matters, 21*(41), 49–56. https://doi.org/10.1016/S0968-8080(13)41690-7

UN. (2016). *The Sustainable Development Goals. 2016 Report*. The United Nations. https://unstats.un.org/sdgs/report/2016/

UN. (2017). *The Sustainable Development Goals. 2017 Report*. The United Nations. https://unstats.un.org/sdgs/report/2017/

UN. (2018). *The Sustainable Development Goals. 2018 Report*. The United Nations. https://unstats.un.org/sdgs/report/2018/

UN. (2019). *The Sustainable Development Goals. 2019 Report*. The United Nations. https://unstats.un.org/sdgs/report/2019/

UN DESA. (2010). *Handbook for Legislation on Violence against Women*. The United Nations Department of Economic and Social Affairs Division for the Advancement of Women. https://www.unwomen.org/en/digital-library/publications/2012/12/handbook-for-legislation-on-violence-against-women

UN Women. (2015). *Monitoring Gender Equality and the Empowerment of Women and Girls in the 2030 Agenda for Sustainable Development: Opportunities and Challenges*. UN Women. https://lac.unwomen.org/en/digiteca/publicaciones/2015/09/monitoreo-genero

UN Women. (2017, November 29). *The Long Road to Justice, Prosecuting Femicide in Mexico*. https://www.unwomen.org/en/news/stories/2017/11/feature-prosecuting-femicide-in-mexico

UN Women. (2018). *Prospects for Ending Child Marriage in Africa: Implications on Legislation, Policy, Culture and Interventions* (Executive Brief). UN Women. https://africa.unwomen.org/en/digital-library/publications/2018/12/child-marriage-study

UN Women, IDLO, World Bank, Task Force on Justice. (2019). *Justice for Women: High Level Group Report*. UN Women. https://www.unwomen.org/en/digital-library/publications/2020/03/justice-for-women-high-level-group-report

UNDP. (2015). *2015 Human Development Report*. United Nations Development Programme. http://hdr.undp.org/sites/default/files/2015_human_development_report.pdf

UNGA. (2012). *Report of the Special Rapporteur on Violence against Women, Its Causes and Consequences; Rashida Manjoo* (A/HRC/26/38). United Nations General Assembly Human Rights Council 20th Session. https://www.unwomen.org/en/docs/2014/5/special-rapporteur-on-violence-against-women-a-hrc-26-38#view

UNGA. (2015). *Report of the Special Rapporteur on Violence against Women, Its Causes and Consequences. Addendum: Mission to the United Kingdom of Great Britain and Northern*

Ireland (A/HRC/29/27/Add.2). United Nations General Assembly Human Rights Council 29th Session. https://www.refworld.org/docid/5583f7254.html

UNGA. (2016). *Report of the Special Rapporteur on Violence against Women, Its Causes and Consequences; Dubravka Šimonović* (A/HRC/32/42/Add.3). United Nations General Assembly Human Rights Council 71st Session. https://digitallibrary.un.org/record/842665?ln=en

UNODC. (2018). *Global Study on Homicide. Gender-Related Killing of Women and Girls*. United Nations Office of Drugs and Crime. https://www.unodc.org/documents/data-and-analysis/GSH2018/GSH18_Gender-related_killing_of_women_and_girls.pdf

US Department of State. (2016). *Country Reports on Human Rights Practices for 2016: Rwanda*. United States Department of State Bureau of Democracy, Human Rights and Labor. https://www.state.gov/reports/2016-country-reports-on-human-rights-practices/rwanda/

WEF. (2016). *The Global Gender Gap Report*. World Economic Forum. http://www3.weforum.org/docs/GGGR16/WEF_Global_Gender_Gap_Report_2016.pdf

WEF. (2017). *The Global Gender Gap Report*. World Economic Forum. https://www.weforum.org/reports/the-global-gender-gap-report-2017

WHO. (2012). *Understanding and Addressing Violence against Women: Femicide*. World Health Organization & Pan-American Health Organization. https://www.who.int/reproductivehealth/topics/violence/vaw_series/en/

World Bank. (2015). *Citizen Security, Law and Justice Brief. VAWG Resource Guide*. The World Bank Group, Global Women's Institute and IDB. https://www.vawgresourceguide.org/sites/vawg/files/briefs/vawg_resource_guide_citizen_security_brief_april_2015.pdf

World Bank. (2017). *World Development Report 2017: Governance and the Law*. The World Bank Group. https://www.worldbank.org/en/publication/wdr2017

Zamora, G., Koller, T. S., Thomas, R., Manandhar, M., Lustigova, E., Diop, A., & Magar, V. (2018). Tools and approaches to operationalize the commitment to equity, gender and human rights: Towards leaving no one behind in the sustainable development goals. *Global Health Action, 11*(sup1), 75–81. https://doi.org/10.1080/16549716.2018.1463657

Zwingel, S. (2005). From intergovernmental negotiations to (sub) national change: A transnational perspective on the impact of CEDAW. *International Feminist Journal of Politics, 7*(3), 400–424. https://doi.org/10.1080/1461674050016118

8

HOW TO MAINSTREAM VAWG ACROSS SECTORS

Two examples from modern slavery and sustainable energy programming

Throughout this volume, we have illustrated that there is a need for a VAWG lens to be embedded across different development sectors. In reviewing the evidence, it is clear that programmes that intend to reduce VAWG must contain multiple components but reducing risk will only be effective if it goes hand in hand with social norm change interventions that target harmful male behaviours and pervasive attitudes towards normalising violence among both men and women. The key argument we make, however, is that given how widespread VAWG is, every opportunity must be seized to make inroads into the reduction of violence. That means that it must be taken into consideration and addressed at all stages of development programming, including inception, implementation, and monitoring and evaluation, regardless of whether the specific intervention is VAWG-focused. This chapter takes the mainstreaming framework presented in Chapter 2 and applies it to two different development sectors: sustainable energy programming and projects aimed at reducing instances of modern slavery. We explore how and where violence intersects with energy programming and how it feeds into modern forms of slavery, and we then demonstrate how, in each case, applying a VAWG Mainstreaming Framework can be utilised and maximised to ensure that opportunities to end violence are not missed.

The chapter is split into two sections beginning with the case study of VAWG and sustainable energy programming with a specific focus on humanitarian energy interventions. This is a particularly useful example because intersections between VAWG and energy are arguably most acute in contexts of forced displacement and in refugee camps. The second section focuses on modern slavery, specifically that which occurs in the Ready-Made Garment (RMG) sector and in commercial sexual exploitation. The second section focuses specifically on Bangladesh and India to show how the sector and country context interact to create unique risks of VAWG, but also potential opportunities for tackling it.

DOI: 10.4324/9780429280603-8

The conclusion summarises how and why taking this approach in these sectors is useful, and points towards some of the potential benefits of the VAWG mainstreaming approach in general.

Case 1: mainstreaming VAWG in sustainable energy programming

How does VAWG intersect with energy issues?

Though there may be many aspects relating to energy that result in an increased vulnerability to violence, two stand out: the collection of fuel (firewood) and poor lighting. Much energy programming has focused on cost-effective and easy to mobilise solutions to energy supply for use in humanitarian situations (e.g. in Kakuma Camp, Kenya) (see Bradley & Liakos, 2019 for a more detailed case study of VAWG and energy). As already discussed in Chapters 4 and 5, the number of factors that influence VAWG in humanitarian settings are numerous. There is some evidence to suggest that reducing trips for firewood collection outside of camp reduces exposure to VAWG risks and that additional lighting may make women and girls feel safer. However, such projects only limit vulnerability in one situation and there is no evidence that they can reduce VAWG incidence or that feeling safer is a reflection of reduced VAWG.

It is important when advocating for a VAWG mainstreaming approach to understand that non-VAWG sectors will only be able to go so far in specifically ending violence. In other words, VAWG cannot be ended through energy projects alone, but by carefully reflecting on activities in a sector, it is possible to maximise opportunity and ensure that no unintended triggers for VAWG occur. As we have argued throughout, programmes to end VAWG are complex and require a focus on long-term mind-set change. That said, the application of a VAWG-sensitive lens in energy programming could well serve to promote a greater sense of control and confidence in women and girls when they no longer fear violence. Improved lighting and cooking methods could be seen as ways of building resilience; if women and girls feel more secure, they may feel more confident to challenge violence or mitigate against the risks of it.

As already discussed elsewhere, the factors that contribute to an increase in VAWG during conflict and humanitarian emergencies are complex and multi-faceted. The relationship between VAWG and energy access in humanitarian emergencies is part of this because lack of access to energy resources is associated with increased exposure to VAWG risk. The increase in exposure to risk is partly a result of the prevailing energy access situation, in particular relating to firewood collection and camp lighting. It has been noted, however, that this context may provide an opportune setting or location for VAWG, but importantly it should not be regarded as its *cause* (CASA Consulting, 2001). Poor lighting in public spaces and the need to collect firewood are among the most frequently reported potential risk factors that contribute to feelings of insecurity among women and girls in camp settings. While the reduction in risks does not automatically result in a reduction of VAWG, collection of firewood clearly presents a significant danger to women and girls. The knock-on impact this will have on the psychological well-being of women and girls, regardless of physical harm (through rape for example), should not be ignored.

This situation is compounded by the widespread reliance on traditional energy sources. There is very little data available on the current energy situation in these types of camps, but it is clear that few refugees or IDPs have access to modern energy services. In most cases, households rely on firewood for cooking and it has been estimated that

> 80 per cent of the 8.7 million refugees and displaced people in camps have absolutely minimal access to energy, with high dependence on traditional biomass for cooking and no access to electricity.
>
> *(Lahn and Graham, 2015)*

Although agencies supply firewood (or other cooking fuels) at some sites, the bulk of the firewood must be collected or bought. Fuelwood collection is primarily carried out by women and girls and involves trips outside the camp. The frequency, distance travelled, and length of each trip depend on the demand for fuel and local fuel availability.

The incidence of VAWG when venturing outside camp settings is well documented in a range of literature on gender and energy access. A recent rapid review carried out for DFID's VAWG helpdesk identified some of the key evidence available on the links between access to different sources of energy at the household and community levels and VAWG in camp-based settings (Parke & Fraser, 2015; see also Gunning, 2014, and evidence on VAWG outside camps can be found in Lahn, 2015; Mercy Corps, 2010; WRC, 2006, 2015). VAWG in general is difficult to measure and is greatly under-reported for several reasons, including lack of safe reporting mechanisms, lack of support, and fear of being ostracised or punished by one's community. In addition, where firewood collection is illegal outside camps, this can further encourage exploitation of girls by host communities and under-reporting. Risks in travelling to get firewood, as highlighted in assessments by the World Food Programme (WFP), are companied by other risks relating to accessing fuel, including domestic violence when there is no fuel for cooking, and transactional sex in exchange for cooking fuel or for money to purchase it (WFP, 2013).

As a result of these concerns, energy issues have begun to be incorporated into global humanitarian responses. The Safe Access to Fuel and Energy (SAFE) initiative was originally established as a protection activity, which intended to:

> ...to reduce exposure to violence, contribute to the protection of and ease the burden on those populations collecting wood in humanitarian settings worldwide, through solutions which will promote safe access to appropriate energy and reduce environmental impacts while ensuring accountability.
>
> *(WFP, 2013)*

Since 2014, it has had a wider cross-sectoral remit, incorporating humanitarian energy needs more broadly. It is led by the SAFE Humanitarian Working Group, a consortium of key partners, including the Food and Agriculture Organisation (FAO), the Global Alliance for Clean Cookstoves, UNHCR, UNICEF, WFP, and Women's Refugee Commission, among others.

New stoves and reduced fuelwood use do not always result in a reduction in fuel collection trips. Thus, in Darfur women still collected wood for sale after the distribution of improved cookstoves. Some studies even suggest that the time saved has fuelled the growth of a secondary market for the sale of firewood (Abdelnour, 2010). It is important to remember that travel outside camps is not restricted to fuelwood collection, but this is the activity that most concerns women.

The review entitled *'Gender-Based Violence in Humanitarian Settings: Cookstoves and Fuels'* produced by the Global Alliance for Clean Cookstoves (GACC, 2016) studied 15 humanitarian energy projects that included reducing GBV as an objective. It provided the following findings:

- Reducing the need to collect firewood does not necessarily bring down the total number of rapes.
- The most prevalent form of VAWG (as already stated) is IPV, not rape in public by a non-partner (which most firewood rapes are classed as) or conflict rape.

Evidence capturing even an increase in rape as a direct result of firewood collection is flimsy at best. Additionally, there is a lack of understanding around which cooking interventions are likely to have the strongest protection impacts. For example, only providing firewood that meets household cooking needs may not address all VAWG related to firewood collection especially if not enough is allocated.

Protection issues, due partly to lack of lighting (along with privacy issues), are frequently cited as barriers to the use of communal WASH facilities and as the rationale for fear of using the communal kitchens. For example, at the Za'atari camp in Jordan, women identified the WASH facilities and kitchens as the most insecure locations, and 24% of participants said safety concerns stopped them using communal kitchens (Serrato, 2014). Women feel unsafe, and incidents of VAWG are reported to take place in poorly lit areas. IOM carried out two rapid assessment surveys and found that VAWG prevalence was very high in two IDP settlements in Somalia, with many of the incidents taking place at night in the dark. Safety issues are affected by lack of lighting and by the design of the facilities and the distance to them. But even poorly designed lighting interventions could increase protection risks. For example, if lighting is provided in a key communal area but the lighting along the route is poor this may result in increased instances of VAWG (Perkins, 2015). Although there is a very likely link between lighting (both handheld lanterns and street lighting) and reducing VAWG risk factors, there is little evidence available since there are no studies that have monitored the incidence of VAWG before and after the introduction of a lighting initiative.

170 How to mainstream VAWG across sectors

One study tried to assess the effectiveness of solar lamps to reduce insecurity and SGBV (sexual and gender-based violence) in Puntland, Somalia, but the low reporting levels of such cases of violence rendered the task almost impossible (DFID, 2014). However, that and other surveys and assessments do show that women often feel safer and appreciate lighting, and there is also a reduced risk of fire-related accidents. For instance, following the pilot launch of its Light Years Ahead initiative, UNCHR carried out a survey in three countries with the findings showing that 60% of respondents feel safer using the bathroom at night (UNHCR, 2012). This isn't always the case; a study undertaken by IRC, which evaluated the impact of the distribution of handheld solar lights on women's and girls' perceptions of their own safety in two Haitian camps, found that women did not feel safer (IRC, 2014). Before and after comparisons in the IRC study found that although 95% of the women and girls reportedly used the lamps, the women's own perception of their safety remained the same or worsened (largely attributable to other broader security issues). The lamps alone did not address the women's primary safety concerns (which included generalised crime, violence and mistrust, including sexual violence and harassment). In the Democratic Republic of the Congo, UNHCR received feedback of an unforeseen consequence that IDPs did not use their solar lamps at night, for fear of revealing their location to rebel groups (IOM, 2011). The IRC study concluded that handheld solar lamps are an important personal resource for women and girls, while the root causes of VAWG are complex and cannot be addressed by a stand-alone distribution of lamps.

Once again, the message emerging clearly highlights that ending VAWG is tied to complex transformations in mind-sets legitimising the use of different forms of violence across contexts. Simply reducing risk (if energy interventions can be shown to do so) will not result in this shift in attitude/perceptions. In summary, most evaluations of energy initiatives conclude that the root causes of VAWG are complex and cannot be addressed by the distribution of energy products. To address VAWG, any alternative energy initiative needs to be part of a much larger long-term risk reduction programme which addresses mind-set changes, social norms, and cultural practices. However, greater awareness of the extent of VAWG and linked feelings of insecurity would greatly improve the sensitivity of energy programming in humanitarian settings and potentially feed into process of change that could positively contribute to improving the daily lives of women and reducing fear of VAWG.

Without doubt the literature presented in this chapter and through the volume highlights the extreme vulnerabilities endured by women and girls in refugee settings. While improved energy will not remove all vulnerabilities, greater sensitivity in energy programming to how it might support a reduction in insecurities are is an important part of supporting interventions that focus specifically on ending VAWG.

We will now present an example of how our mainstreaming VAWG approach could be used to better sensitise energy programming in mitigating VAWG wherever possible. As presented in Chapter 2, we adapt the ecology model adding steer questions that link to the goals of energy programmes. Table 8.1

TABLE 8.1 Applying the ecological model in approaches to respond to energy need

Social ecology level	Meta-question	Factors to think about for operationalisation
Socio-cultural	In what ways are energy needs and the associated activities gendered?	Can these views be seen to increase the vulnerabilities to violence of women and girls? E.g. if firewood collection became a male pursuit would they experience the same level of risk to violence? And, in turn, will reduced risk result in changing mind-sets?
Community	What community mechanisms exist to mitigate VAWG or offer security and protection to victims? E.g. are there reporting mechanisms following fuel collection rape? And to what extent might this provision cover vulnerabilities linked to energy generations/consumption.	How effective are the community mechanisms perceived to be and could they be built upon by the programme? Shaped specifically to energy needs?
Household	What dynamics exist at household level that may support or perpetuate VAWG?	Are there certain intra-/inter-household behaviours that need to be challenged by the programme? Is there opportunity to use the programme to tap into certain change dynamics (e.g. is there evidence that young educated women challenge their parents about the use of violence?). Can they be supported by the programme?
Individual	What room is there for individuals to challenge and change social norms surrounding VAWG? E.g. do women recognise links between vulnerability to violence and energy-related activities?	Can individuals who may be in the minority but wish to see VAWG end tap into wider networks and support structures to mobilise the change they want to see? If the answer is yes can the programme build on them? If it is no can the programme in fact build them?

172 How to mainstream VAWG across sectors

offers examples of the questions that could be used to draw out how energy programming and VAWG might be linked, what opportunities exist for tackling violence, and how programming might potentially contribute to increasing risk for women and girls.

In relation to energy programming, making adaptions by mainstreaming VAWG will not bring instant reductions in violence, but opportunities to reduce harm can be recognised and supported. If this approach were to be taken across development sectors, there would be potential to see a mass shift towards rejecting and challenging VAWG that could in fact drive the achievement of SDG5. At the same time, it could potentially lead to making non-VAWG interventions more effective. We now shift focus to another development sector, that of modern slavery, and similarly offer an example of how VAWG could be mainstreamed into activities for this dual purpose.

Case 2: modern slavery

Modern slavery as a key sector of development

Slavery has long been a recognised global human rights concern, particularly since the 1926 Convention to Suppress the Slave Trade and Slavery, which was an international treaty created under the auspices of the predecessor to the UN, the League of Nations. Since then, there have been numerous international instruments and pieces of national legislation to protect people from slavery and slavery-like conditions.

Over the past two decades, international commitment to ending slavery has expanded to include:

- The ten key principles outlined in the July 2000 UN Global Compact provide businesses with a framework and guidance for corporate sustainability.
- The December 2000 UN Protocol to Prevent, Suppress, and Punish Trafficking in Persons (the Palermo Protocol) was passed as part of the Convention against Transnational Organised Crime.
- The June 2014 International Labour Organisation (ILO) Convention Concerning Forced or Compulsory Labour, employers and workers at the International Labour Conference (ILC), which gave new impetus to the global fight against slavery and slavery-like practices by adopting a Protocol and Recommendation to supplement the Forced Labour Convention.
- The September 2015 UN Sustainable Development Goals (SDGs), which (unlike the MDGs) paid specific attention to the issue of slavery and forced labour

> (Source: all information available at https://www.un.org/
> and https://www.ilo.org/)

Modern slavery now represents a key development sector in its own right, with many global conventions and significant funds dedicated to its eradication.

While the spectrum of activities that now come under the umbrella of 'slavery' are numerous, including overseas labour recruitment, sexual exploitation, and bonded and forced labour in different contexts such as garment and domestic work, the intersections of violence and gender within these are still relatively under-researched. The adoption of the protocols outlined above represents important steps in the international effort to prevent and end modern slavery, but their effectiveness is dependent not only on full ratification by signatory states, but also on the development of systems and mechanisms to support them, as well as their proper implementation. We argue here that in order to do this effectively, it is necessary to incorporate a mainstreaming approach that sensitises actors to the gendered nature of vulnerabilities, which, in turn, mean that some people are more likely to be pushed into slavery than others.

Global estimates of modern slavery obviously depend on what is being measured and how slavery is being defined. That said, data from the ILO and Walk Free Foundation are presented in the most recent Global Slavery Index (GSI, 2018). The key figures from the ILO and Walk Free (2017, p. 5) are as follows: on any given day in 2016, an estimated 40.3 million people were living in modern slavery, including 24.9 million in forced labour and 15.4 million in forced marriage. 89 million people experienced some form of slavery between 2011 and 2016. For every 1,000 people worldwide, there are 5.4 victims of modern slavery. A quarter of people in modern slavery are children. Of those people in forced labour, 16 million are exploited in the private sector, 4.8 million are victims of forced sexual exploitation, and 4 million are forced into labour by state authorities. Women and girls account for 99% of victims in forced commercial sexual exploitation, and 58% in other sectors, making up 71% of all victims of MS (ILO & Walk Free, 2017).

Modern slavery programming and interventions

Modern slavery encompasses a diverse range of interlocking practices, and these must be understood within the complex local, national, regional, and international contexts in which they sit. We know that modern slavery is evolving in response to the changing demands of the global economic context (Kumar, 2014; Phillips, 2011). Understanding how and where demand emerges and feeds into MS is critical for the development of agile and appropriate responses to the changing as well as newly emerging drivers of MS, and the changing face of the individuals, groups, and organisations that commercialise and exploit vulnerable people (LeBaron, Howard, Thibos, & Kyritsis, 2018). However, modern slavery is fundamentally gendered, in terms of the sectors themselves that attract women or men in greater numbers (e.g. there are arguably more women in the poor working conditions of the garment sector, and more women and girls are sexually exploited, but more men are in bonded overseas labour work). Gender also determines what might motivate an individual to move into risky work. ILO-IPEC (2005) reported in early 2000 that girls and young women in the Greater Mekong

Sub-region were attracted to work (which turned out to be commercial sexual exploitation) in towns, as much because of lifestyle opportunities as livelihood opportunities (ILO-IPEC, 2005). This was also shown to some degree in the research of Bradley and Sahariah (2019) looking at the motivations of women in Nepal's informal entertainment sector. Incomes can be higher in occupations that are inherently risky. For women this income can offer a route into greater control and financial empowerment. However, earning an income for many women and girls can come at a cost. Increased exposure to different and multiple forms of violence is a reality for most.

While not an exhaustive list, the UN Office of the High Commissioner for Human Rights (OHCHR) has identified over 90 UN Agencies, Programmes, NGOs, and Foundations working on MS at the global level (OHCHR, 2019). In addition, the End Slavery Now directory, which includes contact details for various national and international actors in the campaign against slavery, lists over 1,000 organisations (ESN, 2019). The INGOs and foundations that have an influence on the modern slavery agenda, at the global level, can be divided into three main categories:

1   those that have a broad focus, part of which involves anti-slavery activities;
2   those that focus on modern slavery, in general; and
3   those that focus only on a particular aspect of modern slavery such as how it affects women or children, or how it relates to labour and migration.

Here, we give an overview of organisations with specific focus on modern slavery, or aspects of it. In general, these organisations work in both the advocacy and implementation fields.

Among the largest of the many organisations with MS-focused activities are Amnesty International, Human Rights Watch, Save the Children, and ILO-IPEC. But there are also many organisations working at the international level that focus specifically on slavery, or on practices that constitute slavery, such as forced labour. The following three examples are organisations that conduct different activities, but all are highly influential: the Walk Free Foundation is part of the Minderoo Foundation. It seeks to contribute to ending MS *'by integrating world class research with direct engagement with some of the world's most influential government, business and religious leaders'*. It is best known for its leading role in developing the Global Slavery Index (GSI), which has become the most often cited source for data on the scope and scale of MS, and on global prevention efforts. Anti-slavery International is the world's oldest human rights organisation. Since it was established in 1839, its focus on slavery has remained consistent, but it has evolved along with the changing landscape of slavery advocacy. Polaris Project is less well-known globally and operates primarily in the USA. It is becoming an influential organisation at the global level in the fight against MS, in part because its work acknowledges that MS is not an issue that is confined to the Global South.

A number of organisations that focus on labour at the international level do significant work relating to modern slavery. These include the ILO, The International Labor Rights Fund, and the Global Workers' Justice Alliance. There are many organisations at the national level conducting a variety of activities relating to modern slavery. In the UK, for example, organisations doing similar work include the Trades Union Congress, Alliance 8.7, and ECPAT International (formerly 'End Child Prostitution and Trafficking'). There are also organisations that address slavery, and particularly trafficking, from a gendered perspective, including the Coalition Against Trafficking in Women (CATW) and the Global Alliance Against Traffic in Women (GAATW).[1]

Many multi-national corporations exert an influence over the global political economy of modern slavery. In recent years, a number of specialist organisations have emerged in the private sector. These operate at the international level with the aim of addressing modern slavery, particularly regarding international supply chains and transparency. Examples of collaborative private sector projects on modern slavery include the Ethical Trading Initiative (ETI), the Thomson Reuters Foundation (TRF), and the Mekong Club. Over the last two decades, the issue of fair labour has gained importance for businesses working in developed markets. Increased Corporate Social responsibility (CSR) led, for example, to the end of child labour in the Pakistan football-stitching industry, reduction in child labour in the Bangladesh garment factories, and development of participatory supplier audits by Levi-Strauss and Marks and Spencer.

Despite these organisations spanning the public, civil society, and commercial sectors, the different forms of violence that emanate from conditions of extreme exploitation are not centrally embedded into approaches to end modern slavery. Yet, personal narratives of those working in modern slavery conditions testify to multiple experiences of violence, with young women and girls suffering the most extreme forms.

Turning now to explore the link between VAWG and modern slavery, we review the situation for women in the RMG sector and the commercial sex industry in Bangladesh and India. Before going further into the analysis of how and why violence intersects with modern slavery, we first summarise what is known about the size of RMG and CSE sectors in the two countries.

The RMG sectors of India and Bangladesh

The textile industry is a major employer in India. According to the Annual Survey of Industries (2016–2018), during the financial year 2016–2017, the textile and wearing apparel sector accounted for 18.1% of all employment in the manufacturing sector. The Indian textile industry in 2019 was estimated to be worth US$ 250 billion; in 2017–2018, the sector contributed 2% to the GDP of India and employed more than 45 million people (IBEF, 2019). In India, and arguably also Bangladesh, liberal economic policies and conservative governments are driving growth in the RMG sector, particularly the informal side of the industry.

In India, the areas of most growth align with the places where large populations of workers reside (e.g. in Bihar). New manufacturing hubs, less visible to global civil society, are emerging where working conditions are poor, and smaller units are now also beginning to emerge in areas where large factories operate. These offer women who have children more flexibility in their working hours, but they pay much less. Conditions here are even worse than elsewhere, and the flexibility they offer is by no means an alternative to better maternity rights and child-care provision (information gathered during fieldwork in India in November 2019).

In Bangladesh, more than 2.2 million women work in the RMG (woven and knit) sector, making it the largest employer of women in the country (Akter, Chhetri, & Rahman, 2019). However, female participation in the RMG sector is decreasing due to the automation of manufacturing. According to data from the Centre for Policy Dialogue, female participation in the RMG sector fell from 64% to 60.8% between 2015 and 2018 (Uddin, 2018). Over 50% of workers in the sector fall outside of direct labour monitoring, and almost 90% of the female work force are sewing operators and helpers (Alam, 2011). Male employees tend to occupy the better paid management and supervisory positions.

CSE in India and Bangladesh

Turning now to commercial sexual exploitation in both countries – while we know that many forms of sex work have traditionally existed in India and Bangladesh, we know relatively little about the day to day lives of those who work in the sector (see Becker et al., 2014). Although male sex workers exist, women and children make up the vast majority of workers in this sector (Bagley, Kadri, Shahnaz, Simkhada, & King, 2017; Shoji & Tsubota, 2018). In terms of record keeping on the number of people caught in cycles of sexual exploitation, in India in 2016 the National Crime Bureau recorded a total of 96,900 cases. Also, in 2016, the Ministry of Women and Child Development reported that 88,908 children were referred to organisations and agencies for support. In India in 2014, according to Becker et al. (2014), 868,000 women were involved in sex work in India and 50,000 children had been trafficked into India from neighbouring countries. In Bangladesh, there are 1.7 million children engaged in labour (BBS, 2013, p. 34). The UN Children's Fund (UNICEF) estimated in 2004 that 10,000 underage girls were sexually exploited for commercial purposes in the country, but other estimates placed the figure as high as 29,000. UNICEF also highlighted that an estimated 1 million street children are at high risk of sexual exploitation (Jackman, 2013). Sex work can also be linked to migration. For example, after eviction from Tanbazar (Narayanganj) brothels, many sex workers migrated to Dhaka and Chattogram city. Some 3,500 sex workers are living in brothels located in Mymensingh, Bagerhat, Jessore, Patuakhali, Faridpur, Jamalpur, Mongla, Daulatdia, and Tangail. Different sources have estimated that there are as many as 150,000 sex workers in Bangladesh (NSWP, 2014).

Legal provisions in India and Bangladesh

India

In terms of legal and institutional provision and support for workers in these sectors, India has a dedicated ministry for textiles and, in the year 2000, launched a National Textile Policy. Another act that seeks to protect workers, including in the RMG sector, is the *Sexual Harassment of Women at Workplace (Prevention, Prohibition and Redressal) Act 2013*. The Act stipulates that employers should form an 'Internal Complaints Committee' to review all complaints of sexual harassment. This Act does not, however, cover home-based workers and has come under much criticism from civil society for being too weak to make a difference to the rights of female workers. The internal committees are also thought to be ineffective. Furthermore, while the government has passed the Act, there are no mechanisms in place to monitor its implementation, and there is no data available on the number (or percentage) of industrial employers that have complied with the Act. Surveys carried out by different CSOs report that very few women in the workplace are aware of the Internal Complaints Committee within their employing organisation, and most have never been through any training or orientation programme on sexual harassment in the workplace (which are the two main components of the Act). In fact, studies on the garment industry reported that the majority of factories in and around Bangalore have no functioning grievance mechanism or Internal Complaints Committee. Somewhat unsurprisingly, given the lack of access to or knowledge of such mechanisms, 82% of female workers who have faced sexual violence did not report it. Similar findings were reported by the Indian National Bar Association who surveyed 6,000 employees, including those from Gurgaon, Delhi, Kolkata, and Noida in 2016. Around 67% of those who had brought a case to the ICC reported that it had not dealt with their complaint fairly (INBA, 2018). The Ministry of Women and Child Development has reported an increase in the number of cases filed under the Act, but this still only amounts to 570 cases in 2017, an increase from 371 in 2014.

In addition to this Act, there are other provisions that support working women: these include the Indian Penal Code 1860, Indecent Representation of Women (Prohibition) Act, the Protection of Children from Sexual Offences (POCSO) Act 2012, and the Information Technology Act 2000. The Juvenile Justice Act (popularly known as the JJ Act) was also passed in the year 2000 and was amended in 2015. This was a progressive law that differentiated between children in need of care and protection (essentially victims, including victims of sexual violence) and children in conflict with the law (essentially those who have committed a crime). The law made separate provisions for managing cases of children in these two categories through the Child Welfare Committees (for children in need of care and protection) and the Juvenile Justice Board (for children in conflict with law). The JJ Act had a broader mandate to intervene in all child-related issues, including sexual violence against children, child marriage, child labour, and other violations of child rights.

In 2012, the Government of India felt the need for a separate law for prevention of sexual offences against children and passed the POCSO Act. This made provisions for setting up special POCSO courts to provide free and supportive environment for child victims of sexual violence and made special provisions for punishments of perpetrators under law. POCSO was recently amended to include the death penalty for sexual offenders against children below 12 years of age. In 2006, the Government also declared marrying a child below 18 years of age as illegal by passing the Child Marriage Prohibition Act. This act was also amended in 2016. The law mandates strict punishments for the person marrying a child with imprisonment and a heavy fine, and it also gives the court powers to declare any child marriage as null and void.

The overarching policy framework for promotion of children's rights in India, as laid out in the National Policy for Children, 2013, is considered by government officials to be highly progressive and it incorporates many of the rights and protections guaranteed under the Constitution of India and the UNCRC. The Integrated Child Protection Scheme (ICPS) of the Government of India is a centrally sponsored scheme aimed at building a protective environment for children in difficult circumstances, as well as other vulnerable children, through Government-Civil Society partnership. It is mandatory for a Child Protection Committee (CPC) to exist in each village. However, a 2017 study by Plan reported that only 17% of the households in nine states were aware of the existence of a CPC in their village, which is perhaps indicative of a gap between policy and practice.

Bangladesh

In Bangladesh, government authorities, including local authorities, BGMEA (Bangladesh Garment Manufacturers Association), BKMEA (Bangladesh Knitwear Manufacturers Association), and stakeholders at the national and international levels, with the involvement of organisations such as the Industrial All Global Union and Clean Clothes Campaign, took bold steps to strengthen occupational safety and health, labour inspection services, skills training, and rehabilitation services. Notably, this long-term plan was supported by the ILO and by global buyers. Action has also been taken to implement a national employment injury scheme.

The following acts and policies cover the RMG sector: The Labour Act 2006, Bangladesh Labour Policy 2012, Bangladesh Labour Rules 2015, and the Health and Safety Policy. According to a Department of Inspection for Factories and Establishments (DIFE) report, 422 factories put in place 50% of the recommended measures in accordance with the Corrective Action Plan (CAPS) and 111 factories put in place 80% of the measure. According to factory reports submitted to DIFE, 29% of recommendations made by CAPS in relation to structural safety, 31% related to electrical safety, and 27% related to fire safety, have been addressed. The government is working with the formal RMG sector bodies – BGMEA and BKMEA – and in factories that are part of the alliance conditions have been noted to have improved.

The government of Bangladesh amended the Labour Law 2006 in July 2013, making it more favourable to ensuring workers' rights, including the right to freedom of association and collective bargaining. In 2017, a new body was formed, the Remediation Coordination Cell (RCC) under DIFE of the Ministry of Labour and Employment (MoLE) with a view to overseeing progress with implementing measures in factories. The number of trade unions in garment factories has increased significantly in recent years, and DIFE has recently launched a free helpline so that workers can register complaints (Uddin, 2018).

The definition of working children and child labour is based on the principles adopted in the Bangladesh Labour Act 2006 (amended in 2013). There is also a National Children Policy 2011 and Children Act 2013. The legal age of employment in Bangladesh is 14, but 12- and 13-year-old children may be engaged in 'light work'. The definition of light work is vague, meaning children under 14 can easily be exploited. In July 2018, the government adopted a National Action Plan to end Child Marriage (2018–2030). The Government passed the Child Marriage Restraint Rules 2018 – instead of banning child marriage it provides rules outlining how it should be performed. The suppression of Violence against Women and Children Act (2000) makes the trafficking of women and children illegal.

Civil society

A key issue in India and Bangladesh is that the prevalence of modern slavery is high while the relative size of the civil society sector, and the capacity of government agencies working on the issue, is very small. In the RMG sector in India, there are two types of CSO: those that work outside of the factory setting and those inside, which actively engage with management. There are many more organisations working outside of factories than there are focusing on bringing change directly by working inside. In Bangladesh, according to the Manusher Jonno Foundation (MJF), there are 32 Federations working in RMG and more than 500 trade unions active at the factory level. Some UN agencies (including ILO, UNICEF, UNFPA), INGOs, and NGOs have been working to address other issues relating to the RMG sector, such as migration and domestic sexual harassment of child workers. In India, organisations exist that provide rehabilitation services but do not campaign specifically on child sexual exploitation. That said, almost all international agencies, including the UN agencies (particularly UNICEF and UN Women), have child rights agendas that include addressing commercial sexual exploitation. In Bangladesh, the Sex Workers Network (SWN) is a platform to raise the voices of sex workers who are campaigning against violence, discrimination, exploitation, and stigmatisation. According to the sex workers' rights organisation PIACT, there are only around 3,200–4,000 sex workers based in brothels who are members of the network, while 100,000 street or hotel workers possess no registration certificate and are therefore not able to access support.

Enforcement of laws and regulations

Legal labour standards have certainly improved in India and Bangladesh, but there has been a lack of commitment in applying them. In India, there is poor enforcement (Connor & Delaney, 2016), and in Bangladesh, this is further compounded by a particularly severe lack of resources combined with high levels of corruption (Brunn & Scherf, 2017). The ILO has acknowledged that there is a need to shift beyond the state and recognise that the private sector is a major contributor to addressing modern slavery (Delaney & Tate, 2015). There is also a lack of understanding that the RMG is divided between a formal and an informal sector, across which working conditions vary enormously. While Tier 1 factories are showing positive signs of adhering to protective legislation in both countries, growth of the sector is reliant on subcontracting to informal factories that do not need to comply. Informal factories are emerging in various forms and locations. They recruit cheap, vulnerable labour in specific parts of the country or are able to retain female workers after childbirth and marriage, even if conditions are poor, by exploiting their need for more flexible working. There is no effective legislation to protect these women. The realities of how the industry is growing in these contexts and the often-stark differences between the formal and informal sectors make the mainstreaming of both VAWG and intersectionality critical.

There is also a significant international aspect to modern slavery, which adds to the complexity of enforcing national level legislation. For example, because India and Bangladesh share a border, they have a shared responsibility to manage modern slavery; the increase in child sex trafficking across the West Bengal border between Bangladesh and India is one area with an extremely urgent need for better collaboration. There is a clear link between sex work and migration, particularly with regard to human trafficking, and both have also been linked to the RMG industry. The extent of this link is demonstrated by prevalent assumption in Bangladesh that female RMG workers are also sex workers (Jewkes, Naved, Rahman, Willan, & Gibbs, 2018). In India, 90% of the trafficking of sex workers happens domestically while only 10% is across international borders. This occurs most often when women are promised economic or marital opportunities (Pandey, 2016). The sex industry is driven by consumer demand, and aside from more research being needed, at the level of practice there is a need to focus on ending poverty and changing social norms relating to the rights and dignity of women and girls (Bagley, Kadri, Shahnaz, Simkhada, & King, 2017). Another study in Bangladesh showed that natural disasters can increase the likelihood of children being trafficked for sex (this highlights yet another intersectional element of VAWG in relation to humanitarian emergencies as discussed in Chapters 4 and 5), meaning that provision of emergency relief and climate resilience programmes can also help protect children from trafficking (Shoji & Tsubota, 2018). Chambers (pers. comm.) has highlighted the seasonal vulnerabilities faced by women and children. In Bangladesh, the 'youth bulge' has also driven an increase in the migration of children, and a corresponding increase in vulnerability to related forms of MS.

Intersections of culture, VAWG, and modern slavery

To understand the causes of high prevalence rates of enslaved women and children, it is also necessary to analyse the gendered norms underpinning these realities. Child marriage is prevalent in both India and Bangladesh, and the practice is linked to poverty and son preference. Girls are given as brides or are sold into slavery from a young age in order to reduce the economic burden on their families. Sons, on the other hand, are prised, not least because of the dowry value they represent (see Bradley, Tomalin, & Subramaniam, 2011). Attempts to introduce legal mechanisms to reverse trends in child marriage hit challenges due to the deeply entrenched cultural and religious views that girl children are less valuable. This view can be seen across levels of society in both countries (Bradley, Tomalin, & Subramaniam, 2011) and generates further barriers to overturning gendered inequalities. The 2011 Indian census reported that 2.2% of children (aged 10–14 years) were married. The proportion was higher for girls (2.86%) compared with boys (1.59%) (Singh, 2017).

In India, there is another specific form of modern slavery child marriage known as 'religious slavery', whereby girls marry a god and become slaves to the temple. This often involves sexual slavery (Androff, 2011) with religious personnel and/or devotees. This is a clear and pertinent example of the intersecting relationship between religion, culture, gender, and poverty, and the overlapping risks of forced marriage, trafficking, and sexual slavery. The extent of the inequalities faced by girls, particularly those born into poor families, highlights the need for activities to be driven by a feminist and rights-based approach. Structural inequalities are not just gendered but are also shaped by caste, class, religion, and ethnicity. In Bangladesh, forced begging by children is rife, for which an estimated 5,000 children per year are abducted, maimed, and forced to beg by 'mafias' and those in positions of power (Helal & Kabit, 2013)

In the RMG sector of India, there is a practice known as 'Sumangali', whereby girls are held captive in hostels while they work in the factory and are not allowed to leave without the permission of the contractor or employer. Girls are also particularly vulnerable to different forms of violence inside factories, at the hands of both male managers and supervisors and their male peers. Fear of violence while travelling to and from work has been recorded in recent research (see, e.g., Bradley, 2020) and young women report that this has a significant and detrimental impact on their well-being and mental health. A 2016 report by Sisters for Change (a UK-based INGO) found that over 60% of the Indian female garment workers interviewed had been intimidated or threatened with violence, and one in seven women had been raped or forced to commit sexual acts. The study goes on to report that only 3.6% of the violence cases resulted in any action being taken by the factories or police). Even within the broad group of 'women and girls' in India, some are, of course, for more vulnerable than others; research that focuses on the impact of the caste system, for example, reveals the extent to which children born into the Dalit groups will suffer the most extreme forms of prejudice and abuse (Children on the Edge, n.d.).

182 How to mainstream VAWG across sectors

Clearly, those caught up in modern slavery in these sectors are highly vulnerable to multiple abuses. However, provision that are in place to address this, both legally and in various forms of advocacy and support, does not necessarily take a holistic approach that understands intersecting vulnerabilities, nor do they challenge the structural drivers of modern slavery effectively.

We argue that by taking a VAWG mainstreaming approach to ending modern slavery opportunities to lift barriers to change could be maximised. So, what would a VAWG mainstreaming approach in modern slavery programming look like? Below we set this out using the same adapted ecology model, which was first introduced in Chapter 2 and applied above to mainstreaming VAWG in the energy sector (Table 8.2).

Conclusion

This chapter set out to provide two concrete examples of how VAWG intersects with other development sectors, sustainable energy and modern slavery, and to demonstrate how embedding a VAWG mainstreaming lens could help to maximise opportunities to challenge, and ultimately end, forms of violence. The chapter looks at how and where the goal of ending VAWG overlaps with the concerns of energy and modern slavery programming. In doing so we identify certain entry points where a more sensitised VAWG approach could make a difference in reducing insecurity and risks that lead to VAWG, or to women and girls living in fear of it.

The adapted ecology model offers a practical straightforward approach, prompting reflection at different levels, which, in turn, encourages development practitioners to question how VAWG may emerge. It then asks how interventions might be tweaked or added in order to do more to specifically end the most common forms of violence that women fear (e.g. rape during firewood collection or in darkness due to poor lighting, work-based harassment, increases in IPV, sexual violence while travelling home after long and late shifts, or child abuse as a result of trafficking). The approach is intended to focus the attention of practitioners on the specific types of violence that intersect most often with the sector focus, and it offers pause points in terms of asking if more can be done within the programme to end VAWG. If it becomes common and expected that policy makers and practitioners will include in their approach considerations of how VAWG might be challenged across sectors, the movement to end it will undoubtedly grow. The country studies offered in this chapter – India and Bangladesh – highlight how even within sectors (in this instance, modern slavery), many other factors relating to culture and religion also mean that some women and girls are more at risk than others. This must also be taken into consideration if programming is to ensure that no one (especially those most vulnerable to VAWG) is left behind.

TABLE 8.2 Applying the ecological model to modern slavery contexts

Social ecology level	Meta-question	Factors to think about for operationalisation
Socio-cultural	In what ways are modern slavery activities gendered? Does gender determine which modern slavery groups are more or less vulnerable to violence? E.g. young girls in the garment sector more likely to be sexually harassed?	In addition to advocacy to reduce modern slavery can mechanisms be put in place to specifically respond to those groups most likely to experience forms of violence either in the workplace or at home or travelling to and from? Can greater space be created for women and girls to share experiences of violence? And in doing so can more be done to support them? And build awareness particularly among employers?
Community	What community mechanisms exist to mitigate VAWG or offer security and protection to victims vulnerable to modern slavery related violence such sexual exploitation? Violence in the workplace and in travelling to and from work and also while in hostels?	How effective are the community mechanisms perceived to be and could they be built upon by the programme? Shaped specifically to challenge violence triggered by modern slavery?
Household	What dynamics exist at household level that may support or perpetuate VAWG?	Are there certain intra-/inter-household behaviours that need to be challenged by the programme (e.g. the devaluing of a girl child leading to child marriage?) Is there opportunity to use the programme to tap into certain change dynamics (e.g. is there evidence that young educated women challenge their parents about the use of violence?). Can they be supported by the programme?
Individual	What room is there for individuals to challenge and change social norms surrounding the violence occurring in relation to modern slavery? E.g. do women recognise links between vulnerability to violence and modern slavery-related activities?	Are there individuals within modern slavery sectors who have leadership qualities and who recognise increased vulnerabilities to VAWG can they be supported in tapping into wider networks and structures to mobilise the change they want to see? If the answer is yes can the programme build on them? If it is no can the programme in fact build them?

184 How to mainstream VAWG across sectors

Note

1 United Nations Office on Drugs and Crime (UNODC); The UN Voluntary Trust Fund; United Nations Children's Fund (UNICEF), International Organization for Migration (IOM), The Inter-Agency Coordination Group against Trafficking in Persons (ICAT).

References

Abdelnour, S. A. (2010). Fuel-efficient stoves for Darfur: The social construction of Subsistence marketplaces in post-conflict settings. *Journal of Business Research, 63*(6), 617–629. https://doi.org/10.1016/j.jbusres.2009.04.027

Akter, N., Chhetri, P., & Rahman, S. (2019). Understanding the usage patterns, practices and decision process of third party logistics outsourcing in Bangladesh. *Journal of Global Operations and Strategic Sourcing, 12*(3), 328–354. https://doi.org/10.1108/JGOSS-08-2018-0027

Alam, K. (2011). *Stitched Up: Women Workers in the Bangladeshi Garment Sector.* War on Want. https://waronwant.org/sites/default/files/Stitched%20Up.pdf

Androff, D. (2011). The problem of contemporary slavery: An international human rights challenge for social work. *International Social Work, 54*(2), 209–222. https://doi.org/10.1177/0020872810368395

Bagley, C., Kadri, S., Shahnaz, A., Simkhada, P., & King, K. (2017). Commercialised sexual exploitation of children, adolescents and women: Health and social structure in Bangladesh. *Advances in Applied Sociology, 7*(04), 137–150. https://doi.org/10.4236/aasoci.2017.74008

BBS. (2013). *Child Labor Survey 2013.* Bangladesh Bureau of Statistics. https://www.ilo.org/ipec/Informationresources/WCMS_IPEC_PUB_28175/lang--en/index.htm

Becker, M. L., McClarty, L. M., Bhattacharjee, P., Blanchard, J. F., Lorway, R. R., Ramanaik, S., Mishra, S., Isac, S., Ramesh, B. M., Washington, R., & Moses, S. (2014). Circumstances, experiences and processes surrounding women's entry into sex work in India. *Culture, Health & Sexuality, 16*(2), 149–163. https://doi.org/10.1080/13691058.2013.845692

Bradley, T., & Liakos, K. (2019). Vulnerability of women and girls in refugee settings: Considerations for energy programming. In O. Grafham (Ed.). *Energy Access and Forced Migration.* Routledge. https://doi.org/10.4324/9781351006941

Bradley, T., & Sahariah, S. (2019). Tales of suffering and strength: Women's experiences of working in Nepal's informal entertainment industry. *International Journal of Gender Studies in Developing Societies, 3*(1), 20–36. https://doi.org/10.1504/IJGSDS.2019.096758

Bradley, T. (2020). *Global Perspectives on Violence against Women and Girls.* London: Zed Press.

Bradley, T., Tomalin, E., & Subramaniam, M. (2011). *Dowry: Bridging the Gap between Theory and Practice.* Zed Press. www.zedbooks.net/shop/book/dowry/

Brunn, C., & Scherf, C. S. (2017). *Case Study on the Governance of Labour Standards in Bangladesh's Garment Industry* (Working Paper 4/2017). Oeko-Institut. https://www.oeko.de/fileadmin/oekodoc/WP-GV-Case-Study-Garment.pdf

CASA Consulting. (2001). *Evaluation of the Dadaab Firewood Project, Kenya.* CASA Consulting. https://www.alnap.org/help-library/evaluation-of-the-dadaab-firewood-project-kenya

Children on the Edge. (n.d.). *The Edge in India: Caste Discrimination in India is Trapping Dalit Communities in a Cycle of Poverty and Exclusion.* Children on the Edge. https://www.childrenontheedge.org/india-education-for-untouchable-dalit-children.html

Connor, T., & Delaney, A. (2016). *Forced Labour in the Textile and Garment Sector in Tamil Nadu, South India: Strategies for Redress* (Non-Judicial Redress Mechanisms Report Series, 13). Corporate Accountability Research. http://www.indianet.nl/pdf/ForcedLabourTextileGarment.pdf

Delaney, A., & Tate, J. (2015). Forced labour and ethical trade in the Indian garment industry. In G. Craig, H. Lewis, & L. Waite (Eds.). *Vulnerability, Exploitation and Migrants* (pp. 244–255). Palgrave Macmillan. https://doi.org/10.1057/9781137460417

DFID. (2014). Review of Non-food Items that Meet the Needs of Women and Girls (June 2014). https://assets.publishing.service.gov.uk/media/57a089a6e5274a27b20001cf/hdq1107.pdf

ESN. (2019). *Trafficking in Persons Report, June 2019*. United States of America Department of State. https://www.endslaverynow.org/act/action-library/download-the-2019-trafficking-in-persons-tip-report

GACC. (2016). *Statement from the Global Alliance for Clean Cookstoves on Malawi Cookstove Study in Lancet*. Global Alliance for Clean Cookstoves. https://www.cleancookingalliance.org/about/news/12-07-2016-statement-from-the-global-alliance-for-clean-cookstoves-on-malawi-cookstove-study-in-lancet.html

GSI. (2018). *Global Slavery Index, 2018*. Walk Free and the Minderoo Foundation. https://www.globalslaveryindex.org/resources/downloads/

Gunning, R. (2014). *The Current State of Sustainable Energy Provision for Displaced Populations: An Analysis* (Research Paper Energy, Environment and Resources December 2014). Chatham House. http://large.stanford.edu/courses/2015/ph240/masri2/docs/gunning.pdf

Helal, A., & Kabit, K. (2013). Exploring the Cruel Business of Begging: The Case of Bangladesh. *Asian Journal of Business and Economics, 3*(3.1).

IBEF. (2019). *Annual Report*. Indian Brand Equity Forum. https://www.ibef.org/annual-report.aspx

ILO & Walk Free. (2017). *Global Estimates of Modern Slavery: Forced Labour and Forced Marriage*. International Labour Organisation and the Walk Free Foundation. https://www.ilo.org/global/publications/books/WCMS_575479/lang--en/index.htm

ILO-IPEC. (2015). *Making History People Power and Participation Mekong Children's Forum on Trafficking*. International Labour Organisation - International Programme on the Elimination of Child Labour. https://www.ilo.org/ipec/Informationresources/WCMS_IPEC_PUB_1304/lang--en/index.htm

INBA. (2018). *Sexual Harassment at Workplace* (Report). Indian Bar Association. https://www.indianbarassociation.org/wp-content/uploads/2017/07/Garima-1INBAs-Book.pdf

IOM. (2011). *MRF Nairobi Bulletin, 5*(11). www.iom.int/jahia/webdav/shared/shared/mainsite/activities/countries/docs/kenya/MRF-Nairobi-Newsletter-May-2011.pdf

IRC. (2014). *Lighting the Way: The Role of Handheld Solar Lamps in Improving Women's and Girl's Perceptions of Safety in Two Camps for Internally Displaced People in Haiti*. International Rescue Committee. http://www.safefuelandenergy.org/files/IRC%20Haiti-Solar-Light-Evaluation-Research-Brief.pdf

Jackman, C. (2013, October 26). Daughters of the brothel. *The Sydney Morning Herald* [online]. https://www.smh.com.au/world/daughters-of-the-brothel-20131021-2vvll.html

Jewkes, R., Naved, R., Rahman, T., Willan, S., & Gibbs, A. (2018). Female garment workers' experiences of violence in their homes and workplaces in Bangladesh: A qualitative study. *Social Science & Medicine, 196*, 150–157. https://doi.org/10.1016/j.socscimed.2017.11.040

Kumar, A. (2014). Interwoven threads: Building a labour countermovement in Bangalore's export-oriented garment industry. *City, 18*(6), 789–807. https://doi.org/10.1080/13604813.2014.962894

Lahn, G., & Grafham, O. (2015). *Heat, Light and Power for Refugees Saving Lives, Reducing Costs*. London: Chatham House. https://www.chathamhouse.org/2015/11/heat-light-and-power-refugees-saving-lives-reducing-costs

LeBaron, G., Howard, N., Thibos, C., & Kyristis, P. (2018). *Confronting Root Causes: Forced Labour in Global Supply Chains*. Open Democracy. https://www.opendemocracy.net/en/beyond-trafficking-and-slavery/confronting-root-causes/

Mercy Corps. (2010, April 23). *In Congo, Saving Trees and Lives*. Mercycorps. www.mercycorps.org/articles/dr-congo/congo-saving-trees-and-lives

NSWP. (2014). *Bangladesh*. Global Network of Sex Work Projects. https://www.nswp.org/country/bangladesh

OHCHR. (2019). *Annual Report 2019: Human Rights-Based Actions Bring Tangible Results*. United Nations Office of the High Commissioner for Human Rights. https://www.ohchr.org/EN/NewsEvents/Pages/Annual-Report-2019.aspx

Pandey, M. (2016). Sex slavery in India: Unpacking the stories of trafficking victims. *Sociology Study, 6*(10), 629–638. https://doi.org/10.17265/2159-5526/2016.10.002

Parke, A., & Fraser, E. (2015). *VAWG and Energy in Camp-Based Settings* (VAWG Helpdesk Research Report No. 94). VAWG Helpdesk. https://www.sddirect.org.uk/media/1197/vawg-helpdesk-report-94-camp-based-settings-vawg-and-energy.pdf

Perkins, S. (2015). *Lighting Impacts SGBV But Not in the Way You Think*. UNHCR. https://www.unhcr.org/innovation/light-impacts-sgbv-but-not-in-the-way-you-think/

Phillips, N. (2011). *Unfree Labour and Adverse Incorporation in Global Production Networks: Comparative Perspectives on Brazil and India* (Working Paper No. 176). Chronic Poverty Research Centre. https://www.files.ethz.ch/isn/133462/176%20Phillips.pdf

Serrato, B. C. (2014). *Refugee Perceptions Study Za'atari Camp and Host Communities in Jordan*. Oxfam GB. https://www.oxfam.org/en/research/refugee-perceptions-study-zaatari-camp-and-host-communities-jordan

Shoji, M., & Tsubota, K. (2018). *Sexual Exploitation of Trafficked Children: Evidence from Bangladesh* (Research Institute Working Paper No. 175). JICA Ogata Research Institute. https://www.jica.go.jp/jica-ri/publication/workingpaper/wp_175.html

Singh, A., Kumar, K., Kumar Pathak, P., Kumar Chauhan, R., & Banerjee, A. (2017). La structure spatiale de la fécondité indienne et ses déterminants. *Population, 72*(3), 525–550. https://doi.org/10.3917/popu.1703.0525

Uddin, M. (2018, December 31). Bangladesh RMG: Gains and Pains in 2018. *The Daily Star* [online]. https://www.thedailystar.net/opinion/perspective/news/bangladesh-rmg-gains-and-pains-2018-1680832

UNHCR. (2012). *Light Years Ahead: Innovative Technology for Better Refugee Protection*. UNHCR. https://www.unhcr.org/4c99fa9e6.pdf

WFP. (2013). *WFP SAFE Project in Kenya, Kakuma: Fuel-Efficient Stoves and Gender-Based Violence*. World Food Programme. http://www.safefuelandenergy.org/files/WFP%20SAFE%20Kenya%20Project%20Summary%20Report.pdf

WRC. (2006). *Finding Trees in the Desert: Firewood Collection and Alternatives in Darfur*. Women's Refugee Commission. https://www.refworld.org/docid/48aa82ec0.html

WRC. (2015). *Call to Action on Protection from Gender-based Violence in Emergencies Road Map 2016–2020*. Women's Refugee Commission. www.womensrefugeecommission.org/gbv/resources/1240-callto-action

9

FUNDING FOR VAWG PREVENTION AND RESPONSE

Gaps and opportunities

Introduction

Funding allocations for any type of action addressing VAWG prevention and response are informed by a range of criteria, such as political imperatives, favoured funding modalities, external factors (such as prioritisation among those who hold the purse strings), plus other perceived or actual calls on finite available resources. Much funding for VAWG prevention and response is categorised in aggregate under 'gender equality', and while total sums may appear huge, further examination throws up issues of concern. As the Organisation for Economic Co-operation and Development (OECD) website states:

> Support to programmes specifically dedicated to gender equality and women's empowerment as their principal objective remains consistently low. In 2016–2017, funding for dedicated programmes remained low at 4% and 62% of aid remained gender blind.[1]

This final chapter examines topics considered throughout this volume, addressing the inadequacy of funding dedicated to VAWG prevention and response in both development and humanitarian emergency assistance. We discuss the existing funding modalities, the often enormous challenges involved in identifying and tracking such funding, and the emerging new players in the gender equality and VAWG fields. The chapter ends by considering where next for VAWG funding advocacy.

Funding for gender equality vis-à-vis VAWG prevention and response

While the total global amount for 'gender equality' may seem extremely generous, experts are unanimous that earmarked, dedicated allocations for VAWG prevention and response are extraordinarily inadequate and too often fail

DOI: 10.4324/9780429280603-9

188 Funding for VAWG prevention and response

to reach organisations that might otherwise make notable contributions to such work. It can be extremely difficult to disentangle VAWG-specific funds from the all too broad 'gender equality' marker developed by the OECD-Development Assistance Committee (OECD-DAC).[2]

Two recent studies sought to disaggregate the amounts allocated to VAWG prevention and response. Estimates are based on OECD-DAC members' overall official development assistance (ODA) contributions vis-à-vis sums specifically allocated to gender equality; VAWG prevention funds are calculated as a proportion of those. Just over USD 400 million per annum were allocated between 2014 and 2019 to prevention of VAWG (and, crucially, to wider initiatives too); that translates to less than 0.002% of total ODA (The Equality Institute, 2019). This funding gap/shortfall is seen as a limiting action on VAWG, especially when so few of the available funds reach CSOs in the Global South (Wilton Park, 2019).

When programmes and projects listed under the broad banner of 'gender equality' are examined, many challenges emerge. A recent comprehensive review of initiatives labelled as addressing gender equality objectives identified that achievements were limited, and many opportunities had been wasted. It also underscored the lack of clarity surrounding action on gender and VAWG prevention in particular. The findings suggest that there is a lack of quality (not least because of almost universal failure to apply OECD minimum criteria for gender marking) and mismarking of projects, which results in further challenges in tracking spend vis-à-vis reach and impact (Grabowski & Essick, 2020).

Much remains extremely muddled in terms of gender equality funding (let alone for VAWG work), and the *Gender Financing Project* (Center for Global Development) is seeking to shed light on this. But the fact that donors are not obliged to report and specify spend remains a significant hurdle to clarity, and to evaluation of quality of intervention.

Some current major initiatives supporting VAWG prevention and response[3]

In the multilateral sphere, the **UN Trust Fund**, administered by UN Women, is a major provider of funds. According to the Association for Women's Rights in Development's (AWID) 2019 report, it has disbursed approximately USD 128 million to 462 initiatives across 139 countries and territories since its inception in 1996.

The current largest bilateral donors in terms of funds dedicated to VAWG actions are the UK, the USA, and Australia. A significant programme funded by the UK Government is the *What Works to Prevent Violence Against Women and Girls* programme (What Works: phase I ran between 2016 and early 2020; phase II was scheduled to begin in late 2020).[4] GBP 25 million was allocated to fund research and innovation studies and impact evaluations across the globe. The intention was to provide the most robust possible evidence base and corpus of best practice; this will continue in phase II. *What Works* consists of three components: a global programme, a focus on conflicts and crises (humanitarian emergencies), and assessing the economic costs of VAWG. *What Works* partnered with many different organisations and entities, including university departments and women's rights organisations (WROs) and civil society organisations (CSOs) in both the Global South and Global North, as well as international non-governmental organisations (INGOs) such as the International Rescue Committee (IRC).

The **Spotlight Initiative** was launched in 2017, as a global, six-year partnership between the UN and the European Union (the EU). It places SDGs 5 and 16 at the core of its efforts. Activities are to be transformative, rights-based, and address the underlying causes of VAWG and harmful practices, while targeting social norms. At present, there are 24 country-level programmes under Spotlight. Funding, while significant, is defined as starter capital ('seed money') only, given the extent of the challenge if VAWG is truly to be eliminated.

> The initial €uro 500 million...provided by the European Union will help to target the most prevalent forms of violence - wherever they exist. But if we are really going to call time on gender-based violence – once and for all - then we need all of our partners to act, now.
>
> *(EU & UN, 2018, p. 7)*

Of course, size of fund is not the sole criterion for quality of intervention; small sums, if used for well-targeted, truly accountable, and evidence-based interventions, can provide invaluable lessons, and this learning can be leveraged for scaling up. However, large sums dedicated to VAWG actions can undoubtedly facilitate more wide ranging interventions and achieve more prominence in terms of visibility. Yet even when 'traditional' donors use well-understood funding modalities and channels, access to financial resources too often remains all too challenging for key VAWG prevention and gender equality actors (see AWID, 2019).

Nonetheless, the current significant funding streams and approaches suggest greater opportunity for genuinely local organisations to receive support and to provide evidence of the value of their work. Even so, such sums are invariably dwarfed by overall ODA. For instance, while the total ODA allocations by the Dutch Government for 2017–2018 were USD 5.6 billion, the *Leading from the South* fund, launched in 2017, has had €40 million earmarked to support women's organisations in Africa, the Middle East, Asia and the Pacific, and Latin America and the Caribbean. The funds are managed by regional women's funds, e.g. the Fondo de Mujeres del Sur (O'Donnell, 2020).

While acknowledging such programmes, we must bear in mind the very many, small-scale, modestly (and all too often underfunded) initiatives being undertaken at sub-national level across the world. These rarely receive the same degree of attention as large interventions, unless the smaller projects inform advocacy or link into a bigger programme as an implementing or research partner.

Yet, many such small projects are essential components of VAWG prevention and are often the main or only recourse for survivors and those at risk at community level.

Another factor with significant consequences for VAWG prevention activities is that certain geographical locations appear less prioritised than others. A Pacific region study found that two out of three women in the region will experience violence in their lifetimes – twice the global average. Yet, funding does not reflect need or take full account of local expertise and advocacy action. Less than 1% of funding is currently allocated to women's organisations in the Pacific region (Fiji Women's Fund, 2019).

New players in the field of VAWG prevention and response

Funds for both VAWG prevention and overall gender equality have been increasingly allocated to private-public partnerships (PPPs), to for-profit organisations such as Chemonics and FHI 360 and to INGOs. Such allocations can be at the expense of national and sub-national CSOs, whose internal budgets for advocating for more funds will be limited and for which writing funding proposals to several donor sources may well be challenging.

> Members of the OECD-DAC provided USD 35.5 billion in aid to gender equality in 2014; this was an all-time high. Around 28% - nearly USD 10 billion - went to civil society organisations (CSOs). The majority of this aid supported... INGOs or CSOs based in the donor country. In 2014, 8% of gender focused aid to civil society went directly to CSOs in developing countries. Little was reported as going directly to women's rights organisations... Small amounts of money can stimulate learning and innovation, but they do not enable vital expansion, scale-up and strengthening of organisational and operational capacity.
>
> *(OECD, 2016, p. 4)*

In this arena, funding has increasingly been channelled to PPPs; this approach is now widespread and is often strongly supported by donors, especially international and multilateral institutions such as the OECD, the World Bank, and the UN agencies.

Research has begun to indicate that there exists an imbalance between allocations to 'women's organisations in the developing world' and funds supporting PPPs and INGOs (O'Donnell, 2020).[5] While each type of organisation will no doubt bring specific expertise to bear, there will always be the need (and the ethical imperative) to work with local organisations on issues of VAWG. PPPs are promoted by bilateral donors and international financial institutions, not least as a mechanism to deliver the SDGs. Yet, it can be argued that such support challenges women's rights principles under *Agenda 2030* (Eurodad, GADN, & FEMNET, 2019).

Practitioners and advocates have given critical attention to the types of private organisation entering into PPPs, as well as to the services provided, user fees, robustness of accountability mechanisms, and the overall amounts allocated to the private sector. So far, more has been written about the increasing prevalence of PPPs in the broader 'gender equality' field than in VAWG prevention and response specifically, but general concerns are shared. One example of such concerns is the introduction or expansion of user fees under PPP-managed interventions (health services, for example, such as those supporting VAWG survivors), which may very well reduce access for the poorest, reduce services to the more marginalised, or those who are harder to reach. These and other barriers may have profound and detrimental implications for survivors (see, e.g., Mackintosh et al., 2016; Woodroffe & Meeks, 2019).

> *Public services play a pivotal role in the pursuit of gender equality, and the increasing use of… [PPPs] in their provision has set off alarm bells… critics raise concerns that PPPs will provide poorer quality services and drain governments of resources, with little evidence of the promised efficiency gains beyond those created by user fees or cuts in labour costs….*
>
> [The] *forms of PPPs which have given rise to most controversy are those where private sector companies replace the state as the provider of traditional public services or social infrastructure.*
>
> *(GADN, 2020, pp. 1 & 2)*

One shorthand description sometimes applied to the function of a PPP is 'privatise the profit, socialise the cost' – in other words, users of services as well as governments will ultimately (and it is argued, disproportionally) pay, while profits return to the private partner. There is growing disquiet about whether the PPP modality represents the best approach for something as challenging and multifaceted as VAWG prevention and response.

Research conducted into 'new actors' and 'new money' for women's rights and gender equality found that 170 'corporate sector initiatives' had access to USD 14.6 billion pledged to interventions scheduled to be implemented between 2005 and 2020 to 'support women and girls'. Some 11% of this amount (ca. USD 1.6 billion) is stated to have been targeted at VAWG work. The potential dangers of new players entering the sector are significant. For example, such organisations may not possess adequate understanding of the challenges, complexities, or long-term social norm change required to have a long-term and sustainable impact on VAWG (AWID, 2013).

Inherent in the possibility (and increasingly, reality) of such organisations receiving significant percentages of funding is that national and sub-national WROs, VAWG prevention CSOs, and other smaller scale, less easily visible, and less promoted entities will receive further reduced funding and support. In addition to this, the 2019 report by The Equality Institute questions the quality of many initiatives under the new funding dispensation, with 'simplistic', even 'unethical', initiatives receiving funding.

Using SDG indicator 5.c.1 to increase knowledge on VAWG prevention and response funding?

One potential means of achieving greater clarity on funding flows, objectives achieved, and monies wasted or misspent (overall for gender-focused projects, potentially including specific VAWG prevention initiatives), and to provide information to advocate for more appropriately targeted funding, is to apply the relevant SDG indicator: 5.c.1 (*Proportion of countries with systems to track and make public allocations for gender equality and women's empowerment*). Governments should report against 5.c.1, but to date (2020) only a minority appear to have done so. Despite the lack of reporting so far, the particular importance of 5.c.1 lies in the global acceptance that financing for gender equality is necessary (Elson, 2017). However, it is a general indicator that does not specify tracking of allocations at national and sub-national levels.

Funding for humanitarian emergency assistance

Funding for humanitarian emergency assistance has until recently been based chiefly on multilateral UN and IRC and Red Crescent Movement (RCM) appeals, as well as on single country and private sector and philanthropic entities' responses to specific emergencies. Such funding is intended for emergencies and for protracted humanitarian crises. There is no obligation for any organisation (multilateral, bilateral, private, or any other) to report on humanitarian emergency expenditure to the UN OCHA Financial Tracking Service (OCHA FTS) or to OECD-DAC.

In 2018, international humanitarian funding as reported was USD 28.9 billion, covering all types of response and funding channels on which data are available (Development Initiatives, 2019). Funding from private and philanthropic entities is estimated to be significantly increasing from a modest base, but such funds are difficult to track.

Sources of funding for humanitarian emergency assistance

CERF – the Central Emergency Response Fund – was set up by the UN in 2005. It has two core 'windows': for rapid response and for underfunded emergencies. The CERF website notes that:

> ...since its inception in 2006, 126 UN Member States and observers, as well as regional Governments, corporate donors, foundations and individuals, made it possible for humanitarian partners to deliver over $5.5 billion in life-saving assistance in over 100 countries and territories.

Significant funds can be provided by the organisation: *'As of mid-November 2019, CERF had allocated more than USD 494 million to support urgent needs in 47 countries and territories'* (UN OCHA, 2019b, p. 84).

Country-based Pooled Funds (CBPFs) are multi-donor humanitarian funding mechanisms, established by the UN Emergency Relief Co-ordinator and managed through UN OCHA at country level (UN OCHA, 2017, 2020). Through this, '*Contributions from donors are collected into single, unearmarked funds to support local humanitarian efforts. The 18 CBPFs that were active in 2019 received US$956 million*' (UN OCHA, 2020, p. 1).

The Grand Bargain: at the World Humanitarian Summit (the WHS) in May 2016, 18 donor countries and 16 entities (including the UN and the ICRC) signed a 'Grand Bargain', the core rationale for which appears to be that if all partners become more transparent and accountable as to funds allocated and spent, then delivery should become more efficient (ICVA, 2017; see also Chapter 4).

This initiative is widely acknowledged as a potential game changer for humanitarian response, but the jury remains out regarding its usefulness for VAWG-specific interventions. The IASC hosts the Grand Bargain Secretariat, and as of 2019, there were 61 signatories (24 states, 11 UN Agencies, five inter-governmental organisations and Red Cross movements and 21 NGOs). The Grand Bargain has serious potential for strength and reach: in 2017, 80% of all global humanitarian contributions came from its signatories. It has 51 commitments to improve efficiency and effectiveness in delivering international assistance in humanitarian emergencies.

Signatories to the Grand Bargain commit to annual self-reporting on progress, which is complemented with an annual independent report (Metcalfe-Hough, Fenton, & Poole, 2019; Metcalfe-Hough, Poole, Bailey, & Belanger, 2018). As such, the Grand Bargain is among the more transparent of the international humanitarian funding mechanisms. However, there is no requirement for any entity to report funding and expenditure on humanitarian emergency assistance (indeed, any type of development assistance).

To what extent does the Grand Bargain address VAWG?

The initial declaration, '*The Grand Bargain - a shared commitment to better serve people in need*', makes no reference to VAWG or GBV, and 'gender' receives three superficial mentions. Neither the 2018 nor the 2019 independent report refers to GBV or VAWG. As such, the potential for the Grand Bargain to make VAWG prevention and gender equality in humanitarian emergencies more than an 'optional extra' continues to be debated (see ActionAid UK & CARE International, 2018).

It is unclear if any work is underway to ensure that the Grand Bargain integrates a VAWG focus into funding modalities and requirements. But in light of the weight of evidence on VAWG in humanitarian emergencies (see Chapters 5 and 6), it is clearly unacceptable that a mechanism developed in 2016 does not include any VAWG prevention and response and does not have an overall gender equality focus in its 51 commitments or the original ten work streams. It is a pertinent example of why a VAWG Mainstreaming Framework across development and humanitarian aid sectors is so crucial at this time.

A defence of the Grand Bargain might be that it is primarily a fund-raising mechanism and applies a voluntary, self-reporting approach, seeking to improve the efficiency and effectiveness of humanitarian action. However, the Grand Bargain has lofty intentions and links together many key stakeholders. The lack of attention to VAWG and gender equality represents a grave gap and missed opportunities for focused efficiency, effectiveness, and co-operation in funding streams, programming, implementation, and development of the evidence base.

The **Global Acceleration Instrument** was set up in 2015 (renamed the **Women's Peace and Humanitarian Fund** in 2017). The WPHF is a UN, member state, and civil society pooled funding mechanism designed to be fast, flexible, and responsive in humanitarian emergencies, and supportive of WPS actions. It is stated to be linked to the localisation and the 'humanitarian-development nexus' Grand Bargain work streams. However, few data on its effectiveness are available.

REAP: the Risk-informed Early Action Partnership is a new initiative launched in September 2019. REAP seeks to anticipate and mitigate the impacts of extreme weather and 'climate disasters' (naturally occurring hazards). One billion people could theoretically benefit from REAP. While documentation is to date limited, there appear to be no references to VAWG-specific aspects of extreme weather events or planning for dedicated funding streams. Information is unavailable as to how REAP actions intend to avoid duplication or dilution of funding allocations and flows vis-à-vis CERF and/or the Grand Bargain, for example.

Is funding for VAWG/GBV in humanitarian emergencies adequate?

One estimate is that less than 1% of all funding for humanitarian emergencies worldwide is currently specifically dedicated to 'sexual and gender-based violence prevention and response activities' (UN OCHA, 2019a). It is unclear, however, whether that includes any part of 'unearmarked' funds intended for humanitarian assistance but with a greater flexibility of use. In 2018, 2.6% of all funding for humanitarian emergencies was unearmarked, representing USD 521 million. It is difficult to ascertain how (and indeed, if) this might contribute to tackling VAWG: a major report by Development Initiatives, for example, provides no information on the extent to which any of that 2.6% was in support of VAWG programming and does not once refer to any tracking of dedicated (or indeed unearmarked) funding allocated to VAWG or GBV (Development Initiatives, 2019).

Despite the lack of transparency regarding how funds are spent, the balance of available evidence demonstrates that funding for VAWG programming is not remotely matching need. Existing and new initiatives, renewed commitments, targets, and guidance appear not to have resulted in adequate funding (and actual disbursements, rather than merely pledges). This is despite the very considerable work that has been undertaken to bring to the fore the urgent need to prevent and respond to VAWG.

One significant challenge when attempting to disentangle funding allocations that are dedicated to VAWG-specific interventions in humanitarian emergency situations is that different actors use different words and terms. Thus, 'gender equality' may or may not be an umbrella term that encompasses VAWG prevention and response, and questions also remain regarding what exactly 'GBV' might cover, as well as what such ambiguity might mean in terms of delivery of support (see, e.g., COFEM, 2017).

Tracking allocations

The ways in which funding is channelled and the modalities used will have an impact on what is supported and indeed reported, but close and disaggregated tracking of expenditures on VAWG prevention and response activities in humanitarian emergencies on a global level is not available.

The **IASC Gender Marker** was introduced in 2009; it coded the extent to which humanitarian projects supported gender-equitable access to services. Projects coded as '2b' concentrated specifically on VAWG. The Gender Marker has since been replaced by the **Gender with Age Marker** (GAM), to be applied during design and monitoring of humanitarian interventions (IASC, 2018a, 2018b). GenCap focuses on gender equality for women, girls, men, and boys; to date, it is not clear how much it will separately consider issues of VAWG. It was only in 2016 that GBV funding became a separate sub-cluster area within the UN OCHA FTS. Funds for work on VAWG prevention and response and GBV will presumably remain as programmatic activities under the broader FTS heading of 'protection', health, education, and other sectors – and, therefore, challenging to identify, disaggregate, and track.

The 2018 CERF Annual Review describes the percentage of its funding stream that addresses 'GBV'. The quotation below illustrates that though there has been a somewhat increased commitment, monitoring it is hampered by all too generalised categories that make tracking VAWG-specific funding streams so challenging.

> Gender was systematically mainstreamed across CERF interventions in 2018, with nearly three quarters of all CERF-funded projects (275) indicating strong gender mainstreaming (IASC Gender Marker 2a). A total of 80 projects (21 per cent) were marked 2b indicating a targeted gender action.
>
> *(UN OCHA & CERF, 2019, p. 27)*

COFEM looked at CBPF monies allocated specifically to 'GBV' under the overall banner of 'protection'. It found that GBV interventions (however defined) received at best 30% of funding from the 2014–2016 CBPF funds, which

196 Funding for VAWG prevention and response

translates to a maximum total of 3% overall of CBPF monies (COFEM, 2017). Other reviews similarly found that the extreme shortfall between need and funding continues, with actual amounts and percentages very hard to determine, primarily due to the absence of disaggregated data (ActionAid, IRC, & WRC, 2019; IRC, 2019).

To conclude this section, it is important to note that there are numerous programmes listed under 'gender equality' that include a VAWG component across all development assistance, including humanitarian aid. These components will usually not be separately budgeted and are seldom separately evaluated. Different definitions – including GBV, VAWG, SGBV – and the lack of disaggregated data make it difficult to track funding, expenditures, robustness of data, and crucially any positive impacts on the lives of survivors and those at risk. What is clear, though, is that even with an optimistic analysis of the limited data available, funding to prevent VAWG and to support survivors remains inadequate.

What is to be done – how to allocate funds where they will be best used?

Here, we return to discussing all funding for VAWG, across both development in general and humanitarian emergency assistance.

The core principle of the SDGs is to *Leave no-one behind*, and paragraph 20 of the *2030 Agenda for Sustainable Development*, agreed by all country signatories, makes explicit reference to the elimination of all forms of discrimination and violence against women and girls. This would suggest that greater opportunities currently exist for increased and more effective funding to be allocated to wider gender equality and to more tailored VAWG prevention interventions. Yet, this is not the case.

The need is argued for a 'feminist funding ecosystem': transformational change to funding and disbursement systems, including funding channels, allocations, priorities, favoured partnerships, and other levers of influence and power (AWID, 2019; see also COFEM Tip Sheets and other documentation, e.g. COFEM, 2017; see further the WILPF website). Calls are also increasing for more robust tracking of funds and for greater accountability, i.e. for donors of any description, recipients of funds, and those with oversight of expenditures.

Advocating for VAWG prevention and response funding

There is increasingly targeted advocacy for ring-fenced VAWG prevention funding, but our discussion above highlights how much remains to be done if this is to be achieved. It is sobering that despite decades of work dedicated to informing and educating communities, politicians, and organisations about the urgent need to fund VAWG prevention, sums allocated continue to fall far short. Colossal effort has been invested in increasing awareness of VAWG, in

Funding for VAWG prevention and response **197**

establishing legal provisions that seek to end impunity and immunity of perpetrators, and in pushing for greater and more targeted support. And yet, the extent to which current funding fails to match need is a stark reminder of how much more of this type of advocacy is needed. It also indicates how seemingly low on the priority list VAWG prevention and response actions must be for many donors and implementing organisations, whether funding or working on humanitarian emergency response or on development programmes.

Many questions arise when considering how best to advocate for greater support to VAWG prevention: thus, many activists rightly emphasise that funds should be used to achieve genuinely transformational change, with a clear agenda based on feminist principles and women's rights. Such an agenda will at times be potentially discomforting for some who make financial decisions, which may, in turn, have implications for levels of funding for such work. At the time of writing (2020), only Sweden, Canada, and Mexico have adopted explicitly feminist foreign/development assistance policies (see also Chapter 1); yet, governments that are signatories to CEDAW have committed to transformative work to achieve gender equality.

Constant vigilance against backlash and reactionary attitudes and behaviour is required; such retrogressive steps will inevitably have detrimental impacts on funding. Erosion of women's rights can be seen across the globe, and this worrying trend has only been exacerbated in 2020 and 2021 as a result of the Covid-19 pandemic (as discussed further in the Conclusions of this book).

The new funding landscape, with increased opportunity for PPPs and for-profit implementers, as well as for philanthropic organisations such as The Bill and Melinda Gates Foundation (see, e.g., Girard, 2019), has perhaps reduced opportunities to fund truly transformational initiatives on VAWG prevention and response. Concerns over how best to 'fit' advocacy and proposals to what funders 'want' might weaken messaging and reduce space for truly transformative interventions. Thus, it is necessary to scrutinise how funding decisions are made and how resources are allocated to ensure that donor preferences do not result in reduced opportunities and funding for organisations that seek transformational, feminist solutions to VAWG and gender inequality. Embedding a VAWG Mainstreaming Framework within the decision-making processes of organisations that make funding decisions across development and humanitarian sectors will be a critical tool in preventing this.

Notes

1 The OECD Development Co-operation Directorate: development finance statistics. Available at: http://www.oecd.org/dac/financing-sustainable-development/development-finance-data/

2 The DAC *gender equality policy marker* web page states: 'The marker is a qualitative statistical tool to record development activities that target gender equality as a policy objective. The gender equality policy marker is used by DAC members as part of annual reporting…to the DAC, to indicate for each aid activity whether it targets

gender equality as a policy objective…Some philanthropists, private sector organisations, non-DAC donors and other actors have started monitoring their development activities using the policy marker. The data based on the marker provide a measure of the development finances that DAC members and other actors allocate in support of gender equality' (OECD, 2019).

3 Data for the discussion on funders are drawn from AWID (2013, 2019), Eurodad, GADN, and FEMNET (2019), GADN (2020), O'Donnell (2020), The Equality Institute (2019), Wilton Park (2019), and OECD-DAC web sources, available at: www.oecd.org

4 Both authors of this book have worked on the independent evaluation of phase I of *What Works*. All comments here and elsewhere in the book are solely our own views.

5 O'Donnell's data are from *Aid in Support of Gender Equality and Women's Empowerment: Donor Charts*. Available at: https://www.oecd.org/dac/financing-sustainable-development/development-finance-topics/Aid-to-gender-equality-donor-charts-2019.pdf

References

ActionAid, IRC, & WRC. (2019). *Statement by Action Aid, International Rescue Committee and Women's Refugee Commission at the Ending Sexual Violence in Humanitarian Crisis Conference, Oslo, May 24, 2019*. ActionAid, International Rescue Committee & Women's Refugee Commission. https://reliefweb.int/report/world/statement-action-aid-international-rescue-committee-and-women-s-refugee-commission

ActionAid UK & Care International. (2018). *Not What She Bargained For? Gender and the Grand Bargain*. https://www.actionaid.org.uk/publications/not-what-she-bargained-for

AWID. (2013). *New Actors, New Money, New Conversations: A Mapping of Recent Initiatives for Women and Girls*. Association for Women's Rights in Development. https://www.awid.org/publications/new-actors-new-money-new-conversations

AWID. (2019). *Toward a Feminist Funding Ecosystem*. Association for Women's Rights in Development. https://www.awid.org/publications/toward-feminist-funding-ecosystem-framework-and-practical-guide

COFEM. (2017). *Funding: Whose Priorities? Feminist Perspectives on Addressing Violence against Women and Girls Series* (Paper No. 4.). Coalition of Feminists for Social Change. https://raisingvoices.org/wp-content/uploads/2013/03/Paper-4-COFEM.final_.sept2017.pdf

Development Initiatives. (2019). *Global Humanitarian Assistance Report 2019*. DI Ltd. https://devinit.org/resources/global-humanitarian-assistance-report-2019/

Elson, D. (2017). *Measuring Sustainable Development Goal Indicator 5.c.1. Discussion Paper* (for Expert Group Meeting 27–28 March 2017). UN Women. https://gender-financing.unwomen.org/en/resources/d/i/s/discussion-paper-on-measuring-sustainable-development-goal-indicator-5c1

EU & UN. (2018). *Spotlight Initiative Annual Report July 2017- March 2018*. European Union and United Nations: Spotlight Initiative. https://gender-financing.unwomen.org/en/resources/d/i/s/discussion-paper-on-measuring-sustainable-development-goal-indicator-5c1

Eurodad, GADN, & FEMNET. (2019). *Can Public-Private Partnerships Deliver Gender Equality?* Eurodad, Gender and Development Network and African Women's Development and Communication Network (FEMNET). https://gadnetwork.org/gadn-resources/new-briefing-can-public-private-partnerships-deliver-gender-equality

Fiji Women's Fund. (2019). *Where Is the Money for Women and Girls in Asia and the Pacific? Mapping Funding Gaps, Opportunities and Trends*. Fiji Women's Fund and Urgent

Action Fund for Women's Human Rights, Asia and Pacific. https://www.uafanp.org/ckeditor_assets/attachments/96/Full-report-UAF-FWF-14Feb2020.pdf

GADN. (2020). *The Impact of PPPs on Gender Equality and Women's Rights*. Gender and Development Network. https://gadnetwork.org/gadn-resources/the-impact-of-ppps-on-gender-equality-and-womens-rights

Girard, F. (2019). Philanthropy for the women's movement, not just 'empowerment'. *Stanford Social Innovation Review* (online paper, Autumn 2019). https://ssir.org/articles/entry/philanthropy_for_the_womens_movement_not_just_empowerment

Grabowski, A., & Essick, P. (2020). *Are They Really Gender Equality Projects?* (Oxfam Research Reports) Oxfam. https://doi.org./10.21201/2020.5655

IASC (GenCap). (2018a). *Gender with Age Marker: Overview*. Inter-Agency Standing Committee Gender Standby Capacity Project, Norwegian Refugee Council and UN OCHA. https://fscluster.org/sites/default/files/documents/gam_overview_.pdf

IASC (GenCap). (2018b). *The IASC Gender with Age Marker (GAM)*. Inter-Agency Standing Committee Gender Standby Capacity Project, Norwegian Refugee Council and UN OCHA. https://interagencystandingcommittee.org/other/content/iasc-gender-age-marker-gam-2018

ICVA. (2017). *The Grand Bargain: Everything You Need to Know* (ICVA Briefing Paper, February 2017). International Council of Voluntary Agencies. http://agendaforhumanity.org/sites/default/files/The%20Grand%20Bargain_Everything%20You%20Need%20to%20Know%20(ICVA)_0.pdf

IRC. (2019). *Where Is the Money? How the Humanitarian System Is Failing In Its Commitments to End Violence against Women and Girls*. International Rescue Committee. https://www.rescue.org/report/wheres-money-how-humanitarian-system-failing-fund-end-violence-against-women-and-girls

Mackintosh, M., Channon, A., Karan, A., Selvaraj, S., Cavagnero, E., & Zhao, H. (2016). What is the private sector? Understanding private provision in the health systems of low-income and middle-income countries. *The Lancet, 388*(10044), 596–605. http://doi.org/10.1016/S0140-6736(16)00342-1

Metcalfe-Hough, V., Fenton, W., & Poole, L. (2019). *Grand Bargain Annual Independent Report 2019*. Overseas Development Institute; Humanitarian Policy Group. https://www.odi.org/publications/11387-grand-bargain-annual-independent-report-2019

Metcalfe-Hough, V., Poole, L., Bailey, S., & Belanger, J. (2018). *Grand Bargain Annual Independent Report 2018*. Overseas Development Institute; Humanitarian Policy Group. https://www.odi.org/publications/11135-grand-bargain-annual-independent-report-2018

O'Donnell, M. (2020). *From Principles to Practice: Strengthening Accountability for Gender Equality in International Development* (CGD Note, Jan 2020). Center for Global Development. https://www.cgdev.org/publication/principles-practice-strengthening-accountability-gender-equality-international

OECD. (2016). *Donor Support to Southern Women's Rights Organisations: OECD Findings*. Organisation for Economic Co-Operation and Development Assistance Committee; Network on Gender Equality (GenderNet). https://www.oecd.org/dac/gender-development/donor-support-to-southern-women-s-rights-organisations.htm

OECD. (2019). *DAC Gender Equality Policy Marker*. OECD-DAC. https://www.oecd.org/dac/gender-development/dac-gender-equality-marker.htm

The Equality Institute. (2019). *Global Scoping of Advocacy and Funding for the Prevention of Violence against Women and Girls*. https://www.equalityinstitute.org/projects/global-scoping-of-advocacy

200 Funding for VAWG prevention and response

UN OCHA. (2017). *Operational Handbook for Country-Based Pooled Funds (Version 1.2)*. UN Office for the Co-ordination of Humanitarian Affairs. https://www.unocha.org/sites/unocha/files/Operational_Handbook_for_OCHA_CBPFs_Version1.2.pdf

UN OCHA. (2019a). *Gender-Based Violence: A Closer Look at the Numbers*. UN Office for the Co-ordination of Humanitarian Affairs. https://www.unocha.org/story/gender-based-violence-closer-look-numbers

UN OCHA. (2019b). *Global Humanitarian Overview 2020*. UN Office for the Co-Ordination of Humanitarian Affairs. https://www.unocha.org/sites/unocha/files/GHO-2020_v9.1.pdf

UN OCHA. (2020). *About CBPFs*. UN Office for the Co-ordination of Humanitarian Affairs. https://www.unocha.org/sites/unocha/files/AboutCBPFs_2020_20200107_EN.pdf

UN OCHA & CERF. (2019). *CERF 2018 Annual Report*. UN Office for the Co-Ordination of Humanitarian Affairs and the Central Emergency Response Fund. https://cerf.un.org/document/cerf-2018-annual-report

Wilton Park. (2019). *Building a Shared Agenda on Prevention of Violence against Women and Girls* (WP 1657). Wilton Park, in Partnership with DFID and Wellspring Philanthropic Trust. https://www.wiltonpark.org.uk/wp-content/uploads/WP1657-Report.pdf

Woodroffe, J., & Meeks, J. (2019). *Push No-One Behind: How Current Economic Policy Exacerbates Gender Inequality* (GADN/FEMNET Briefing). The African Women's Development and Communication Network. https://gadnetwork.org/gadn-resources/push-no-one-behind-how-current-economic-policy-exacerbates-gender-equality

CONCLUSION

The Covid-19 pandemic and implications for VAWG prevention and response and gender equality[1]

Here, we discuss some of the potential implications of the Covid-19 pandemic with reference to key themes that resonate throughout this book. There is visible failure to date to take co-ordinated, aligned, and focused action at national and international levels to address VAWG, sexual and reproductive health, and wider gender equality issues – issues that have continued and worsened during the pandemic. This failure exemplifies the lack of will to act among too many key decision-makers. Yet again, VAWG and gender equality are revealed as unimportant for too many of those who have the power to act, despite the deluge of pious words promising action and change (see, e.g., Bhatia, 2020; UN ECOSOC, 2020).

A recent paper by O'Donnell (2020a) sets out the 'pathways' linking the Covid-19 pandemic (as well as earlier pandemics) with VAWG, and an August 2020 article in *The Lancet* has provided data on the impacts on countless women and girls during 2020, as well as pointed out how challenging it will be just to restore previous interventions, let alone build back better. Other analyses have noted the following observations:

- UN Women has described VAWG as the 'shadow pandemic' and increases in such violence have been experienced in every country that has collected data (e.g. in Colombia, a 175% increase has been reported during lockdown);
- UNFPA has estimated that there could be 7 million unintended pregnancies worldwide;
- 9.5 million vulnerable women and girls could have lost access to contraception and safe abortion in 2020, a disruption that could result in as many as 2.7 million unsafe abortions and 11,000 pregnancy-related deaths;
- access to medical abortion services in some countries (e.g. India) has virtually ended; and

DOI: 10.4324/9780429280603

- many countries closed or re-purposed sexual and reproductive health services (including VAWG response service delivery) during national lockdowns, because they were not classed as essential (Cousins, 2020).

Such failures need to be balanced against the decades of dedicated advocacy and action by activists, practitioners, and organisations across the globe. Truth has been spoken to power about VAWG, including by many who themselves hold power, as well as by those without power but with immense commitment and will.

Protecting VAWG prevention and response, and gender equality gains: the need for a feminist global health agenda

Recent evidence has shown that early demands and/or hopes for VAWG prevention during the pandemic would not translate into action. This is not unique to Covid-19, but instead is characteristic of an increasingly recognised relationship between disease outbreaks, violence, and gender. For example, the impacts of Ebola on women and children and on health systems and delivery in West Africa (including increased rates of IPV and child marriage, post-VAWG health and psychosocial care, lack of sexual and reproductive, maternal, neonatal, and child health care, lack of access to family planning and safe abortion) have been apparent since 2014. Yet, very little was done to address such gender inequalities during that emergency or subsequently, or in later crises such as the cholera outbreak in Yemen which began in 2016 (see Menendez, Lucas, Munguambe, & Langer, 2015; O'Donnell, 2020a, 2020b; Smith, 2019; UNICEF, 2018). These mistakes and their impacts have been repeated, and indeed have been amplified considerably in terms of geographical spread, during the global Covid-19 pandemic (Fraser, 2020; Hussein, 2020; UKSRHR Network, 2020).

For these reasons, it is essential that a global public health agenda that is both feminist and gender equal is established.[2] This was abundantly clear before the pandemic and is even more necessary now in order to address its many negative outcomes. Covid-19 economic support and build back policies that genuinely address gender issues are just as essential, and there must be feminist perspectives on opportunities for gender-transformative action in global public health emergencies.

There are many individual health and economic risks bound up with Covid-19, and all come with gender implications. Health, social care, and other essential service workers, both men and women, in 'normal' times, are considered low skilled, but they have become recognised as 'essential' (no doubt temporarily). WHO estimates that 70% of all health and social care workers worldwide are female; they may, therefore, be more exposed to the risk of contracting the virus because physical (social) distancing is impossible in many essential service occupations. Women's risks of unemployment are often likely to be higher because they work in large numbers in retail, the food industry, and hospitality, all of which are sectors experiencing widespread disruption and closures. Informal workers face particularly grave consequences, including a lack of social protection safety nets (see, e.g., APHRC & ICRW, 2020b; Fraser, 2020; GH, 5050).

VAWG as a 'shadow pandemic'

UN Women (2020) has shown that since the pandemic began, VAWG – and especially IPV – has intensified. For instance, emergency calls linked to domestic violence increased by 25% in Argentina after its lockdown began; in France, such reports rose by 30%. There are similar patterns in the UK, the USA, Singapore, and elsewhere: women and girls have no escape from those who perpetrate violence and support services have been overwhelmed. Femicide rates have risen in Mexico. Demand for emergency shelter places has increased. Self-isolation, lockdown, working from home: all such factors increase the risk of IPV. Other stress factors undoubtedly include loss of income, loss of work, worries over money, challenges to mental and physical health, substance abuse, lack of health and social care, and other safety nets.

UNFPA projected that the Covid-19 pandemic will drive 31 million new cases of GBV (by the end of 2020) and cause a one-third reduction in progress towards ending GBV by 2030.

This represents a truly global challenge for all women and girls, perhaps most acutely for those who are already most vulnerable and/or at the intersection of more than one vulnerability (e.g. those with disabilities, living in IDP camps, or from a religious minority). Disruption to education across the world has potentially dire consequences for all children, and for girls in particular, this lack of access to school may become permanent in many situations, driven by socio-economic imperatives. Emerging evidence indicates that girls may be seen increasingly as commodities for forced marriage; they might also be removed permanently from school to engage in wage labour and/or care of family members (see, e.g., Evans, 2020; GBV AoR, 2020; Lokot & Avakyan, 2020; Spotlight Initiative, 2020; UN Women, 2020; Wenham, Smith, & Morgan, 2020). Adolescent girls who often fall between child protection and interventions focused on protection of adult women may be at risk of being overlooked: tailored, specific services need to be continued and expanded (Plan International, 2020; SCF, 2020).

Women's participation in Covid-19 decision-making

Decision-makers across the globe have not prioritised issues of VAWG and gender equality during the pandemic and applying a gender perspective in the context of Covid-19 has been patchy.

Below are a few examples (gleaned from UN, INGOs, and other sources) of why balanced representation and attention to issues of gender are crucial if the short- and long-term impacts of Covid-19 on women and girls are to be mitigated.

204 Conclusion

- There have been various cases of Covid-19 emergency legislation that ignores or walks back previous gains. For example, in India, we have seen regressive laws introduced condemning workers to longer hours at lower pay.
- Measures to address social protection (income and other safety nets) are too often gender-blind (see, e.g., Gentilini, Almenfi, & Orton, 2020).
- There are reports of re-allocation of funds to fight Covid-19 from otherwise pressing VAWG issues. For example, in Ethiopia, funds earmarked to fight FGM have reportedly been diverted.
- There is widespread lack of gender-focused action to support workers, including the huge numbers of women in the informal economy.
- There is failure to acknowledge, let alone address, care burdens that have fallen even more disproportionately on women in 2020 and 2021.
- There is failure to understand the differential needs of female health and social care workers (e.g. Personal Protective Equipment being designed and made to male size specifications).

For these reasons and many more, a genuine gender perspective is required in order to understand and then address the various elements of the pandemic. Here, women's inclusion in decision-making is an essential part of the response. Much support has been put in place by women's rights organisations and other groups in many countries, including Kyrgyzstan, the Democratic Republic of the Congo, Nigeria, Iraq, India, and elsewhere. Such organisations work on key issues, including providing factual information and provision of services and safe spaces. But even where organisations like these lead the way in practical action, they are too often not asked to participate in debate and decision at national and international levels (see, e.g., CARE International, 2020, which undertook rapid research in 30 countries; Encarnacion, 2020).

Equitable decision-making cannot be solely or chiefly at the community level, where, for instance, invaluable public health work has been done in South Africa and elsewhere by volunteers and activists; it must also take place in contexts where major decisions are made (GADN, 2020). In some countries and institutions, this is happening, but not extensively enough: women's under-representation in high-level decision-making continues to be starkly insufficient.

> In several countries around the globe, women are at the helm of effective and inclusive COVID-19 response efforts, though they are frequently under-represented at the highest levels of decision-making in sectors that are directly impacted by the COVID-19 pandemic.
>
> *(Freizer, Azcona, Berevoescu, & Cookson, 2020, p. 3)*

Disaggregated data

Disaggregated collection and gender analysis are essential for an overview of how the Covid-19 pandemic is evolving across the world and the relative impacts on different groups of people. At the very least, all countries should collect sex-disaggregated data. Age and location data are also crucial to understand the demographic profile of the virus and to track differences in rural and urban places of residence, high-income vs low- and middle-income countries, migrants and refugees, for example. Yet, evidence shows that only 75 countries from a total of 175 providing data are collecting sex-disaggregated data.[3] Without collection of disaggregated data, it will be impossible to develop evidence-based and gender-transformative Covid-19 policy, or to address VAWG in this or any future public health emergency.

UN Women, the IRC, CARE International, and a wide range of national CSOs have called for Covid-19 gender impact assessments and analysis (BMGF, 2020; Encarnacion, 2020; Fuhram & Rhodes, 2020; IRC, 2020), but there is also acknowledgement of the general and specific risks involved in VAWG data collection. These include potentially exposing the respondent to yet more violence, concerns over inability to keep physical distance, potential for violence against the researcher, and lack of confidentiality if using remote data collection methods (UN Women & WHO, 2020).

Covid-19, humanitarian emergencies, and VAWG

As of November 2020, the severe implications of Covid-19 in terms of humanitarian emergency had become apparent, but robust data remain severely limited.[4] People at risk from naturally occurring or man-made hazards, refugees, and internally displaced persons (whether living in precarious environments, camps, or in host communities) will face potentially dire consequences should Covid-19 reach them, their hosts, and those working to support them.

Precarious environments (such as land recently inundated due to floods) and camps will often be profoundly insanitary, with minimal opportunities for effective WASH (water, sanitation and hygiene) or for physical distancing. It was only in April 2020 that Rohingya refugees in what is now the world's largest refugee camp, outside Cox's Bazaar in Bangladesh, had internet connections restored – this will have given people at least the chance of having access to genuine information about how to avert infection and protect themselves and their loved ones. IRC describes the situation in stark terms: there is a direct impact of Covid-19 on already weak systems; there is a secondary impact on humanitarian responses and already fragile environments (IRC, 2020).

Of course, it is not only refugees and IDPs who potentially will be profoundly affected by Covid-19 in conflict, post-conflict, and fragile state environments: the same will be the case for the great majority of those living in poverty, in informal settlements, reliant on day labour and living on less than USD 2 a day. Cross-border workers and economic migrants will have seen restrictions on movement with direct financial challenges; remittances from such workers will have reduced significantly.

206 Conclusion

People experiencing forced migration during the pandemic have been described as the 'furthest behind'; they face often insurmountable barriers to assistance. VAWG survivors who are refugees or IDPs may become even more vulnerable. Reduced health and psychosocial care services, lack of access to any police or legal services, physical distancing when seeking support (yet lack of such distancing in camp environments), inadequate WASH facilities, increased commodification of girls, reversion to harmful social norms (such as marrying off a VAWG survivor to the perpetrator): all such impacts have happened and continue (IFRC, 2020; IRC, 2020; RWC & University of Birmingham, 2020).

Evidence from the Ebola epidemic and elsewhere indicates that rates of VAWG increase during public health emergencies as systems buckle and priorities shift. As such, the Covid-19 pandemic represents a high-risk context in which women and girls may experience increased incidence in VAWG, and this may include violence from the very people tasked with keeping them safe, such as those enforcing lockdowns (GAPS UK, 2020).

Box 10.1   Covid-19 and VAWG in the context of humanitarian emergency

Refugees and IDPs living in camps endure cramped conditions with often minimal privacy and absence of sanitation; in addition, many female refugees and IDPs always face restrictions on their movement, based on social norms. While such restrictions might conceivably protect against infection, it brings challenges in terms of prolonged proximity to potential/existing perpetrators whose propensity to violence might be increased due to tensions linked to the pandemic.

Restrictions on women's and girls' movements may also be due to curfews or physical distancing measures – these too might limit access to VAWG prevention and support activities.

Programmes that support women and girls, and VAWG survivors in humanitarian emergencies are likely to have been disrupted, paused, or otherwise affected – this may well have a knock-on effect on women and girls' opportunities for support, safe spaces, health and other services and redress.

Female and child-headed refugee and IDP households may be especially vulnerable to infection, because they will need to balance self-protection against the need to earn money or food in kind – when livelihoods are squeezed, women and children might turn to precarious activities such as sex work or be more vulnerable to coercion and trafficking.

Overviews of the potential impacts of the pandemic on Yemen and Iraq, countries already reeling from years of conflict, indicate the magnitude of the challenge in terms of addressing VAWG (including extreme spikes in rates of child marriage) while also grappling with Covid-19. Challenges, including famine, lack of any social protection safety nets, or lack of access to clean water, compound the gravity of the situation in so many countries now experiencing the double impacts of an existing humanitarian emergency and the ongoing pandemic (GBV AoR, 2020).

Lockdown – and undoubtedly other impacts of restrictions, such as reductions in earnings – have clearly exacerbated VAWG challenges, with emerging evidence from many countries (not only those already experiencing some form of humanitarian emergency) of increased rates of VAWG (especially IPV) and deaths of women and girls. As such, it is imperative that a VAWG Mainstreaming Framework, as described throughout this book, be integrated into Covid-19 response during and after the pandemic.

How to address VAWG and gender inequality during Covid-19?

Key VAWG issues that need to be addressed swiftly and flexibly during the pandemic (and beyond) include:

- Ensuring that women (including refugees and IDPs) are included in short- and longer-term government, donor partner (bilateral and multilateral), and civil society planning specific to VAWG programming – this includes active participants as well as potential recipients of assistance. This is especially essential, given the overwhelmingly male dominance of Covid-19 response decision-making.
- Ensuring that existing VAWG programming remains funded and that all actions that can continue safely are able to do so.
- Ensuring that VAWG prevention work remains active and that those vulnerable to VAWG, including coercion into sex work and trafficking, continue to be protected.
- Ensuring that governments, donor partners, and civil society organisations examine whether the pandemic throws up new needs for those in danger of, or surviving, VAWG; governments and donor partners should respond with speedy and flexible funding and support being channelled to tried and tested CSOs that are willing and able to work.
- Seeking to ensure that health, education, and other key programming continue and that any VAWG components are not neglected.
- Ensuring that any Covid-19 humanitarian emergency programming specific to VAWG has comprehensive gender analysis as a key component, that all data collected are disaggregated, and that findings are used to inform ongoing activities, with ethical principles being adhered to throughout.

Concluding remarks

Many vulnerabilities have been deepened and new ones have emerged as a consequence of Covid-19. At a time when everyone is vulnerable, it has become critical to apply models that help to make visible who is most at risk and why. A number of key questions can help to determine the availability of resilience options during a crisis of this kind, including:

1. Are people able to maintain food security and meet their basic needs (shelter, health care, etc.)?
2. Are 'decent' livelihood opportunities available?
3. Has it become necessary to use damaging or dangerous coping strategies in order to survive?
4. Is support (from anyone – the government, police, donor-funded projects, CSOs, etc.) available and/or accessible?
5. And how do the answers to the above questions affect rates of VAWG and action to prevent and respond to it?

These questions allow specific groups or individuals to be located on a vulnerability continuum, which, in turn, provides an indication of which groups to target with interventions and which types of interventions and/or support will mitigate risk most effectively and build resilience.

Ending on a positive note

To end these Conclusions on a possibly more positive note: gender theory argues that social norms can be and are contested and transformed, sometimes markedly, in times of crisis. This position links into a view of gender as 'performance', developed originally by Butler (2006) – that gender roles, relations, structures of power are never entirely immutable and that because such norms are produced through social interactions, there is always potential, however limited, for positive change.

As West and Zimmerman (1987, 2009) (see also Butler, 2004; Legerski & Cornwall, 2010) suggest, men and women and those who self-identify otherwise 'do' gender on a daily basis, through the use of social behaviours and signalling and in their engagement with each other; people may also 'undo' gender, as either an act of conscious resistance or often in response to a cataclysmic event. Covid-19 is such an event: in contexts where there is 'undoing of gender', there may be an opportunity to reshape social norms and gender roles and relations – even, just possibly, for the better, despite all the emerging evidence that suggests otherwise. When faced with the grim realities of gender discrimination and violence as detailed through this volume, it is critical that in responding the development sector, women and girls are understood as active agents in shaping their own futures. The term 'girl-led approach' is gaining popularity as a means of ensuring that the rights and voices of the next generation are front and centre. In reality, this has to mean protecting and preventing violence through the building of an enabling environment for these voices to be heard.

Conclusion **209**

The image on the front cover of this book is a painting of a group of women: artists in South Sudan who embroider bedsheets. The art form is known as *Milaya*. Girls from a young age, as soon as they can thread and use a needle, begin to learn their craft. They are mentored and taught by their mothers, grandmothers, and older sisters. In research into art heritage and resilience in South Sudan (see www.genderfocus.org), interviews and story circles with *Milaya* artists revealed multiple reasons and motivations for the art form. It is usually bedsheets that are embroidered, and they are often given as marriage gifts, sometimes forming part of the bride price agreement between families. The bedsheets can fetch a sizeable sum of money and women talk of being able to pay for school fees and feed their children by selling them. This is a critical income, given that many women live as single mothers in the absence of husbands who have been displaced or killed by the conflicts. A sense of self-worth and independence is clearly derived from being able to generate an income through this art form. The link between economic engagement and self-confidence has been explored (for example, in Bradley, 2020), and noted as an important dimension in ending violence. However, *Milaya* is much more than just a source of income.

Many of the women spoken with during the research talked of the embroidered sheets as expressions and gifts of love given to other women at marriage. The sheets carry emotional attachments and are seen as a way of projecting individual identity. Each woman can recognise the unique work of another through the specifics of the design and the colours used. The women also shared the importance of the time spent together while embroidering and teaching the next generation. The stories they shared illustrated the help and support they give each other through and in these spaces.

The positive image of agency revealed through these stories provides nuance to the otherwise unremittingly harsh statistics in this volume that indicate the extent of violence endured by women and girls in South Sudan. In particular, the high level of intimate partner violence is not the sole identifier for survivors; the strength and determination shared by the *Milaya* artists demonstrates their agency. What this example of self-determination, as well as the others given throughout this volume, shows us is the importance of approaching VAWG – and more specifically ending it – with a positive perception of the power and agency women and girls have to make a difference in their lives on their own terms. Interventions, then, need to begin with an understanding of the personal and collective experiences of violence and the coping strategies deployed by women and girls. The visions they have for themselves need to be at the forefront of programming and central to decision-making, which means listening to and including women and girls in development planning and implementation, regardless of sector, which can be facilitated through the VAWG Mainstreaming Framework. With this in mind, we end with the voice of one *Milaya* artist in Juba who shared the inspiration for her art as follows:

I embroider the beauty that is my head, the flowers and the colours I see when I shut my eyes. I do not embroider the dead brown tree.

210 Conclusion

Notes

1 There have been literally tens of thousands of publications in 2020 addressing Covid-19. We base our discussion here on tried and tested resources and data sources across the world. This text has been updated throughout 2020 and in the first half of 2021.
2 See the call for a feminist Covid-19 policy by the *Feminist Alliance for Rights*: http://feministallianceforrights.org/blog/2020/03/20/action-call-for-a-feminist-covid-19-policy/. Also see the Centre for Feminist Foreign Policy, with its dissection of what is not being done during the pandemic to address gender inequality and its impacts, such as increased rates of VAWG: https://centreforfeministforeignpolicy.org/. The *Feminist Response to Covid-19* represents another valuable resource at https://www.feministcovidresponse.com/. Also see Davies and Harman (2019).
3 The Global Health 5050, APHRC and ICRW website at https://globalhealth5050.org/the-sex-gender-and-covid-19-project/ provides a sex-disaggregated data tracker specific to Covid-19. See further GH 5050, APHRC, and ICRW (2020a, 2020b).
4 Our work on Covid-19 and VAWG in humanitarian emergencies has been informed by a number of key documents, but this is a very fast-moving field and there will doubtless be many more publications. The documents produced will provide an increasingly nuanced picture of the impact of Covid-19 as projections and potential implications become clearer and as actual experiences and ramifications come to be known. See CARE International (2020), Ravallion (2020), GAPS UK (2020), Fraser (2020), GBV AoR (2020), IFRC (2020), IRC (2020), UN DGC (2020), UNFPA (2020).

References

Bhatia, A. (2020). *Five Things Governments Can Do Now.* UN Women. https://www.unwomen.org/en/news/stories/2020/3/news-women-and-covid-19-governments-actions-by-ded-bhatia

BMGF. (2020). *Covid-19: A Global Perspective. 2020 Goalkeepers Report.* Bill and Melinda Gates Foundation. https://www.gatesfoundation.org/goalkeepers/report/2020-report/ - Global Perspective

Bradley, T. (2020). *Global Perspectives on Ending Violence against Women and Girls.* Zed Books.

Butler, J. (2004). *Undoing Gender.* New York and London: Routledge. https://doi.org/10.4324/9780203499627

Butler, J. (2006). *Gender Trouble: Feminism and the Subversion of Identity.* New York and London: Routledge. https://doi.org/10.4324/9780203824979

CARE International. (2020). *Gender Implications of Covid-19 Outbreaks in Development and Humanitarian Settings.* https://insights.careinternational.org.uk/publications/gender-implications-of-covid-19-outbreaks-in-development-and-humanitarian-settings

Cousins, S. (2020). Covid-19 has "devastating" effect on women and girls. *The Lancet, 396*(10247), 301–302. https://doi.org/10.1016/S0140-6736(20)31679-2

Davies, E., & Harman, S. (2019). Why it must be a feminist global health agenda. *The Lancet, 393*(10171), 601–603. https://doi.org/10.1016/S0140-6736(18)32472-3

Encarnacion, J. (2020). *Guidance Note: Rapid Gender Assessment Surveys on the Impacts of Covid-19. Guidance Document.* https://data.unwomen.org/publications/guidance-rapid-gender-assessment-surveys-impacts-covid-19

Evans, D. (2020). *How Will Covid-19 Affect Women and Girls in Low and Middle-Income Countries?* Center for Global Development. https://www.cgdev.org/blog/how-will-covid-19-affect-women-and-girls-low-and-middle-income-countries

Fraser, E. (2020). *Impact of Covid-19 Pandemic on Violence against Women and Girls* (Research Report 284). VAWG Help Desk. https://www.sddirect.org.uk/media/1881/vawg-helpdesk-284-covid-19-and-vawg.pdf

Freizer, S., Azcona, G., Berevoescu, I., & Cookson, T. P. (2020). *Covid-19 and Women's Leadership: From an Effective Response to Building Back Better* (Policy Brief 18). UN Women. https://www.unwomen.org/en/digital-library/publications/2020/06/policy-brief-covid-19-and-womens-leadership

Fuhram, S., & Rhodes, F. (2020). *Where Are the Women? The Conspicuous Absence of Women in Covid-19 Response Teams and Plans, and Why We Need Them.* CARE International. https://insights.careinternational.org.uk/publications/why-we-need-women-in-covid-19-response-teams-and-plans

GADN. (2020). *Ensuring Women's Equal Participation and Leadership in Covid-19 Decision-Making.* Gender and Development Network. https://gadnetwork.org/gadn-resources/covid-19-amp-womens-participation-and-leadership

GAPS UK. (2020). *Call to Action: Now and the Future. COVID-19 and Gender Equality, Global Peace and Security.* Gender Action for Peace and Security UK. https://gaps-uk.org/covid-19-and-gender-equality-global-peace-and-security/

GBV AoR. (2020). *Guidance Note on GBV Service Provision during the Time of COVID-19* [specific to Iraq]. GBV Sub-Cluster. https://reliefweb.int/report/iraq/guidance-note-gbv-service-provision-during-time-covid-19-march-2020

Gentilini, I., Almenfi, M., & Orton, I. (2020). *Social Protection and Jobs Responses to COVID-19: A Real-Time Review of Country Measures.* World Bank Social Protection and Jobs Global Practice. https://openknowledge.worldbank.org/handle/10986/33635

GH 5050, APHRC & ICRW. (2020a). *Gender and Sex-Disaggregated Data: Vital to Inform an Effective Response to COVID-19.* Global Health 5050, African Population and Health Research Center, & the International Center for Research on Women. https://globalhealth5050.org/wp-content/themes/globalhealth/covid/media/ ISSUE BRIEF - Sex-Disaggregated Data & COVID-19- Sept 2020.pdf?1

GH 5050, APHRC & ICRW. (2020b). *Men, Sex, Gender and COVID-19.* Global Health 5050, African Population and Health Research Center, & the International Center for Research on Women. https://globalhealth5050.org/the-sex-gender-and-covid-19-project/men-sex-gender-and-covid-19/

Hussein, J. (2020). COVID-19: What Implications for Sexual and Reproductive Health and Rights Globally? *Sexual and Reproductive Health Matters, 28*(1). https://doi.org/10.1080/26410397.2020.1746065

IFRC. (2020). *How to Consider Protection, Gender and Inclusion in the Response to Covid-19: Technical Guidance Note.* International Federation of Red Cross and Red Crescent Societies. https://media.ifrc.org/ifrc/wp-content/uploads/sites/5/2020/03/Technical-guidance-note-for-PGI-and-health-staff-30March20.pdf

IRC. (2020). *Covid-19 in Humanitarian Crises: A Double Emergency.* International Rescue Committee. https://www.rescue.org/report/covid-19-humanitarian-crises-double-emergency

Legerski, E., & Cornwall, M. (2010). Working class job loss, gender and the negotiation of household labor. *Gender and Society, 24*(4), 447–474. https://doi.org/10.1177/0891243210374600

Lokot, M., & Avakyan, Y. (2020). Intersectionality as a lens to the COVID-19 pandemic: Implications for sexual and reproductive health in development and humanitarian contexts. *Sexual and Reproductive Health Matters, 28*(1). https://doi.org/10.1080/26410397.2020.1764748

Menendez, C., Lucas, A., Munguambe, K., & Langer, A. (2015). Ebola crisis: The unequal impact on women and children's health. *The Lancet Global Health, 3*(3). https://doi.org/10.1016/S2214-109X(15)70009-4

O'Donnell, M. (2020a). *Preventing a 'Return to Normal': Addressing Violence against Women during Covid-19*. Center for Global Development. https://www.cgdev.org/blog/preventing-return-normal-addressing-violence-against-women-during-covid-19

O'Donnell, M. (2020b). *Playing the Long Game: How a Gender Lens Can Mitigate Harm Caused by Pandemics*. Center for Global Development. https://www.cgdev.org/blog/playing-long-game-how-gender-lens-can-mitigate-harm-caused-pandemics

Pearce, A. (2020). *Disability Considerations in GBV Programming during the Covid-19 Pandemic*. UNFPA. https://reliefweb.int/report/world/disability-considerations-gbv-programming-during-covid-19-pandemic

Plan International. (2020). *Living under Lockdown: Girls and Covid-19*. Plan International. https://plan-international.org/publications/living-under-lockdown

Ravallion, M. (2020). *Pandemic Policies in Poor Places* (CGD Note). Center for Global Development. https://www.cgdev.org/publication/pandemic-policies-poor-places

RWC & University of Birmingham. (2020). *Forced Migration, Sexual and Gender-Based Violence and Covid-19. Understanding the Impact of Covid-19 on Forced Migrant Survivors of SGBV*. Refugee Women Connect and University of Birmingham, Institute for Research into Superdiversity (IRIS). https://www.birmingham.ac.uk/research/superdiversity-institute/covid19-forced-migration-sexual-gender-violence/index.aspx

SCF. (2020). *Beyond the Shadow Pandemic. Protecting a Generation of Girls from GBV through Covid-19 to Recovery*. Save the Children USA and Save the Children Fund International. https://resourcecentre.savethechildren.net/library/beyond-shadow-pandemic-protecting-generation-girls-gender-based-violence-through-covid-19

Smith, J. (2019). Overcoming the 'tyranny of the urgent': Integrating gender into disease outbreak preparedness and response. *Gender and Development, 27*(2), 355–369. https://doi.org/10.1080/13552074.2019.1615288

Spotlight Initiative. (2020). *Key Messages: Violence against Women and Girls and Covid-19*. https://www.spotlightinitiative.org/es/node/18605

UKSRHR Network. (2020). *Five Recommendations for Action: Covid-19*. UK Sexual and Reproductive Health and Rights Network. https://frontlineaids.org/wp-content/uploads/2020/04/UKSRHR-Covid-19-Briefing.pdf

UN DGC. (2020). *UN Working to Ensure Vulnerable Groups Not Left Behind in Covid-19 Response*. UN Department of Global Communications https://www.un.org/en/un-coronavirus-communications-team/un-working-ensure-vulnerable-groups-not-left-behind-covid-19

UN ECOSOC. (2020). *Progress towards the Sustainable Development Goals. Report of the Secretary-General*. 2020. United Nations Economic and Social Council. https://sustainabledevelopment.un.org/content/documents/26158Final_SG_SDG_Progress_Report_14052020.pdf

UN Women. (2020). *The Shadow Pandemic: Violence against Women and Girls and COVID-19*. UN Women. https://www.unwomen.org/en/news/in-focus/in-focus-gender-equality-in-covid-19-response/violence-against-women-during-covid-19

UN Women & WHO. (2020). *Violence against Women and Girls. Data Collection during Covid-19*. UN Women & World Health Organization. https://www.unwomen.org/en/digital-library/publications/2020/04/issue-brief-violence-against-women-and-girls-data-collection-during-covid-19

UNFPA. (2020). *Impact of the COVID-19 Pandemic on Family Planning and Ending Gender-based Violence, Female Genital Mutilation and Child Marriage: Interim Technical Note*. United Nations Population Fund. https://www.unfpa.org/pcm/node/24179

UNICEF. (2018). *UNICEF Helpdesk. GBV in Emergencies. Emergency Responses in Public Health Outbreaks.* UNICEF Helpdesk: Gender Based Violence in Emergencies. https://www.sddirect.org.uk/media/1617/health-responses-and-gbv-short-query-v2.pdf

Wenham, C., Smith, J., & Morgan, R. (2020). Covid-19: The gendered impacts of the outbreak. *The Lancet, 395*(10227), 846–848. https://doi.org/10.1016/S0140-6736(20)30526-2

West, C., & Zimmerman, D. (1987). Doing gender. *Gender and Society, 1*(2), 125–151. https://doi.org/10.1177/0891243287001002002

West, C., & Zimmerman, D. (2009). Accounting for doing gender. *Gender and Society, 23*(1), 112–122. https://doi.org/10.1177/0891243208326529

INDEX

Note: **Bold** page numbers refer to figures; *italic* page numbers refer to tables; and page numbers followed by "n" denote endnotes.

2016–2020 Road Map, The 83

accountability 168–169
Addis Ababa, SDG meeting, 2019 73
adolescent girls 107, 203
advocacy 8, 11–12, 196–197
African Union Maputo Protocol on the Rights of Women in Africa 143
agency 1, 41; positive image of 208–209
Agenda for Sustainable Development, 2030 105, 190, 196
aid architecture 98–100, 103
alcohol consumption, male 62, 68, 71
Amnesty International 174
Anti-slavery International 174
AoR GBV Handbook 85–86, 86–87
Argentina 203; Femicide Observatory 146
Association for Women's Rights in Development 188
Aurat Foundation Study 27
Australia, workplace harassment 5
authority structures 21–22

Bain, A. 104
Ball, L. 18
Bangladesh 11, 107; children's rights 179; civil society sector 179; commercial sexual exploitation 176, 179, 180; Labour Law 2006 179; legal protection mechanisms 178–179; Remediation

Coordination Cell 179; RMG sector 175–176, 178–179, 179, 180; textile industry 175–176
behavioural dimensions 20
Beijing +25 142
Beijing Conference, 1995 6, 82
Beijing Declaration and Platform for Action 82, 142
Belem do Para Convention 146
Bill and Melinda Gates Foundation 197
Bourdieu, P. 19–20
Bradley, T. 18, 19, 20, 174
bullying 4

Call to Action, 2013 83, 86–87, 101, 104
capacity development support 100
CARE International 74, 205
CARE Zambia 26
Caribbean, the, femicide rates 146
caste, and intimate partner violence 62–63, 70–71
CEDAW Committee 123
Central Emergency Response Fund 192, 195
Centre for Policy Dialogue 176
change interventions 45, **47**, 49–50, 52
child labour 176, 177–178, 179
child marriage 3–4, 145, 181
child trafficking 3
children's rights 177–178

216 Index

Cluster system 81–82
Colombia, Venezuelan refugees 73–74, 74
colonialism 21–22
coloniality, of power 21–22
commercial sexual exploitation 176, 179, 180
community leaders 71
conflict and post-conflict situations 10; evidence gaps 106; Nepal 27; South Sudan 27–28; *see also* Women, Peace, and Security (WPS) Agenda
conflict-related sexual violence 121, 125–126, 143; definition 119; initiatives to counter 129–131
Connell, R. 20
Convention on the Elimination of All Forms of Discrimination against Women 140–141, 150, 197; Committees 141; effectiveness 141; General Recommendations 141
Convention to Suppress the Slave Trade and Slavery 172
cooking interventions 169
Coordinated Response to Sexual and Gender Based Violence in Zambia project 26
corporate social responsibility 175
corruption 26
Costa Rica 146
Country-based Pooled Funds 193
courage 1
Covid-19 pandemic 7, 201–208; decision-making 203–204; disaggregated data 204–205; forced migration 205–206; funding 204; gender impact assessments 205; gender implications 202–203; as humanitarian emergency 205–207; impacts 201–202; intimate partner violence 203; lockdowns 207; resilience options 208; shadow pandemic 201, 203; VAWG issues 207; VAWG rates 206
co-working 86–87
cyber-harassment 5

Darfur 169
decision-making, women's inclusion 203–204
Democratic Republic of the Congo 75, 170
Dennis Mukwege Foundation 142
Department for International Development (UK); *What Works to Prevent Violence Research and Innovation Programme* 2, 16, 36, 37, 39–40, 104, 133n5, 188–189

development aid 24
development and humanitarian emergency sectors 1, 8
development programming 15
development projects 38
disarmament 122, 127, 128
discrimination 40
displacement 9, 28, 53n2, 58–71, 73, 79, 107
domestic violence 144–145
dowry deaths 146
due diligence principle 144
Durevall, D. 51

Ebola 202, 206
ecological model 16–17, **16**, **17**, 20–21, 24, 30, 36, 182; humanitarian emergencies 108, *109*, 110; modern slavery *183*; sustainable energy programming *171*; VAWG Mainstreaming Framework 41–42, **44**, *44*, 45
Economic Commission for Latin America and the Caribbean 146
economic engagement 209
education 79–80, 203
empowerment 7, 40–41, *40*
enabling environment 45, **46**, 49, 51–52; building 208–209
End Slavery Now directory 174
energy programming 167–172; access 167–168; cooking interventions 169; ecological model 170, *171*, 172; focus 167; incidence of VAWG 168; lighting initiatives 169–170; risk factors 167–168; Safe Access to Fuel and Energy (SAFE) initiative 168–169; WASH facilities 169
environment, enabling 45, **46**, 49, 51–52; building 208–209
environmental displacement 9
Equality Institute 191
ethical requirement 102–103
Ethical Trading Initiative 175
European Convention on Preventing Violence against Women and Domestic Violence 143
European Union 5, 26, 189
evidence, evidence-base and evidence-based understanding 39–40, 103–108, 99–100
extremism, preventing and countering violent 128

Fast, L. 99–100
female genital mutilation 4, 18, 25
female representation 150
femicide 10–11, 145–146, 149

feminism, and gender 8–9
feminist approaches 15–16
feminist funding ecosystem 196
firewood collection 167–169
five Ps, the 144
forced displacement 9, 76, 182
forced marriage 203
forced migration 105, 110n5, 205
forced sexual intercourse 4, 60, 67, 70
France 203
Freizer, S. 204
Fulu, E. 42
funding and funding allocations 45,
    187–197; accountability 191; advocacy
    196–197; contributions 188; Covid-19
    pandemic 204; criteria 187; feminist
    funding ecosystem 196; for gender
    equality 187–188; geographical priorities
    190; humanitarian emergencies 11,
    80–81, 87, 99, 192–195; imbalance 190;
    inadequacy of 11, 22, 187–188; initiatives
    188–190; private-public partnerships
    190–191; SDG indicator: 5.c.1 192;
    targeting 189, 196; tracking 195–196;
    transparency 194–195; women's rights
    190, 191; WPS Agenda 124–125, 132

GADN 191
GBV Accountability Framework 83, 84
GBV Area of Responsibility 82, 101
GBV myths 77–78
gender: and feminism 8–9; insensitivity to
    64–65; as performance 208; undoing 208
gender-based violence 9–10
Gender-based Violence Information
    Management System 105, 110n8
*Gender-Based Violence in Humanitarian
    Settings* (GACC) 169
gender blind approaches 100, 110n1
Gender Development Index 150
gender discrimination 208
gendered experiences, intersectionality
    of 126
gender equality 7, 11, 26, 35, 38, 119, 120,
    124–125, 143; Covid-19 pandemic 201;
    funding 187–188; Rwanda case study
    149–154
gender equality policy marker 197–198n1
gender equity 38
gender expertise, use of 127–128
Gender Financing Project (Center for Global
    Development) 188
gender inequality 23, 26, 35, 38, 88n8
Gender Inequality Index 27

gender mainstreaming 1–2, 6–7, 15
gender (male) bias 147–148
Gender Marker 195
gender marking 187–188
gender policy 40
gender power relations 6
gender programming 1
gender relations, individuals' perceptions 53
gender stereotypes 16
Gender with Age Marker 195
geographical priorities 190
Ghana 24–28; Domestic Violence and
    Victim Support Unit - DOVVSU) 25;
    Domestic Violence Act 25; security
    risks 29
girl-led approach 208
Global Acceleration Instrument 125, 194
Global Alliance for Clean Cookstoves 169
Global Gender Gap 26
Global Gender Gap Report 150
global health agenda, feminist, need for
    202–203
globalization 42
Global Slavery Index 173
Grafham, O. 168
Grand Bargain initiative 87, 193, 193–194
Guatemala 122
*Guidelines for Integrating Gender-Based
    Violence Interventions in Humanitarian
    Action* (IASC) 78
Guimond, M. 104

habitus 19–20
Hague, W. 130, 131
*Handbook for coordinating GBV interventions
    in emergencies* (GBV AoR –GPC) 77–78
Harper, C. 18
hegemonic control 21–22
Heise, L. **17**
hierarchies of humanity 100
HIV 3, 35, 47, 50–53, 74, 79, 149
HIV/Aids 9
holistic approach 6
honour killings 146
humanitarian aid architecture 10
humanitarian emergencies 7, 9, 9–10, 30,
    72–87, 98–110; aid architecture 98–100,
    103; Beijing Conference, 1995 82; Call
    to Action, 2013 83, 86–87; capacity
    development support 100; Cluster system
    81–82; cooking interventions 169; Covid-
    19 pandemic as 205–207; co-working
    86–87; definition 75; ecological model
    108, *109*, 110; education impacts 79–80;

218 Index

energy access 167–168; evidence-base 103–108; evidence-based understanding 99–100; evidence gaps 106–108; funding 11, 80–81, 87, 99, 192–195; GBV Area of Responsibility 82; gender blind approaches 100; IASC 81–82; implementation structures 99; insecurity 72; Inter-Agency Standing Committee (IASC) GBV Guidelines 74, 84, 85, 86–87; intersectionality 102; intimate partner violence 74, 78–79, 107–108; lighting initiatives 170; localisation 100–102; man-made 75; maternal deaths 79; migration indicator 73; milestones of action 81–87; multi-partner focus 73; multi-partner initiatives 80–81; naturally occurring 75, 107–108; numbers affected 76–77, **77**; policy and practice priorities 98; Real-Time Accountability Partnership (RTAP) 83–84; refugees 73–74; response 74, 84–87; social norm change 102–103; suffering 72; targeted focus 78; terminology 75; triggers 73; Typhoon Haiyan 84–87; UN Security Council Resolution 1325 82; VAWG impacts 78–80; VAWG in 77–80; Venezuelan refugee case study 73–74; World Humanitarian Summit, 2016 87; WPS Agenda 72
humanitarianism, new approaches to 99
human rights 19
Human Rights Watch 174
human trafficking 3
hygiene 8

IASC Gender Marker 195
ideologies 21
ILO-IPEC 173–174
implementation structures 99
income 62
Indashyikirwa programme, Rwanda 154
Independent Commission for Aid Impact (UK) 37, 131
India 11; child marriage 181; children's rights 177–178; Child Welfare Committees 177; civil society sector 179; commercial sexual exploitation 176; Covid-19 pandemic 204; femicide 146; legal protection mechanisms 177–178; National Policy for Children 177–178; National Textile Policy 177; religious slavery 181; RMG sector 175–176, 177–178, 179, 181; Sexual Harassment of Women at Workplace (Prevention,

Prohibition and Redressal) Act 2013. 177; Sumangali 181; textile industry 175–176
inequality 21–22; gender 23, 26, 35, 38, 88n8
innovation 103
insecurity 72
Integrated Women's Development Programme, Nepal 37, 48–50
Inter-Agency Standing Committee (IASC) 81–82, 84; GBV Guidelines 74, 84, 85, 86–87; *Gender Handbook* 88n8
Inter-American Convention of Belem Do Para on the Prevention, Punishment, and Eradication of Violence against Women 143
internal displacement 58–71; causes 59; field sites 59; forms of violence 58; and intimate partner violence 58, 60–64, 67–69; levels of violence 60, 67; methods 60; Myanmar 58, 59, 66–70; Nepal 58, 59, 59–66; sampling strategy 60; stakeholder interviews 65–66; as trigger 70
internally displaced persons 76–77, **77**, 205
International Criminal Court 10, 123, 142
International Labor Rights Fund Global Workers' Justice Alliance 175
International Labour Organization 173, 175, 180
Inter-parliamentary Union 5
intersectionality 22; of gendered experiences 126; humanitarian emergencies 102, and IPV 63
intervention and mechanism process 41, **42**
intimate partner violence 209; and caste 62–63, 70–71; Covid-19 pandemic 203; evidence gaps 107–108; gender (male) bias 148; and HIV 51; humanitarian emergencies 74, 78–79, 107–108; and income 62; and internal displacement 58, 60–64, 67–69; intersectional dimensions 63; levels 60, 67; and literacy levels 63, 69; and male alcohol consumption 62, 68, 71; Myanmar 67–69; Nepal 60–64; and poverty 68; prevalence 3, 50–51; rates 50, 51; reporting rates 61; societal barriers 153–154; stakeholder interviews 65; support 64–65, 71; triggers 61–64, 68–69, 70, 71
Iraq 206
IRC 74, 80, 192, 205

Jamaica 122
jealousy, male 62

Johnson, K. 25
joint working 131–132
Jordan 79, 169
justice, access to 42–43, *44*, 45–46

Kabeer, N. 40–41
Kangas, A. 120
Kenya 11
Kishor, S. 25
knowledge, attitudes, and practice (KAP)
    strategy 18
knowledge collection 41–42, **42**, **43**, *43*
knowledge, decolonisation of 22

Lahn, G. 168
land ownership 151
Latin America, femicide rates 146
*Latin American Model Protocol for the
    investigation of gender-related killing*
    (OHCHR) 146
Latvia 122
law, rule of 10–11
laws and legislation 5–6, 25–26, 144–145,
    147, 151–152
Leading from the South fund 189
legal context 140–156; Beijing Declaration
    and Platform for Action 142; CEDAW
    140–141; due diligence principle 144;
    femicide case study 145–146; gaps
    147–148; gender (male) bias 147–148;
    instruments addressing VAWG 144;
    International Criminal Court 142; laws
    144–145; regional commitments 143;
    Rome Statue 142; Rwanda case study
    149–154; and social norms 147–148;
    Sustainable Development Goals 143–
    144; UN Action Team of Experts 143;
    United Kingdom 148–149; Vienna World
    Conference on Human Rights 142
lighting initiatives 169–170
Light Years Ahead initiative 170
Lindskog, A. 51
literacy levels 63
localisation 100–102, 127
Lugones, M. 21–22, 22

male attitudes and behaviours: changing 38;
    to forced sexual intercourse 70
Manjoo, R. 146
Mannell, J. 6, 7
Marcus, R. 18
marginalisation 1, 7
Marsh, M. 104
Martin, Z. 20

masculinity 19, 30, 128
maternal deaths 79
maternity entitlements 153
medical support 45
Meer, S. 6
Mekong Club 175
men: alcohol consumption 62, 68, 71;
    breadwinning status 20; jealousy 62
mental health services 110
Mexico, femicide rates 146
micro finance 9
Miedema, S. 42
migration indicator 73
Milaya 209
Minimum Initial Service Package (MISP)
    110n5
mobilisers/advocates 49, 50
modern slavery 11, 172–182; children
    176, 177–178, 179, 180; commercial
    sexual exploitation 176, 179, 180;
    commitment to end 172; cultural
    factors 181–182; definition 173; ecology
    model *183*; extent 173; gendered
    173–174; international aspect 180;
    as key development sector 172–173;
    legal protection mechanisms 177–
    179; legislation 180; motivations of
    women 174; Nepal 174; private sector
    organisations 175; programming and
    interventions 173–175; recruitment
    180; religious slavery 181; RMG sector
    175–176, 177–179; sex workers 176
Monitoring, Analysis and Reporting
    Arrangements 105–106
Moser, C., & Moser, A. 6
mother-in-law perpetration 67–68, 71
multidimensional violence 2
multi-partner initiatives 80–81
Multi-Partner Trust Fund 129–131, 132
Myanmar 9; field sites 66; internal
    displacement 58, 59, 66–70;
    intersectional dimensions 69; intimate
    partner violence 67–69; literacy levels
    69; male alcohol consumption 68;
    participants 66, *66*; poverty 68; support
    69–70; women's organisations 69–70

National Action Plans 121–123, 126–128
naturally occurring hazards 59, 75, 76, 84,
    102, 107, 194
Nepal 9, 24–28, 71; April 2015 earthquake
    59; castes 62–63; constitution 2015 48;
    Domestic Violence Act 27; Domestic
    Violence and Punishment Act 49;

220 Index

field sites 59; Gender Inequality Index 27; gender issues 64–65; income 62; Integrated Women's Development Programme 37, 48–50; internal displacement 58, 59, 59–66; intersectional dimensions 63; intimate partner violence 60–64; levels of VAWG 25, 27; levels of violence 60; literacy levels 63; male alcohol consumption 62; methods 60; modern slavery 174; prevalence rate 49, 50; reporting rates 61; sampling strategy 60; security risks 29; stakeholder interviews 65–66; support 64–65; women's organisations 65

new humanitarian aid architecture 99

normalisation, of VAWG 38

norms 9, 17–21; changing 18, 38, 45, **47**, 49–50, 52, 102–103; definition 18; and legal context 147–148; reversing 19; shaping 19–20; sticky 153, 156; underpinning 21

O'Donnell, M. 201

official development assistance (ODA) 188, 189

online harassment 5

Organisation for Economic Co-operation and Development (OECD) 125, 187, 188, 190

Organisation for Economic Co-operation and Development, Development Assistance Committee (OECD-DAC) 190, 192

Pacific Islands' Forum Gender Equality Declaration 143

Pakistan 24–28; levels of VAWG 25, 26–27; security risks 29

Palestine 122

Parliwala, R. 20

partnership 99

patriarchy 128, 148

peace agreements 127

peer networks 64, 69–70, 71

perpetrators 3, 18; mother-in-laws 67–68

Polaris Project 174

policy change 41, **42**

political approach 15

political economy/political analyses(PEA) 22–24, 110n1; case studies 24–28

positive deviants 65

poverty 26, 68, 155, 180, 181, 205

power, coloniality of 21–22

power dynamics 1–2, 15

power quartet, the 40, *40*

power relations 1–2, 6, 19, 21–22

power structures 17–21, 22–23, 24, 40–41, 52

predictors, of violence 39

prevalence: global 3–6; inadequacy of funding 11; IPV 50–1; Nepal 49, 50; rates 14, 18, 38, 49, 50, 152–153

Prevention of Sexual Violence in Conflict Initiative (PSVI) 10, 104, 118, 130–131, 132

private-public partnerships 101, 190–191

programme design 42–43, *44*

prosecutions 25

psychological violence 5

Quijano, A. 21–22

rape 11, 28, 67, 79, 119, 149

Read-Hamilton, S. 104

Real-Time Accountability Partnership (RTAP) 83–84, 101

Red Crescent Movement 192

Reference Group on Gender in Humanitarian Action 82

Refugee (Geneva) Convention, 1951 88n4

refugees 11, 73–74; Covid-19 pandemic 205; definition 88n4; evidence gaps 106–107; legal protections 88n4; transit countries 79

religious slavery 181

reporting rates, intimate partner violence 61

resilience 1

resilience options 208

restorative justice approaches 148

Risk-informed Early Action Partnership (REAP) 11, 194

role models 19

Rome Statue 142

Rwanda 11, 119–120; child-headed households 149; Constitution 151; female representation 150; gender budgeting 151; *Gender Development Index* rating 150; gender equality case study 149–154; the genocide 149; government initiatives 150; *Indashyikirwa* programme 154; intimate partner violence 153–154; Labour Law 13/2009 151; Land Law 43/2013 151; national gender machinery 150; prevention and response laws 151–152; societal barriers 153–154, 156; status of women 149; VAWG rates 152–153

Safe Access to Fuel and Energy (SAFE) initiative 168–169
safe houses 45
SAFE Humanitarian Working Group 169
Sahariah, S. 174
sanitation 8
SASA! 52
Save the Children 174
scaling up interventions 14
school-related gender-based violence 4
security risks 29–30
self-confidence 209
self-worth 40
Sexual and Gender-based Violence: prevention, risk mitigation and response (UNHCR) 78
sexual exploitation 3, 124; commercial 176, 179, 180
sexual harassment, street-based 4
sexual intercourse, forced 60, 67, 70
sexual violence 60
sex workers 176
shadow pandemic, the 201, 203
Sierra Leone 122
Singano, M. S. 101
Sisters for Change 181
slavery *see* modern slavery
social ecology model 8–9
social identity 40
social mobilisers 64, 71
social movements 19, 46
social norms 17–21; changing 18, 38, 45, **47**, 49–50, 52, 102–103; definition 18; and legal context 147–148; reversing 19; shaping 19–20; sticky 153, 156; underpinning 21
South Africa 24–28; Criminal Law Sexual Offenses and Related Matters Act No 32 26; Domestic Violence Act No 116 26; femicide 146; gender equality 26; HIV/ Aids 51; levels of VAWG 25; security risks 29, 29–30
South Sudan 24–28, 28–29, 208–209; levels of VAWG 25, 27–28
SPHERE project 85, 89n9
Spotlight Initiative 189
Sri Lanka 122
Stepping Stones behavioural change programme 21
Stevens, S. 120
street-based sexual harassment 4
structural inequalities 1–2
support networks 49
support services 38
survivor-centric approach 45

Sustainable Development Goal 5 35, 105, 127, 143, 144, 189, 192
Sustainable Development Goal 16 73, 127, 143
Sustainable Development Goals 105, 143–144, 196
Sustainable Development Reports 156n5
sustainable energy programming 167–172; cooking interventions 169; ecological model 170, *171*, 172; focus 167; incidence of VAWG 168; lighting initiatives 169–170; risk factors 167–168; Safe Access to Fuel and Energy (SAFE) initiative 168–169; WASH facilities 169
symbolic violence 20

temporary accommodation 63–64
theoretical approaches 14–31; case studies 24–28; feminist 15–16; political economy analysis (PEA) 22–24; power relations 21–22; sequence 46, **48**; social norms 17–21; traditional values and beliefs 28–29; *see also* ecological model
Thomson Reuters Foundation 175
toilets 8
traditional values and beliefs, and VAWG 28–29
transactional (survival) sex 73–74
Transformative Agenda 81–82
trans-generational perspective 30
triggers, intimate partner violence 62–64, 68–69
Typhoon Haiyan 84–87

Uganda 51, 52
UN Action 10, 118, 132
UN Action against Sexual Violence in Conflict 129–131
UN Action Team of Experts 129–131, 132, 143
UN Action Theory of Change 130
UNCHR 170
UN Declaration on the Elimination of Violence Against Women (DEVAW) 36
UN Declaration on the Rights of the Child 150
UNFPA 203
UN Global Compact 172
UNHCR Regional Refugee and Migrant Response Plan 74, 76, 78
UN High Commissioner for Human Rights 142, 170
UN High Commissioner for Refugees 75
UNICEF 19, 149

United Kingdom: anti-slavery organisations 175; Department for International Development 16, 36, 37, 39–40; Department for International Development (UK) 2, 133n5; Femicide Census 149; Independent Commission for Aid Impact 131; legal context 148–149; NAPs 122; Prevention of Sexual Violence in Conflict Initiative (PSVI) 10, 104, 130–131, 132; rape cases 149; *What Works to prevent VAWG research and innovation* 2, 16, 36, 37, 39–40, 104, 133n5, 188–189

United Nations 24, 29, 189, 192; Special Rapporteur on Violence against Women 142

United States of America, VAWG 5

university students, VAWG 4–5

UN Office for the Co-ordination of Humanitarian Affairs (UN OCHA) 11, 79, 120, 193, 195; Financial Tracking Service 192

UN Office of the High Commissioner for Human Rights (OHCHR) 174

UN Population Fund (UNFPA) 80, 82, 86

UN Security Council: Resolution 1325 10, 82, 118–119, 119, 121, 125, 132; Resolution 1888 129; Resolution 2467 129; WPS Resolutions 121–124; *see also* Women, Peace, and Security (WPS) Agenda

UN Special Representative to the Secretary General for Children and Armed Conflict 123

UN Trust Fund 188

UN Women 5, 82, 123, 130, 132, 188, 201, 203, 205

VAWG: definition 2; ending 1; in humanitarian emergencies 77–80; interpretations of 37–39; normalisation 38, 50; prevalence 3–6, 14, 18, 38, 152–153

VAWG lens 35

VAWG mainstreaming 6–8, 37, 38; energy programming 167–172, *171*; modern slavery 172–182

VAWG Mainstreaming Framework 8, 11, 14–15, 30, 35–53, 102; application 46–53; definitions of violence 36; design stage 41–42, **42**, *43*; ecological model 41–42, **44**, *44*, 45; embedding 45–46, **46**; and empowerment 40–41, *40*; evidence 39–40; intervention and mechanism

process 41, **42**; lens 35, 41–46, **42**, **43**, *43*, **44**, *44*, **46**; male perspectives 38; need for 37, 37–39; operation 9; PEA/PA approach 23–24; programme design 42–43, *44*, 45; targets 35; theory sequence 46, **48**; trans-generational perspective 30

Vienna World Conference on Human Rights 142

violence: definition 2–3, 36; extent 1; geographic distribution 39, 49; and internal displacement 58; levels of, Myanmar 67; levels of, Nepal 60; mother-in-law perpetration 67–68, 71; multidimensional 2; need to be responded to 1; new forms 18; normalisation 71; predictors of 39; psychological 5; sexual 60; socio-cultural interpretation 36; symbolic 20; triggers 62–64, 68–69, 70, 71

visibility 14

vulnerability 48

Walby, S. 6

Walker, L. 16

Walk Free Foundation 173, 174

WASH facilities 169, 206

water, sanitation, and hygiene (WASH) 8

West, C. 208

What Works to prevent VAWG research and innovation 2, 16, 36, 37, 39–40, 104, 133n5, 188–189

women and girls: Covid-19 pandemic decision-making 203–204; definition 155; HIV risk 51; literacy levels 63, 69; lived experience 155–156; male oppression of 15; peer networks 64, 69–70, 71; in Rwanda 149; value 45–46, **47**, 50, 52–53; as victims 126

Women, Peace, and Security (WPS) Agenda 10, 23, 72, 118–132; definitions 119; funding 124–125, 132; gaps 125–126; Global Acceleration Instrument 125; inclusive approach 128; joint working 131–132; NAPs 121–123, 126–128; pillars of 118–119; resources 132; role of civil society 119–120; tensions 132; UN Security Council Resolutions 121–124; Yemen case study 120

Women's International League for Peace and Freedom 23

women's organisations 65, 69–70, 125

Women's Peace and Humanitarian Fund 125, 132, 194

women's rights 6, 119; Beijing Declaration and Platform for Action 142; CEDAW 140–141; erosion of 197; funding 190, 191; International Criminal Court 142; regional commitments 143; Rome Statue 142; Sustainable Development Goals 143–144; UN Action Team of Experts 143; Vienna World Conference on Human Rights 142

workplace, the, harassment and psychological violence 5

World Bank 190

World Conference on Women, 1995 82, 142

World Food Programme 168

World Humanitarian Summit, 2016 80, 87

World Women's Conference, Beijing, 1995 6, 82

Yemen 206; WPS case study 120

Yugoslavia 119–120

Zambia 24–28; Anti-Gender-Based Violence Act 25; gender inequality 26; levels of VAWG 25–26

Zimmerman, D. 208

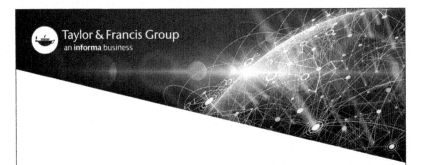